The Posthumous Thomas De Quincey

Thomas De Quincey,
(Editor: Alexander H. Japp)

Alpha Editions

This edition published in 2024

ISBN 9789361471728

Design and Setting By

Alpha Editions

www.alphaedis.com

Email - info@alphaedis.com

Contents

PREFACE.

All that is needful for me to say by way of Preface is that, as in the case of the first volume, I have received much aid from Mrs. Baird Smith and Miss De Quincey, and that Mr. J. R. McIlraith has repeated his friendly service of reading the proofs.

ALEXANDER H. JAPP.

LONDON,
March 1st, 1893.

INTRODUCTION.

All that needs to be said in the way of introduction to this volume will best take the form of notes on the articles which it contains.

I. '*Conversation and S. T. Coleridge.*' This article, which was found in a tolerably complete condition, may be regarded as an attempt to deal with the subject in a more critical and searching, and at the same time more sympathetic and inclusive spirit, than is apparent in any former essay. It keeps clear entirely of the field of personal reminiscence; and if it glances at matters on which dissent must be entered to the views of Coleridge, it is still unvaryingly friendly and reverent towards the subject. It is evidently of a later date than either the 'Reminiscences of Coleridge' in the 'Recollections of the Lakes' series, or the article on 'Coleridge and Opium-Eating,' and may be accepted as De Quincey's supplementary and final deliverance on Coleridge. The beautiful apostrophe to the name of Coleridge, which we have given as a kind of motto to the essay, was found attached to one of the sheets; and, in spite of much mutilation and mixing of the pages with those of other articles, as we originally found them, it was for the most part so clearly written and carefully punctuated, that there can be no doubt, when put together, we had it before us very much as De Quincey meant to publish it had he found a fitting chance to do so. For such an article as this neither *Tait* nor *Hogg's Instructor* afforded exactly the proper medium, but rather some quarterly review, or magazine such as *Blackwood*. We have given, in an appended note to this essay, some corroboration from the poems of Coleridge of the truth of De Quincey's words about the fatal effect on a nature like that of Coleridge of the early and very sudden death of his father, his separation from his mother, and his transference to Christ's Hospital, London.

II. *Mr. Finlay's 'History of Greece.*' This essay is totally different, alike in the advances De Quincey makes to the subject, the points taken up, and the general method of treatment, from the essay on Mr. Finlay's volumes which appears in the Collected Works. It would seem as though De Quincey, in such a topic as this, found it utterly impossible to exhaust the points that had suggested themselves to him on a careful reading of such a work, in the limits of one article; and that, in this case, as in some others, he elaborated a second article, probably with a view to finding a place for it in a different magazine or review. In this, however, he either did not succeed, or, on his own principle of the opium-eater never really finishing anything, retreated from the practical work of pushing his wares with editors even after he had finished them. At all events, we can find no trace of this article, or any part of it, having ever been published. The Eastern Roman Empire was a subject on which he might have written, not merely a couple of review articles, but a volume, as we are sure anyone competent to judge will, on carefully reading these articles, at once admit. This essay, too, was found in a very complete condition, when the various pages had been brought together and arranged. This is true of all save the last few pages, which existed more in the form of notes, yet are perfectly clear and intelligible; the leading thoughts being distinctly put, though not followed out in any detail, or with the illustration which he could so easily have given them.

III. '*The Assassination of Cæsar.*' This was clearly meant to be inserted at the close of the first section of 'The Cæsars,' but was at the last moment overlooked, though without it the text there, as it stands in the Collected Works, is, for De Quincey, perhaps too hurried and business-like.

IV. The little article on '*Cicero*' is evidently meant as a supplementary note to the article on that eminent man, as it appears in the Collected Works. Why De Quincey, when preparing these volumes for the press, did not work it into his text is puzzling, as it develops happily some points which he has there dwelt on, and presents in a very effective and compact style the mingled feelings with which the great Proconsul quitted his office in Cilicia, and his feelings on arriving at Rome.

V. *Memorial Chronology.*—This is a continuation of that already published under the same title in the Collected Works. In a note from the publishers, preceding the portion already given in the sixteenth volume of the original edition, and the fourteenth of Professor Masson's edition, it is said: 'This article was written about twenty years ago [1850], and is printed here for the first time from the author's *MS.* It was his intention to have continued the subject, but this was never done.' From the essay we now present it will be seen that this last statement is only in a modified sense true—the more that the portion published in the Messrs. Black's editions is, on the whole, merely introductory, and De Quincey's peculiar *technica memoria* is not there even indicated, which it is, with some degree of clearness, in the following pages, and these may be regarded as presenting at least the leading outlines of what the whole series would have been.

De Quincey's method, after having fixed a definite accepted point of departure, was to link the memory of events to a period made signal by identity of figures. Thus, he finds the fall of Assyria, the first of the Olympiads, and the building of Rome to date from about the year 777 B.C. That is his starting-point in definite chronology. Then he takes up the period from 777 to 555; from 555 to 333, and so on.

De Quincey was writing professedly for ladies only, and not for scholars; and that his acknowledged leading obstacle was the semi-mythical wilderness of all early oriental history is insisted on with emphasis. The way in which he triumphs over this obstacle is certainly characteristic and ingenious. Though the latter part is fragmentary, it is suggestive; and from the whole a fair conception may be formed of what the finished work would have been had De Quincey been able to complete it, and of the eloquence with which he would have relieved the mere succession of dates and figures.

It is clear that in the original form, though the papers were written for ladies, the phantasy of a definite 'Charlotte' as fair correspondent had not suggested itself to him; and that he had recourse to this only in the final rewriting, and would have applied it to the whole had he been spared to pursue his plan of recast and revision for the Collected Works, as it was his intention to have done. Mrs. Baird Smith remembers very clearly her father's many conversations on this subject and his leading ideas—it was, in fact, a pet scheme of his; and it is therefore the more to be regretted that his final revision only embraced a small portion of the matter which he had already written.

It only needs to be added that, at the time De Quincey wrote, exploration in Assyria and Egypt, not to speak of discovery in Akkad, had made but little way compared with what has now been accomplished, else certain passages in this essay would no doubt have been somewhat modified.

VI. The article entitled '*Chrysomania; or the Gold Frenzy at its Present Stage*', was evidently written after the two articles which appeared in *Hogg's Instructor*. Not improbably it was felt that the readers of *Hogg's Instructor* had already had enough on the Gold Craze, and this it was deemed better not to publish; but it has an interest as supplementing much that De Quincey had said in these papers, and is a happy illustration of his style in dealing with such subjects. Evidently the editor of *Hogg's Instructor* was hardly so attracted by these papers as by others of De Quincey's; for we find that he had excised some of the notes.

VII. '*The Defence of the English Peerage*' is printed because, although it does not pretend to much detail or research, it shows anew De Quincey's keen interest in the events of English history, and his vivid appreciation of the peerage as a means of quickening and reviving in the minds of the people the memorable events with which the earlier bearers of these ancient titles had been connected.

VIII. The '*Anti-Papal Movement*' may be taken to attest once more De Quincey's keen interest in all the topics of the day, political, social, and ecclesiastical.

IX. The section on literature more properly will be interesting to many as exhibiting some new points of contact with Wordsworth and Southey.

X. The articles on the '*Dispersion of the Jews*,' and on '*Christianity as the result of a Pre-established Harmony*,' will, we think, be found interesting by theologians as well as by readers generally, as attesting not only the keen interest of De Quincey in these and allied subjects, but also his penetration and keen grasp, and his faculty of felicitous illustration, by which ever and anon he lights up the driest subjects.

I. CONVERSATION AND S. T. COLERIDGE.

Oh name of Coleridge, that hast mixed so much with the trepidations of our own agitated life, mixed with the beatings of our love, our gratitude, our trembling hope; name destined to move so much of reverential sympathy and so much of ennobling strife in the generations yet to come, of our England at home, of our other Englands on the St. Lawrence, on the Mississippi, on the Indus and Ganges, and on the pastoral solitudes of Austral climes!

What are the great leading vices of conversation as generally managed?—vices that are banished from the best society by the legislation of manners, not by any intellectual legislation, but in other forms of society, and exactly as it approaches to the character of vulgarism, disturbing all approaches to elegance in conversation, and disorganizing it as a thing capable of unity or of progress? These vices are, first, disputation; secondly, garrulity; thirdly, the spirit of interruption.

I. I lay it down as a rule, but still reserving their peculiar rights and exceptions to young Scotchmen for whom daily disputing is a sort of daily bread, that the man who disputes is a monster, and that he ought to be expelled from civilized society. Or could not a compromise be effected for disputatious people, by allowing a private disputing room in all hotels, as they have private rooms for smoking? I have heard of two Englishmen, gentlemanly persons, but having a constitutional *furor* for boxing, who quieted their fighting instincts in this way. It was not glory which they desired, but mutual punishment, given and taken with a hearty goodwill. Yet, as their feelings of refinement revolted from making themselves into a spectacle of partisanship for the public to bet on, they retired into a ball-room, and locked the doors, so that nothing could transpire of the campaigns within except from the desperate rallies and floorings which were heard, or from the bloody faces which were seen on their issuing. A limited admission, it was fancied, might have been allowed to select friends; but the courteous refusal of both parties was always 'No; the pounding was strictly confidential.' Now, pray, gentlemen disputers, could you not make your pounding 'strictly confidential'? My chief reasons for doing so I will mention:

1. That disputing is in bad tone; it is vulgar, and essentially the resource of uncultured people.

2. It argues want of intellectual power, or, in any case, want of intellectual development. It is because men find it easier to talk by disputing than by *not*

disputing that so many people resort to this coarse expedient for calling the wind into the sails of conversation. To move along in the key of contradiction is the cheapest of all devices for purchasing a power that is not your own. You are then carried along by a towing-line attached to another vessel. There is no free power. Always your antagonist predetermines the course of your own movement; and you his. What *he* says, you unsay. He affirms, you deny. He knits, you unknit. Always you are servile to *him*; and he to *you*. Yet even that system of motion in reverse of another motion, of mere antistrophe or dancing backward what the strophe had danced forward, is better after all, you say, than standing stock still. For instance, it might have been tedious enough to hear Mr. Cruger disputing every proposition that Burke advanced on the Bristol hustings; yet even *that* some people would prefer to Cruger's single observation, viz., 'I say *ditto* to Mr. Burke.' Every man to his taste: I, for one, should have preferred Mr. Cruger's *ditto*.[1] But why need we have a *ditto*, a simple *affirmo*, because we have *not* an eternal *nego*? The proper spirit of conversation moves in the general key of assent, but still not therefore of mere iteration, but still each bar of the music is different. Nature surely does not repeat herself, yet neither does she maintain the eternal variety of her laughing beauty by constantly contradicting herself, and quite as little by monotonously repeating herself. Her samenesses are differences.

II. Of the evils of garrulity, which, like the ceaseless droppings of water, will eat into the toughest rock of patience and self-satisfaction, I have spoken at considerable length elsewhere. Its evils are so evident that they hardly call for further illustration. The garrulous man, paradoxical as it may seem to say it, is a kind of pickpocket without intending to steal anything— nay, rather he is fain to please you by placing something in your pocket— though too often it is like the egg of the cuckoo in the nest of another bird.

III. Now, as to *Interruption*, what's to be done? It is a question that I have often considered. For the evil is great, and the remedy occult. I look upon a man that interrupts another in conversation as a monster far less excusable than a cannibal; yet cannibals (though, comparatively with *interrupters*, valuable members of society) are rare, and, even where they are *not* rare, they don't practise as cannibals every day: it is but on sentimental occasions that the exhibition of cannibalism becomes general. But the monsters who interrupt men in the middle of a sentence are to be found everywhere; and they are always practising. Red-letter days or black-letter days, festival or fast, makes no difference to *them*. This enormous nuisance I feel the more, because it is one which I never retaliate. Interrupted in every sentence, I still practise the American Indian's politeness of never interrupting. What, absolutely *never*? Is there *no* case in which I should? If a man's nose, or ear, as sometimes happens in high latitudes, were suddenly and visibly frostbitten, so as instantly to require being rubbed with snow, I conceive it lawful to interrupt that man in the most pathetic sentence, or even to ruin a whole paragraph of his prose. You can never indeed give him back the rhetoric which you have undermined; *that* is true; but neither could he, in the alternative case, have given back to himself the nose which you have saved.

I contend also, against a great casuist in this matter, that had you been a friend of Æschylus, and distinctly observed that absurd old purblind eagle that mistook (or pretended to mistake) the great poet's bald head—that head which created the Prometheus and the Agamemnon—for a white tablet of rock, and had you interrupted the poet in his talk at the very moment when the bird was dropping a lobster on the sacred cranium, with the view of unshelling the lobster, but unaware that at the same time he was unshelling a great poet's brain, you would have been fully justified. An impertinence it would certainly have been to interrupt a sentence as undeniable in its Greek as any which that gentleman can be supposed to have turned out, but still the eagle's impertinence was greater.[2] That would have been your excuse. Æschylus, or my friend the casuist, is not to be listened to in his very learned arguments *contra*.

Short of these cases, nothing can justify an interruption; and such cases surely cannot be common, since how often can we suppose it to happen that an eagle has a lobster to break just at the moment when a tragic poet is walking abroad without his hat? What the reader's experience may have been, of course, is unknown to me; but, for my own part, I hardly meet with such a case twice in ten years, though I know an extensive circle of tragic poets, and a reasonable number of bald heads; eagles certainly not so many—they are but few on my visiting list; and indeed, if that's their way of going on—cracking literary skulls without leave asked or warning given— the fewer one knows the better. If, then, a long life hardly breeds a case in which it is strictly lawful to interrupt a co-dialogist, what are we to think of those who move in conversation by the very principle of interruption? And a variety of the nuisance there is, which I consider equally bad. Men, that do not absolutely interrupt you, are yet continually *on the fret* to do so, and undisguisedly on the fret all the time you are speaking. To invent a Latin word which ought to have been invented before my time, 'non interrumpunt at *interrupturiunt*.' You can't talk in peace for such people; and as to prosing, which I suppose you've a right to do by *Magna Charta*, it is quite out of the question when a man is looking in your face all the time with a cruel expression in his eye amounting to 'Surely, that's enough!' or a pathetic expression which says, '*Have* you done?' throwing a dreadful reproach into the *Have*. In Cumberland, at a farmhouse where I once had lodgings for a week or two, a huge dog as high as the dining-table used to plant himself in a position to watch all my motions at dinner. Being alone, and either reading or thinking, at first I did not observe him; but as soon as I did, and noticed that he pursued each rising and descent of my fork as the poet 'with wistful eyes pursues the setting sun,' that unconsciously he mimicked and rehearsed all the notes and *appoggiaturas* that make up the successive bars in the music of eating one's dinner, I was compelled to rise, and say, 'My good fellow, I can't stand this; will you do me the favour to accept anything on my plate at this moment? And to-morrow I'll endeavour to arrange for your being otherwise employed at this hour than in watching *me*.' It seems a weakness, but I really cannot eat anything under the oppression of an envious *surveillance* like that dog's. A man said to me, 'Oh, what need you care about *him*? He has had *his* dinner long ago.' True, at twelve or one o'clock; but at six he might want another; but, if he thinks so himself, the result is the same. And that result is what the whole South of Frankistan[3] calls the *evil eye*. Wanting dinner, when he sees another person in the very act of dining, the dog (though otherwise an excellent creature) must be filled with envy; and envy is so contagiously allied to malice, that in elder English one word expresses both those dark modifications of hatred. The dog's eye therefore, without any consciousness on his own part, becomes in such a case *an evil eye*: upon me, at least, it fell with as painful an effect as any established eye of that class could do upon the most superstitious Portuguese.

Now, such exactly is the eye of any man that, without actually interrupting one, threatens by his impatient manner as often as one begins to speak. It has a blighting effect upon one's spirits. And the only resource is to say frankly (as I said to the dog), 'Would you oblige me, sir, by taking the whole of the talk into your own hands? Do not for ever threaten to do so, but at once boldly lay an interdict upon any other person's speaking.'

To those who suffer from nervous irritability, the man that suspends over our heads his *threat* of interruption by constant impatience, is even a more awful person to face than the actual interrupter. Either of them is insufferable; and in cases where the tone of prevailing manners is not vigorous enough to put such people down, or where the individual monster, being not *couchant* or *passant*, but (heraldically speaking) *rampant*, utterly disregards all restraints that are not enforced by a constable, the question comes back with greater force than ever, which I stated at the beginning of this article, 'What's to be done?'

I really cannot imagine. Despair seizes me 'with her icy fangs,' unless the reader can suggest something; or unless he can improve on a plan of my own sketching.

As a talker for effect, as a *bravura* artist in conversation, no one has surpassed Coleridge. There is a Spanish proverb, that he who has not seen Seville, has seen nothing. And I grieve to inform the present unfortunate generation, born under an evil star, coming, in fact, into the world a day after the fair, that, not having heard Coleridge, they have *heard*—pretty much what the strangers to Seville have *seen*, which (you hear from the Spaniards) amounts to nothing. *Nothing* is hardly a thing to be proud of, and yet it has its humble advantages. To have heard Coleridge was a thing to remember with pride as a trophy, but with pain as a trophy won by some personal sacrifice. To have heard Coleridge has now indeed become so great a distinction, that if it were transferable, and a man could sell it by auction, the biddings for it would run up as fast as for a genuine autograph of Shakespeare. The story is current under a thousand forms of the man who piqued himself on an interview which he had once enjoyed with royalty; and, being asked what he could repeat to the company of his gracious Majesty's remarks, being an honest fellow he confessed candidly that the King, happening to be pressed for time, had confined himself to saying, 'Dog, stand out of my horse's way'; and many persons that might appear as claimants to the honour of having conversed with Coleridge could perhaps report little more of personal communication than a courteous request from the great man not to interrupt him. Inevitably, however, from this character of the Coleridgean conversation arose certain consequences, which are too much overlooked by those who bring it forward as a model or as a splendid variety in the proper art of conversation. And speaking myself as personally a witness to the unfavourable impression left by these consequences, I shall not scruple in this place to report them with frankness.

At the same time, having been heretofore publicly misrepresented and possibly because misunderstood as to the temper in which I spoke of Coleridge, and as though I had violated some duty of friendship in uttering a truth not flattering after his death, I wish so far to explain the terms on which we stood as to prevent any similar misconstruction. It would be impossible in any case for me to attempt a Plinian panegyric, or a French *éloge*. Not that I think such forms of composition false, any more than an advocate's speech, or a political partisan's: it is understood from the beginning that they are one-sided; but still true according to the possibilities of truth when caught from an angular and not a central station. There is even a pleasure as from a gorgeous display, and a use as from a fulness of unity, in reading a grand or even pompous laudatory oration upon a man like Leibnitz, or Newton, which neglects all his errors or blemishes. This abstracting view I could myself adopt as to a man whom I had learned to know from books, but not as to one whom I knew also from personal intercourse. His faults and his greatness are then too much intertwisted.

There is still something unreal in the knowledge of men through books; with which is compatible a greater flexibility of estimate. But the absolute realities of life acting upon any mind of deep sincerity do not leave the same liberty of suppression or concealment. In that case, the reader may perhaps say, and wherever the relations of the writer to a deceased man prescribe many restraints of tenderness or delicacy, would it not be better to forbear speaking at all? Certainly; and I go on therefore to say that my own relations to Coleridge were not of that nature. I had the greatest admiration for his intellectual powers, which in one direction I thought and think absolutely unrivalled on earth; I had also that sort of love for him which arises naturally as a rebound from intense admiration, even where there is little of social congeniality. But, in any stricter sense of the word, *friends* we were not. For years we met at intervals in society; never once estranged by any the slightest shadow of a quarrel or a coolness. But there were reasons, arising out of original differences in our dispositions and habits, which would probably have forever prevented us, certainly *did* prevent us, from being confidential friends. Yet, if we had been such, even the more for that reason the sincerity of my nature would oblige me to speak freely if I spoke at all of anything which I might regard as amongst his errors. For the perfection of genial homage, one may say, in the expression of Petronius Arbiter, *Præcipitandus est liber spiritus*, the freedom of the human spirit must be thrown headlong through the whole realities of the subject, without picking or choosing, without garbling or disguising. It yet remains as a work of the highest interest, to estimate (but for that to display) Coleridge in his character of great philosophic thinker, in which character he united perfections that never *were* united but in three persons on this earth, in himself, in Plato (as many suppose), and in Schelling, viz., the utmost expansion and in some paths the utmost depths of the searching intellect with the utmost sensibility to the powers and purposes of Art: whilst, as a creator in Art, he had pretensions which neither Plato nor Schelling could make. His powers as a Psychologist (not as a Metaphysician) seem to me absolutely unrivalled on earth. And had his health been better, so as to have sustained the natural cheerfulness towards which his nature tended, had his pecuniary embarrassments been even moderately lightened in their pressure, and had his studies been more systematically directed to one end—my conviction is that he would have left a greater philosophic monument of his magnificent mind than Aristotle, or Lord Bacon, or Leibnitz.

With these feelings as to the pretensions of Coleridge, I am not likely to underrate anything which he did. But a thing may be very difficult to do, very splendid when done, and yet false in its principles, useless in its results, memorable perhaps by its impression at the time, and yet painful on the whole to a thoughtful retrospect. In dancing it is but too common that an intricate *pas seul*, in funambulism that a dangerous feat of equilibration, in the Grecian art of *desultory* equitation (where a single rider governs a plurality of horses by passing from one to another) that the flying contest with difficulty and peril, may challenge an anxiety of interest, may bid defiance to the possibility of inattention, and yet, after all, leave the jaded spectator under a sense of distressing tension given to his faculties. The sympathy is with the difficulties attached to the effort and the display, rather than with any intellectual sense of power and skill genially unfolded under natural excitements. It would be idle to cite Madame de Staël's remark on one of these meteoric exhibitions, viz., that Mr. Coleridge possessed the art of monologue in perfection, but not that of the dialogue; yet it comes near to hitting the truth from her point of view. The habit of monologue which Coleridge favoured lies open to three fatal objections: 1. It is antisocial in a case expressly meant by its final cause for the triumph of sociality; 2. It refuses all homage to women on an arena expressly dedicated to their predominance; 3. It is essentially fertile in *des longueurs*. Could there be imagined a trinity of treasons against the true tone of social intercourse more appalling to a Parisian taste?

In a case such as this, where Coleridge was the performer, I myself enter less profoundly into the brilliant woman's horror, for the reason that, having originally a necessity almost morbid for the intellectual pleasures that depend on solitude, I am constitutionally more careless about the luxuries of conversation. I see them; like them in the rare cases where they flourish, but do not require them. Not sympathizing, therefore, with the lady's horror in its intensity, I yet find my judgment in harmony with hers. The evils of Coleridgean talk, even managed by a Coleridge, were there, and they fixed themselves continually on my observation:

I. It defeats the very end of social meetings. Without the excitement from a reasonable number of auditors, and some novelty in the composition of his audience, Coleridge was hardly able to talk his best. Now, at the end of some hours, it struck secretly on the good sense of the company. Was it reasonable to have assembled six, ten, or a dozen persons for the purpose of hearing a prelection? Would not the time have been turned to more account, even as regarded the object which they had substituted for *social* pleasure, in studying one of Coleridge's printed works?—since there his words were stationary and not flying, so that notes might be taken down, and questions proposed by way of letter, on any impenetrable difficulties; whereas in a stream of oral teaching, which ran like the stream of destiny, impassive to all attempts at interruption, difficulties for ever arose to irritate your nervous system at the moment, and to vex you permanently by the recollection that they had prompted a dozen questions, every one of which you had forgotten through the necessity of continuing to run alongside with the speaker, and through the impossibility of saying, 'Halt, Mr. Coleridge! Pull up, I beseech you, if it were but for two minutes, that I may try to fathom that last sentence.' This in all conversation is one great evil, viz., the substitution of an alien purpose for the natural and appropriate purpose. Not to be intellectual in a direct shape, but to be intellectual through sociality, is the legitimate object of a social meeting. It may be right, medically speaking, that a man should be shampooed; but it cannot be right that, having asked him to dine, you should decline dinner and substitute a shampooing. This a man would be apt to call by the shorter name of a *sham*.

II. It diminishes the power of the talking performer himself. Seeming to have more, the man has less. For a man is never thrown upon his mettle, nor are his true resources made known even to himself, until to some extent he finds himself resisted (or at least modified) by the reaction of those around him. That day, says Homer, robs a man of half his value which sees him made a slave. But to be an autocrat is as perilous as to be a slave. And supposing Homer to have been introduced to Coleridge (a supposition which a learned man at my elbow pronounces intolerable—'It's an anachronism, sir, a base anachronism!' Well, but one may *suppose* anything, however base), Homer would have observed to me, as we came away from the *soirée*, 'In my opinion, our splendid friend S. T. C. would have been the better for a few kicks on the shins. That day takes away half of a man's talking value which raises him into an irresponsible dictator to his company.'

III. It diminishes a man's power in another way less obvious, but not less certain. I had often occasion to remark how injurious it was to the impression of Coleridge's finest displays where the minds of the hearers had been long detained in a state of passiveness. To understand fully, to sympathise deeply, it was essential that they should react. Absolute inertia produced inevitable torpor. I am not supposing any indocility, or unwillingness to listen. Generally it might be said that merely to find themselves in that presence argued sufficiently in the hearers a cheerful dedication of themselves to a dutiful patience.

The mistake, in short, is to suppose that the particular power of talk Coleridge had was a *nuance* or modification of what is meant by conversational power; whereas it was the direct antithesis: it differed diametrically. So much as he had of his own peculiar power, so much more alien and remote was he from colloquial power. This remark should be introduced by observing that Madame de Staël's obvious criticism passes too little unvalued or unsearched either by herself or others. She fancied it an accidental inclination or a caprice, or a sort of self-will or discourtesy or inattention. No; it was a faculty in polar opposition to the true faculty of conversation.

Coleridge was copious, and not without great right, upon the subject of Art. It is a subject upon which we personally are very impatient, and (as Mrs. Quickly expresses it) peevish, as peevish as Rugby in his prayers.[4] Is this because we know too much about Art? Oh, Lord bless you, no! We know too little about it by far, and our wish is—to know more. But *that* is difficult; so many are the teachers, who by accident had never any time to learn; so general is the dogmatism; and, worse than all, so inveterate is the hypocrisy, wherever the graces of liberal habits and association are supposed to be dependent upon a particular mode of knowledge. To know nothing of theology or medicine has a sort of credit about it; so far at least it is clear that you are not professional, and to that extent the chances are narrowed that you get your bread out of the public pocket. To be sure, it is still possible that you may be a stay-maker, or a rat-catcher. But these are out-of-the-way vocations, and nobody adverts to such narrow possibilities. Now, on the other hand, to be a connoisseur in painting or in sculpture, supposing always that you are no practising artist, in other words, supposing that you know nothing about the subject, implies that you must live amongst *comme-il-faut* people who possess pictures and casts to look at; else how the deuce could you have got your knowledge—or, by the way, your ignorance, which answers just as well amongst those who are not peevish. We, however, *are* so, as we have said already. And what made us peevish, in spite of strong original *stamina* for illimitable indulgence to all predestined bores and nuisances in the way of conversation, was—not the ignorance, not the nonsense, not the contradictoriness of opinion—no! but the false, hypocritical enthusiasm about objects for which in reality they cared not the fraction of a straw. To hear these bores talk of educating the people to an acquaintance with what they call 'high art'! Ah, heavens, mercifully grant that the earth may gape for us before *our* name is placed on any such committee! 'High art,' indeed! First of all, most excellent bores, would you please to educate the people into the high and mysterious art of boiling potatoes. We, though really owning no particular duty or moral obligation of boiling potatoes, really *can* boil them very decently in any case arising of public necessity for our services; and if the art should perish amongst men, which seems likely enough, so long as *we* live, the public may rely upon it being restored. But as to women, as to the wives of poor hard-working men, not one in fifty can boil a potato into a condition that is not ruinous to the digestion. And we have reason to know that the Chartists, on their great meditated outbreak, having hired a six-pounder from a pawnbroker, meant to give the signal for insurrection at dinner-time, because (as they truly observed) cannon-balls, hard and hot, would then be plentiful on every table. God sends potatoes, we all know; but *who* it is that sends the boilers of potatoes, out of civility to the female sex, we decline to say.

Well, but this (you say) is a digression. Why, true; and a digression is often the cream of an article. However, as you dislike it, let us *re*gress as fast as possible, and scuttle back from the occult art of boiling potatoes to the much more familiar one of painting in oil. Did Coleridge really understand this art? Was he a sciolist, was he a pretender, or did he really judge of it from a station of heaven-inspired knowledge? A hypocrite Coleridge never was upon any subject; he never affected to know when secretly he felt himself ignorant. And yet, of the topics on which he was wont eloquently to hold forth, there was none on which he was less satisfactory—none on which he was more acute, yet none on which he was more prone to excite contradiction and irritation, if that had been allowed.

Here, for example, is a passage from one of his lectures on art:

'It is sufficient that philosophically we understand that in all imitations two elements must coexist, and not only coexist, but must be perceived as existing. Those two constituent elements are likeness and unlikeness, or sameness and difference, and in all genuine creations of art there must be a union of these disparates. The artist may take this point of view where he pleases, provided that the desired effect be perceptibly produced, that there be likeness in the difference, difference in the likeness, and a reconcilement of both in one. If there be likeness to nature without any check of difference, the result is disgusting, and the more complete the delusion the more loathsome the effect. Why are such simulations of nature as wax-work figures of men and women so disagreeable? Because, not finding the motion and the life all we expected, we are shocked as by a falsehood, every circumstance of detail, which before induced you to be interested, making the distance from truth more palpable. You set out with a supposed reality, and are disappointed and disgusted with the deception; whilst in respect to a work of genuine imitation you begin with an acknowledged total difference, and then every touch of nature gives you the pleasure of an approximation to truth.'

In this exposition there must be some oversight on the part of Coleridge. He tells us in the beginning that, if there be 'likeness to nature without any check of difference, the result is disgusting.' But the case of the wax-work, which is meant to illustrate this proposition, does not at all conform to the conditions; the result is disgusting certainly, but not from any want of difference to control the sameness, for, on the contrary, the difference is confessedly too revolting; and apparently the distinction between the two cases described is simply this—that in the illegitimate case of the wax-work the likeness comes first and the unlikeness last, whereas in the other case this order is reversed. But that distinction will neither account *in fact* for the difference of effect; nor, if it *did*, would it account upon any reason or ground suggested by Coleridge for such a difference. Let us consider this case of wax-work a little more vigilantly, and then perhaps we may find out both why it is that some men unaffectedly *are* disgusted by wax-work; and secondly, why it is that, if trained on just principles of reflective taste, all men *would* be so affected.

As a matter not altogether without importance, we may note that even the frailty of the material operates to some extent in disgusting us with wax-work. A higher temperature of the atmosphere, it strikes us too forcibly, would dispose the waxen figures to melt; and in colder seasons the horny fist of a jolly boatswain would 'pun[5] them into shivers' like so many ship-biscuits. The grandeur of permanence and durability transfers itself or its expression from the material to the impression of the artifice which moulds it, and crystallizes itself in the effect. We see continually very ingenious imitations of objects cut out in paper filigree; there have been people who showed as much of an artist's eye in this sort of work, and of an artist's hand, as Miss Linwood of the last generation in her exquisite needlework; in both cases a trick, a *tour-de-main*, was raised into the dignity of a fine art; and yet, because the slightness of the material too emphatically proclaims the essential perishableness of the result, nobody views such modes of art with more even of a momentary interest than the morning wreaths of smoke ascending so beautifully from a cottage chimney, or cares much to preserve them. The traceries of hoar frost upon the windows of inhabited rooms are not only beautiful in the highest degree, but have been shown in several French memoirs to obey laws of transcendental geometry, and also to obey physical laws of startling intricacy. These lovely forms of almighty nature wear the grandeur of mystery, of floral beauty, and of science (immanent science) not always fathomable.[6] They are anything but capricious. Solomon in all his glory was not arrayed like *them*; and yet, simply because the sad hand of mortality is upon them, because they are dedicated to death, because on genial days they will have passed into the oblivion of graves before the morning sun has mounted to his meridian, we do not so much as honour them with a transient stare from the breakfast-table. Ah, wretches that we are, the horrid carnalities of tea and toast, or else the horrid bestialities in morning journals of Chartists and Cobdenites at home, of Red Ruffians abroad, draw off our attention from the chonchoids and the cycloids pencilled by the Eternal Geometrician! and these celestial traceries of the dawn, which neither Da Vinci nor Raphaello was able to have followed as a mimic, far less as a rival, we regard as a nuisance claiming the attentions of the window-cleaner; even as the spider's web, that might absorb an angel into reverie, is honoured amongst the things banned by the housemaid. But *the* reason why the wax-work disgusts is that it seeks to reproduce in literal detail the traits that should be softened under a general diffusive impression; the likeness to nature is presented in what is essentially fleeting and subsidiary, and the 'check of difference' is found also in this very literality, and not in any effort of the etherealizing imagination, as it is in all true works of art; so that the case really stands the exact opposite of that which Coleridge had given in his definition.[7]

To pass from art to style. How loose and arbitrary Coleridge not infrequently was in face of the laws on that subject which he had himself repeatedly laid down! Could it be believed of a man so quick to feel, so rapid to arrest all phenomena, that in a matter so important as that of style, he should have nothing loftier to record of his own merits, services, reformations, or cautions, than that he has always conscientiously forborne to use the personal genitive *whose* in speaking of inanimate things? For example, that he did not say, and could not have been tempted or tortured into saying, 'The bridge *whose* piers could not much longer resist the flood.' Well, as they say in Scotland, some people are thankful for small mercies. We—that is, you, the reader, and ourselves—are *persons*; the bridge, you see, is but a *thing*. We pity it, poor thing, and, as far as it is possible to entertain such a sentiment for a bridge, we feel respect for it. Few bridges are thoroughly contemptible; and we make a point, in obedience to an old-world proverb, always to speak well of the bridge that has carried us over in safety, which the worst of bridges never yet has refused to do. But still there *are* such things as social distinctions; and we conceive that a man and a 'contributor' (an *ancient* contributor to *Blackwood*), must in the herald's college be allowed a permanent precedency before all bridges whatsoever, without regard to number of arches, width of span, or any other frivolous pretences. We acknowledge therefore with gratitude Coleridge's loyalty to his own species in not listening to any compromise with mere things, that never were nor will be raised to the peerage of personality, and sternly refusing them the verbal honours which are sacred to us humans. But what is the principle of taste upon which Coleridge justifies this rigorous practice? It is—and we think it a very just principle—that this mechanic mode of giving life to things inanimate ranks 'amongst those worst mimicries of poetic diction by which imbecile writers fancy they elevate their prose.' True; but the same spurious artifices for giving a fantastic elevation to prose reappear in a thousand other forms, from some of which neither Coleridge nor his accomplished daughter is absolutely free. For instance, one of the commonest abuses of pure English amongst our Scottish brethren, unless where they have been educated out of Scotland, is to use *aught* for *anything*, *ere* for *before*, *well-nigh* for *almost*, and scores besides. No home-bred, *i.e.* Cockney Scotchman, is aware that these are poetic forms, and are as ludicrously stilted in any ear trained by the daily habits of good society to the appreciation of pure English—as if, in Spenserian phrase, he should say, '*What time* I came home to breakfast,' instead of '*When* I came home.' The *'tis* and *'twas*, which have been superannuated for a century in England, except in poetic forms, still linger in Scotland and in Ireland, and these forms also at intervals look out from Coleridge's prose. Coleridge is also guilty at odd times (as is Wordsworth) of that most horrible affectation, the *hath* and *doth* for *has* and *does*. This is really criminal. But amongst all barbarisms known to man, the very worst—and this also, we are sorry to say, flourishes as rankly as weeds in Scotch prose, and is to be found in Coleridge's writings—is the use of the *thereof, therein, thereby, thereunto*. This monstrous expression of imperfect civilization, which for one hundred and fifty years has been cashiered by cultivated Englishmen as *attorneys' English*, and is absolutely frightful unless in a lease or conveyance, ought (we do not scruple to say) to be made indictable at common law, not perhaps as a felony, but certainly as a misdemeanour, punishable by fine and imprisonment.

In nothing is the characteristic mode of Coleridge's mind to be seen more strikingly than in his treatment of some branches of dramatic literature, though to that subject he had devoted the closest study. He was almost as distinguished, indeed, for the points he missed as for those he saw. Look at his position as regards some questions concerning the French drama and its critics, more particularly the views of Voltaire, though some explanation may be found in the fact, which I have noticed elsewhere, that Coleridge's acquaintance with the French language was not such as to enable him to read it with the easy familiarity which ensures complete pleasure. But something may also be due to his deep and absorbed religious feeling, which seemed to incapacitate him from perceiving the points where Voltaire, despite his scepticism, had planted his feet on firm ground. Coleridge was aware that Voltaire, in common with every Frenchman until the present generation, held it as a point of faith that the French drama was inapproachable in excellence. From Lessing, and chiefly, from his *Dramaturgie*, Coleridge was also aware, on the other hand, upon what erroneous grounds that imaginary pre-eminence was built. He knew that it was a total misconception of the Greek unities (excepting only as regards the unity of fable, or, as Coleridge otherwise calls it, the *unity of interest*) which had misled the French. It was a huge blunder. The case was this: Peculiar embarrassments had arisen to the Athenian dramatists as to time and place, from the chorus—out of which chorus had grown the whole drama. The chorus, composed generally of men or women, could not be moved from Susa to Memphis or from one year to another, as might the spectator. This was a fetter, but, with the address of great artists, they had turned their fetters into occasions of ornament. But, in this act of beautifying their narrow field, they had done nothing to enlarge it. They had submitted gracefully to what, for *them*, was a religious necessity. But it was ridiculous that modern dramatists, under no such necessity (because clogged with no inheritance of a personal chorus), should voluntarily assume fetters which, having no ceremonial and hallowed call for a chorus, could have no meaning. So far Coleridge was kept right by his own sagacity and by his German guides; but a very trifle of further communication with Voltaire, and with the writers of whom Voltaire was speaking, would have introduced him to two facts calculated a little to raise Voltaire in his esteem, and very much to lower the only French writer (viz., Racine) whom he ever thought fit to praise. With regard to Voltaire himself he would have found that, so far from exalting the French poetic literature *generally* in proportion to that monstrous pre-eminence which he had claimed for the French drama, on the contrary, from this very drama, from the very pre-eminence, he drew an argument for the general inferiority of the French poetry. The French drama, he argued, was confessedly exalted amongst the French themselves beyond any other section of their literature. But why? Why was this? If the drama had prospered disproportionately under public favour, what caused that favour? It was, said Voltaire, the social nature of the French, with their consequent interest in whatever assumed the attire of conversation or dialogue; and, secondly, it was the peculiar strength of their language in that one function, which had been nursed and ripened by this preponderance of social habits. Hence it happened that the drama obtained at one and the same time a greater *interest* for the French, and also (by means of this culture given to conversational forms) most unhappily for his lordship's critical discernment of flavours, as well as his Greek literature, happens to be a respectable Joe Miller from the era of Hierocles, and through *him* probably it came down from Pythagoras. Yet still Voltaire was very far indeed from being a 'scribbler.' He had the graceful levity and the graceful gaiety of his nation in an exalted degree. He had a vast compass of miscellaneous knowledge; pity that it was so disjointed, *arena sine calce*; pity that you could never rely on its accuracy; and, as respected his epic poetry, 'tis true 'tis pity, and pity 'tis 'tis true, that you are rather disposed to laugh than to cry when Voltaire solemnly proposes to be sublime. His *Henriade* originally appeared in London about 1726, when the poet was visiting this country as a fugitive before the wrath of Louis the Well-beloved; and naturally in the opening passage he determined to astonish the weak minds of us islanders by a flourish on the tight-rope of sublimity. But to his vexation a native Greek (viz., a Smyrniot), then by accident in London, called upon him immediately after the publication, and, laying his finger on a line in the exordium (as it then stood), said, 'Sare, I am one countryman of Homer's. He write de Iliad; you write de Henriade; but Homer vos never able in all de total whole of de Iliad to write de verse like dis.' Upon which the Greek showed him a certain line.

Voltaire admired the line itself, but in deference to this Greek irony, supported by the steady advice of his English friends, he finally altered it. It is possible to fail, however, as an epic poet, and very excusable for a Frenchman to fail, and yet to succeed in many other walks of literature. But to Coleridge's piety, to Coleridge's earnest seeking for light, and to Coleridge's profound sense of the necessity which connects from below all ultimate philosophy with religion, the scoffing scepticism of Voltaire would form even a stronger repulsion than his puerile hostility to Shakespeare. Even here, however, there is something to be pleaded for Voltaire. Much of his irreligion doubtless arose from a defective and unimpassioned nature, but part of it was noble, and rested upon his intolerance of cruelty, of bigotry, and of priestcraft—but still more of these qualities not germinating spontaneously, but assumed fraudulently as masques. But very little Coleridge had troubled himself to investigate Voltaire's views, even where he was supposing himself to be ranged in opposition to them.

A word or two about those accusations of plagiarism of which far too much has been made by more than one critic; we ourselves having, perhaps, been guilty of too wantonly stirring these waters at one time of our lives; and in the attempt to make matters more clear, only, it may be, succeeded in muddying them. Stolberg, Matthison, Schiller, Frederika Brun, Schelling, and others, whom he has been supposed to have robbed of trifles, he could not expect to lurk[8] in darkness, and particularly as he was actively contributing to disperse the darkness that yet hung over their names in England. But really for such bagatelles as were concerned in this poetic part of the allegation—even Bow Street, with the bloodiest Draco of a critical reviewer sitting on the bench, would not have entertained the charge. Most of us, we suppose, would be ready enough to run off with a Titian or a Correggio, provided the coast were clear, and no policemen heaving in sight; but to be suspected of pocketing a silver spoon, which, after all, would probably turn out to be made of German silver—faugh!— we not only defy the fiend and his temptations generally, but we spit in his face for such an insinuation. With respect to the pretty toy model of Hexameter and Pentameter from Schiller, we believe the case to have arisen thus: in talking of metre, and illustrating it (as Coleridge often did at tea-tables) from Homer, and then from the innumerable wooden and cast-iron imitations of it among the Germans—he would be very likely to cite this little ivory bijou from Schiller; upon which the young ladies would say: 'But, Mr. Coleridge, we do not understand German. Could you not give us an idea of it in some English version?' Then would he, with his usual obligingness, write down his mimic English echo of Schiller's German echo. And of course the young ladies, too happy to possess an autograph from the 'Ancient Mariner,' and an autograph besides having a separate interest of its own, would endorse it with the immortal initials 'S. T. C.,' after which an injunction issuing from the Court of Chancery would be quite unavailing to arrest its flight through the journals of the land as the avowed composition of Coleridge. They know little of Coleridge's habits who suppose that his attention was disposable for cases of this kind. Alike, whether he were unconsciously made by the error of a reporter to rob others, or others to rob him, he would be little likely to hear of the mistake—or, hearing of it by some rare accident, to take any pains for its correction. It is probable that such mistakes sometimes arose with others, but sometimes also with himself from imperfect recollection; and *that*, owing chiefly to his carelessness about the property at issue, so that it seemed not worth the requisite effort to vindicate the claim if it happened to be *his*, or formally to renounce it if it were not. But, however this might be, his daughter's remark remains true, and is tolerably significant, that the people whom (through anybody's mistake) he seems to have robbed were all pretty much in the sunshine of the world's regard; there was no attempt to benefit by darkness or twilight, and an intentional robber must have known that the detection was inevitable.

A second thing to be said in palliation of such plagiarisms, real or fancied, intentional or not intentional, is this—that at least Coleridge never insulted or derided those upon whose rights he is supposed to have meditated an aggression.

Coleridge has now been dead for more than fifteen years,[9] and he lived through a painful life of sixty-three years; seventy-eight years it is since he first drew that troubled air of earth, from which with such bitter loathing he rose as a phœnix might be supposed to rise, that, in retribution of some treason to his immortal race, had been compelled for a secular period to banquet on carrion with ghouls, or on the spoils of *vivisection* with vampires. Not with less horror of retrospect than such a phœnix did Coleridge, when ready to wing his flight from earth, survey the chambers of suffering through which he had trod his way from childhood to gray hairs. Perhaps amongst all the populous nations of the grave not one was ever laid there, through whose bones so mighty a thrill of shuddering anguish would creep, if by an audible whisper the sound of earth and the memories of earth could reach his coffin. Yet why? Was he not himself a child of earth? Yes, and by too strong a link: *that* it was which shattered him. For also he was a child of Paradise, and in the struggle between two natures he could not support himself erect. That dreadful conflict it was which supplanted his footing. Had he been gross, fleshly, sensual, being so framed for voluptuous enjoyment, he would have sunk away silently (as millions sink) through carnal wrecks into carnal ruin. He would have been mentioned oftentimes with a sigh of regret as that youthful author who had enriched the literature of his country with two exquisite poems, 'Love' and the

'Ancient Mariner,' but who for some unknown reason had not fulfilled his apparent mission on earth. As it was, being most genial and by his physical impulses most luxurious; yet, on the other hand, by fiery aspirations of intellect and of spiritual heart being coerced as if through torments of magical spells into rising heavenwards for ever, into eternal commerce with the grander regions of his own nature, he found this strife too much for his daily peace, too imperfect was the ally which he found in his will; treachery there was in his own nature, and almost by a necessity he yielded to the dark temptations of opium. That 'graspless hand,' from which, as already in one of his early poems (November, 1794) he had complained—

'Drop friendship's priceless pearls as hour-glass sands,'

was made much *more* graspless, and in this way the very graces of his moral nature ministered eventually the heaviest of his curses. Most unworldly he was, most unmercenary, and (as somebody has remarked) even to a disease, and, in such a degree as if an organ had been forgotten by Nature in his composition, disregardful of self. But even in these qualities lay the baits for his worldly ruin, which subsequently caused or allowed so much of his misery. Partly from the introversion of his mind, and its habitual sleep of reverie in relation to all external interests, partly from his defect in all habits of prudential forecasting, resting his head always on the pillow of the *present*—he had been carried rapidly past all openings that offered towards the creation of a fortune before he even heard of them, and he first awoke to the knowledge that such openings had ever existed when he looked back upon them from a distance, and found them already irrecoverable for ever.

Such a case as this, as soon as it became known that the case stood connected with so much power of intellect and so much of various erudition, was the very ideal case that challenges aid from the public purse. Mrs. Coleridge has feelingly noticed the philosophic fact. It was the case of a man lame in the faculties which apply to the architecture of a fortune, but lame through the very excess in some other faculties that qualified him for a public teacher, or (which is even more requisite) for a public stimulator of powers else dormant.

A perfect romance it is that settles upon three generations of these Coleridges; a romance of beauty, of intellectual power, of misfortune suddenly illuminated from heaven, of prosperity suddenly overcast by the waywardness of the individual. The grandfather of the present generation, who for us stands forward as the founder of the family, viz., the Rev. John Coleridge; even *his* career wins a secret homage of tears and smiles in right of its marvellous transitions from gloom to sudden light, in right of its entire simplicity, and of its eccentric consistency. Already in early youth, swimming against a heady current of hindrances almost overwhelming, he had by solitary efforts qualified himself for any higher situation that might offer. But, just as this training was finished, the chances that it might ever turn to account suddenly fell down to zero; for precisely then did domestic misfortunes oblige his father to dismiss him from his house with one solitary half-crown and his paternal benediction. What became of the half-crown is not recorded, but the benediction speedily blossomed into fruit. The youth had sat down by the roadside under the mere oppression of grief for his blighted prospects. But gradually and by steps the most unexpected and providential, he was led to pedagogy and through this to his true destination—that of a clergyman of the English church—a position which from his learning, his devotion, and even from his very failings—failings in businesslike foresight and calculation—his absence of mind, his charitable feelings, and his true docility of nature, he was fitted to adorn; and, indeed, but for his eccentricities and his complete freedom from worldly self-seeking, and indifference to such considerations as are apt to weigh all too little with his fellows of the cloth, he might have moved as an equal among the most eminent scholars and thinkers. Beautiful are the alternate phases of a good parish priest—now sitting at the bedside of a dying neighbour, and ministering with guidance and consolation to the labouring spirit—now sitting at midnight under the lamp of his own study, and searching the holy oracles of inspiration for light inexhaustible. These pictures were realized in J. Coleridge's life.

Mr. Wordsworth has done much to place on an elevated pedestal a very different type of parish priest—Walker of Seathwaite. The contrast between him and John Coleridge is striking; and not only striking but apt, from some points of view, to move something of laughter as well as tears. The strangest thing is that, if some demon of mischief tempts us, a hurly-burly begins again of laughter and mockery among that ancient brotherhood of hills, like Handel's chorus in 'l'Allegro' of 'laughter holding both his sides.'

'Old Skiddaw blowsHis speaking-trumpet; back out of the cloudsOn Glaramara, "*I say, Walker*" rings;And Kirkstone "goes it" from his misty head.'

The Rev. Walker, of Seathwaite, it is recorded, spent most of his time in the parish church; but doing what? Why, spinning; *always* spinning wool on the steps of the altar, and only *sometimes* lecturing his younger parishioners in the spelling-book. So passed his life. And, if you feel disposed to say, '*An innocent life!*' you must immediately add from Mr. Wordsworth's 'Ruth,' '*An innocent life, but far astray!*' What time had he for writing sermons? The Rev. John Coleridge wrote an exegetical work on the Book of Judges; we doubt whether Walker could have spelt *exegetical*. And supposing the Bishop of

Chester, in whose diocese his parish lay, had suddenly said, 'Walker, *unde derivatur "exegesis"*?' Walker must have been walked off into the corner, as a punishment for answering absurdly. But luckily the Bishop's palace stood ninety and odd miles south of Walker's two spinning-wheels. For, observe, he had *two* spinning-wheels, but he hadn't a single Iliad. Mr. Wordsworth will say that Walker did something besides spinning and spelling. What was it? Why, he read a little. A *very* little, I can assure you. For *when* did he read? Never but on a Saturday afternoon. And *what* did Walker read? Doubtless now it was Hooker, or was it Jeremy Taylor, or Barrow? No; it was none of these that Walker honoured by his Saturday studies, but a magazine. Now, we all know what awful rubbish the magazines of those days carted upon men's premises. It would have been indictable as a nuisance if a publisher had laid it down *gratis* at your door. Had Walker lived in *our* days, the case would have been very different. A course of *Blackwood* would have braced his constitution; his spinning-wheel would have stopped; his spelling would have improved into moral philosophy and the best of politics. This very month, as the public is by this time aware, Walker would have read something about himself that *must* have done him good. We might very truly have put an advertisement into the *Times* all last month, saying, 'Let Walker look into the next *Blackwood*, and he will hear of something greatly to his advantage.' But alas! Walker descended to Hades, and most ingloriously as *we* contend, before *Blackwood* had dawned upon a benighted earth. We differ therefore by an inexpressible difference from Wordsworth's estimate of this old fellow. And we close our account of him by citing two little sallies from his only known literary productions, viz., two letters, one to a friend, and the other to the Archbishop of York. In the first of these he introduces a child of his own under the following flourish of rhetoric, viz., as 'a pledge of conjugal endearment.' We doubt if his correspondent ever read such a bit of sentiment before. In the other letter, addressed to the Metropolitan of the province, Walker has the assurance to say that he trusts the young man, his son (*not* the aforesaid cub, the pledge of conjugal endearment) will never disgrace the *paternal* example, *i.e.*, Walker's example. Pretty strong *that*! And, if exegetically handled, it must mean that Walker, junr., is to continue spinning and spelling, as also once a week reading the *Town and Country Magazine*, all the days of his life. Oh, Walker, you're a very sad fellow! And the only excuse for you is, that, like most of your brethren in that mountainous nook of England, so beautiful but so poor, you never saw the academic bowers of either Oxford or Cambridge.

Both in prose and verse, much prose and a short allowance of verse, has Wordsworth celebrated this man, and he has held him aloft like the saintly Herbert[10] as a shining model of a rural priest. We are glad, therefore, for Wordsworth's sake, that no judge from the Consistorial Court ever happened to meet with Walker when trudging over the Furness Fells to Ulverston with a *long* cwt. (120 lb. avoirdupois) of wool on his back, a thing which he did in all weathers. The wool would have been condemned as a good prize, and we much fear that Walker's gown would have been stripped over his head; which is a sad catastrophe for a pattern priest. Mr. John Coleridge came much nearer to Chaucer's model of a *Parish* Priest, whilst at the same time he did honour to the Academic standard of such a priest. He loved his poor parishioners as children confided to his pastoral care, but he also loved his library. But, on the other hand, as to Walker, if ever *he* were seen burning the midnight oil, it was not in a gentleman's study—it was in a horrid garret or cock-loft at the top of his house, disturbing the 'conjugal endearments' of roosting fowl, and on a business the least spiritual that can be imagined. By ancient usage throughout this sequestered region, which is the Savoy of England (viz., Cumberland, Westmoreland, and Furness) all accounts are settled annually at Candlemas, which means the middle of February. From Christmas, therefore, to this period the reverend pastor was employed in making out bills, receipts, leases and releases, charges and discharges, wills and codicils to wills for most of the hardworking householders amongst his flock. This work paid better than spinning. By this night work, by the summer work of cutting peats and mowing grass, by the autumnal work of reaping barley and oats, and the early winter work of taking up potatoes, the reverend gentleman could average seven shillings a day besides beer. But meantime our spiritual friend was poaching on the manors of the following people—of the chamber counsel, of the attorney, of the professional accountant, of the printer and compositor, of the notary public, of the scrivener, and sometimes, we fear, of the sheriff's officer in arranging for special bail. These very uncanonical services one might have fancied sufficient, with spinning and spelling, for filling up the temporal cares of any one man's time. But this restless Proteus masqueraded through a score of other characters—as seedsman, harvester, hedger and ditcher, etc. We have no doubt that he would have taken a job of paving; he would have contracted for darning old Christopher's silk stockings, or for a mile of sewerage; or he would have contracted to dispose by night of the sewage (which the careful reader must not confound with the sewerage, that being the ship and the sewage the freight). But all this coarse labour makes a man's hands horny, and, what is worse, the starvation, or, at least, impoverishment, of his intellect makes his mind horny; and, what is worst of all in a clergyman, who is stationed as a watchman on a church-steeple expressly to warn all others against the all-besetting danger of worldliness, such an incessant preoccupation of the heart by coarse and petty cares makes the spiritual apprehensiveness and every organ of spiritual sensibility more horny than the hoofs of a rhinoceros.

Kindliness of heart, no doubt, remained to the last with Mr. Walker, *that* being secured by the universal spirit of brotherly and social feeling amongst the dalesmen of the lake district. He was even liberal and generous, if we may rely upon the few instances reported by W. W. His life of heroic money-getting had not, it seems, made his heart narrow in that particular direction, though it must not be forgotten that the calls upon him were rare and trivial. But however *that* may have been, the heart of stone had usurped upon the heart of flesh in all that regarded the spiritualities of his office. He was conscientious, we dare say, in what related to the *sacramentum militaire* (as construed by himself) of his pastoral soldiership. He would, perhaps, have died for the doctrines of his church, and we do not like him the worse for having been something of a bigot, being ourselves the most malignant of Tories (thank Heaven for all its mercies!). But what tenderness or pathetic breathings of spirituality *could* that man have, who had no time beyond a few stray quarters of an hour for thinking of his own supreme relations to heaven, or to his flock on behalf of heaven? How could that man cherish or deepen the motions of religious truth within himself, whose thoughts were habitually turned to the wool market? Ninety and odd years he lived on earth labouring like a bargeman or a miner. Assuredly he was not one of the *fainéans*. And within a narrow pastoral circle he left behind him a fragrant memory that will, perhaps, wear as long as most reputations in literature. Nay, he even acquired by acclamation a sort of title, viz., the posthumous surname of the *wonderful*; pointing, however, we fear, much less to anything in himself than to the unaccountable amount of money which he left behind him—unaccountable by comparison with any modes of industry which he practised, all of which were indomitably persevering, but all humble in their results. Finally, he has had the honour (which, much we fear, men far more interesting in the same situation, but in a less homely way, never *would* have had) of a record from the pen of Wordsworth. We and others have always remarked it as one of the austere Roman features in the mind of Wordsworth, that of all poets he has the least sympathy, effeminate or not effeminate, with romantic disinterestedness. He cannot bear to hear of a man working by choice for nothing, which certainly *is* an infirmity, where at all it arises from want of energy or of just self-appreciation, but still an amiable one, and in certain directions a sublime one. Walker had no such infirmity. He laboured in those fields which ensure instant payment. Verily he *had* his reward: ten per cent., at least, beyond all other men, without needing to think of reversions, either above or below. The unearthly was suffocated in *him* by the earthly. Let us leave him, and return to a better man, viz., to the Rev. John Coleridge, author of the *Quale-quare-quidditive* case—a man equal in simplicity of habits and in humility, but better in the sight of God, because he laboured in the culture of his higher and not his lower faculties.

Mr. John Coleridge married a second time; and we are perplexed to say *when*. The difficulty is this: he had by his second wife ten children. Now, as *the* Coleridge, the youngest of the flock, was born in 1772, the space between that year and 1760 seems barely adequate to such a succession of births. Yet, on the other hand, *before* 1760 he could not probably have seen his second wife, unless, indeed, on some casual trip to Devonshire. Her name was Anne Bowden; and she was of a respectable family, that had been long stationary in Devonshire, but of a yeomanly rank; and people of that rank a century back did not often make visits as far as Southampton. The question is not certainly of any great importance; and we notice it only to make a parade of our chronologic acumen. Devilish sly is Josy Bagstock! It is sufficient that her last child was her illustrious child; and, if S. T. C.'s theory has any foundation, we must suppose him illustrious *because* he was the last. For he imagines that in any long series of children the last will, according to all experience, have the leonine share of intellect. But this contradicts our own personal observation; and, besides, it seems to be unsound upon an *à priori* ground, viz., that to be the first child carries a meaning with it: *that* place in the series has a real physiologic value; and we have known families in which, from generation to generation, the first-born child had physical advantages denied to all that followed. But to be the last child must very often be the result of accident, and has in reality no meaning in any sense known to nature. The sixth child, let us suppose, is a blockhead. And soon after the birth of this sixth child, his father, being drunk, breaks his neck. That accident cannot react upon this child to invest him with the privileges of absolute juniority. Being a blockhead, he will remain a blockhead. Yet he is the youngest; but, then, nature is no party to his being such, and probably she is no party (by means of any physical change in the parents) once in a thousand births to a case of absolute and predeterminate juniority.

Whether with or without the intention of nature, S. T. C. was fated to be the last of his family. He was the tenth child of the second flock, and possibly there might have been an eleventh or even a twentieth, but for the following termination of his father's career, which we give in the words of his son. 'Towards the latter end of September, 1781, my father went to Plymouth with my brother Francis, who was to go out as' (a) 'midshipman under Admiral Graves—a friend of my father's. He settled Frank as he wished, and returned on the 4th of October, 1781. He arrived at Exeter about six o'clock, and was pressed to take a bed there by the friendly family of the Harts; but he refused, and, to avoid their entreaties, he told them that he had never been superstitious, but that the night before he had had a dream, which had made a deep impression on him. He dreamed that Death had appeared to him, as he is commonly painted, and had touched him with his dart. Well, he returned home; and all his family, *I* excepted, were up. He told my mother his dream; but he was in good health and high spirits; and there was a bowl of punch made, and my father gave a long and particular account of his travels, and that he had placed Frank under a religious captain, and so forth. At length he went to bed, very well and in high spirits. A short time after he had lain down, he complained of a pain to which he was subject. My mother got him some peppermint water, which he took; and after a pause he said, "I am much better now, my dear!" and lay down again. In a minute my mother heard a noise in his throat, and spoke to him; but he did not answer, and she spoke repeatedly in vain. Her shriek awaked me, and I said, "Papa is dead!" I did not know of my father's return, but I knew that he was expected. How I came to think of his death, I cannot tell; but so it was. Dead he was. Some said it was gout in the heart; probably it was a fit of apoplexy. He was an Israelite without guile, simple, generous; and, taking some Scripture texts in their literal sense, he was conscientiously indifferent to the good and evil of this world.'

This was the account of his father's sudden death in 1781, written by S. T. Coleridge in 1797. 'Thirty years afterwards' (but after 1781 or after 1797?), says Mr. H. N. Coleridge, 'S. T. C. breathed a wish for such a death, "if," he added, "like him I were an Israelite without guile!" and then added, "The image of my father, my revered, kind, learned, simple-hearted father, is a religion to me."'

In his ninth year, therefore, thus early and thus suddenly, Coleridge lost his father; and in the result, though his mother lived for many a year after, he became essentially an orphan, being thrown upon the struggles of this world, and for ever torn from his family, except as a visitor when equally he and they had changed. Yet such is the world, and so inevitably does it grow thorns amongst its earliest roses, that even that dawn of life when he had basked in the smiles of two living parents, was troubled for *him* by a dark shadow that followed his steps or ran before him, obscuring his light upon every path. This was Francis Coleridge, one year older, that same boy whom his father had in his last journey upon earth accompanied to Plymouth.

We shall misconceive the character of Francis if we suppose him to have been a boy of bad nature. He turned out a gallant young man, and perished at twenty-one from over exertion in Mysore, during the first war with Tippoo Sahib. How he came to be transferred from the naval to the land service, is a romantic story, for which, as it has no relation to *the* Coleridge, we cannot find room.

In that particular relation, viz., to *the* Coleridge, Francis may seem at first to have been unamiable, and especially since the little Samuel was so entirely at the mercy of his superior hardiness and strength; but, in fact, his violence arose chiefly from the contempt natural to a bold adventurous nature for a nursery pet, and a contempt irritated by a counter admiration which he could not always refuse. 'Frank,' says S. T. C., looking back to these childish days, 'had a violent love of beating me; but, whenever *that* was superseded by any humour or circumstances, he was always very fond of me, and used to regard me with a strange mixture of admiration and contempt. Strange it was not; for he hated books, and loved climbing, fighting, playing, robbing orchards, to distraction.'

In the latter part of 1778, when S. T. C. was six years old, and recently admitted to King's School at Ottery, he and his brother George (that brother to whom his early poems were afterwards dedicated) caught a putrid fever at the same time. But on this occasion Frank displayed his courageous kindness; for, in contempt of orders to the contrary, and in contempt of the danger, he stole up to the bedside of little Samuel and read Pope's 'Homer' to him. This made it evident that Frank's partiality for thumping S. T. C. did really arise very much out of a lurking love for him; since George, though a most amiable boy, and ill of the same fever in another room, was left to get well in the usual way, by medicine and slops, without any thumping certainly, but also without any extra consolations from either Iliad or Odyssey. But what ministered perpetual fuel to the thumping-mania of Francis Coleridge was a furor of jealousy—strangely enough not felt by him, but felt *for* him by his old privileged nurse. She could not inspire her own passions into Francis, but she could point his scorn to the infirmities of his rival. Francis had once reigned paramount in the vicarage as universal pet. But he had been dethroned by Samuel, who now reigned in his stead. Samuel felt no triumph at that revolution; Francis no anger. But the nurse suffered the pangs of a baffled stepmother, and looked with novercal eyes of hatred and disgust upon little Sam that had stolen away the hearts of men and women from one that in *her* eyes was a thousand times his superior. In that last point nurse was not so entirely wrong, but that nine-tenths of the world (and therefore, we fear, of our dearly-beloved readers) would have gone along with her, on which account it is that we have forborne to call her 'wicked old nurse.' Francis Coleridge, her own peculiar darling, was memorable for his beauty. All the brothers were handsome—'remarkably handsome,' says S. T. C., 'but *they*,' he adds, 'were as inferior to Francis as *I* am to *them*.'[11]

Reading this and other descriptions of Frank Coleridge's beauty (in our Indian army he was known as the *handsome Coleridge*), we are disposed to cry out with Juliet,

'Beautiful tyrant! fiend angelical!Dove-feathered raven!'

when we find how very nearly his thoughtless violence had hurried poor S. T. C. into an early death. The story is told circumstantially by Coleridge himself in one of the letters to Mr. Poole; nor is there any scene more picturesque than this hasty sketch in Brookes's 'Fool of Quality.' We must premise that S. T. C. had asked his mother for a particular indulgence requiring some dexterity to accomplish. The difficulty, however, through *her* cautious manipulations, had just been surmounted, when Samuel left the room for a single instant, and found upon his return that the beautiful Francis had confounded all Mama's labours, and had defeated his own enjoyment. What followed is thus told by Samuel nearly twenty years after: 'I returned, saw the exploit, and flew at Frank. He pretended to have been seriously hurt by my blow, flung himself upon the ground, and there lay with outstretched limbs.' This is good comedy: the pugnacious Frank affecting to be an Abel, killed by a blow from Cain such as doubtless would not have 'made a dint in a pound of butter.' But wait a little. Samuel was a true penitent as ever was turned off for fratricide at Newgate. 'I,' says the unhappy murderer, 'hung over him mourning and in great fright;' but the murdered Frank by accident came to life again. 'He leaped up, and with a hoarse laugh gave me a severe blow in the face.' This was too much. To have your grief flapped back in your face like a wet sheet is bad, but also and at the same time to have your claret uncorked is unendurable. The 'Ancient Mariner,' then about seven years old, could not stand this. 'With *his* cross-bow'—no, stop! what are we saying? Nothing better than a kitchen knife was at hand—and 'this,' says Samuel, 'I seized, and was running at him, when my mother came in and took me by the arm. I expected a whipping, and, struggling from her, I ran away to a little hill or slope, at the bottom of which the Otter flows, about a mile from Ottery. There I stayed, my rage died away; but my obstinacy vanquished my fears, and taking out a shilling book, which had at the end morning and evening prayers, I very devoutly repeated them, thinking at the same time with a gloomy inward satisfaction how miserable my mother must be. I distinctly remember my feelings when I saw a Mr. Vaughan pass over the bridge at about a furlong's distance, and how I watched the calves in the fields beyond the river. It grew dark, and I fell asleep. It was towards the end of October, and it proved a stormy night. I felt the cold in my sleep, and dreamed that I was pulling the blanket over me, and actually pulled over me a dry thorn-bush which lay on the ground near me. In my sleep I had rolled from the top of the hill till within three yards of the river, which flowed by the unfenced edge of the bottom. I awoke several times, and, finding myself wet and cold and stiff, closed my eyes again that I might forget it.

'In the meantime my mother waited about half an hour, expecting my return when the *sulks* had evaporated. I not returning, she sent into the churchyard and round the town. Not found! Several men and all the boys were sent out to ramble about and seek me. In vain. My mother was almost distracted, and at ten o'clock at night I was cried by the crier in Ottery and in two villages near it, with a reward offered for me. No one went to bed; indeed, I believe half the town were up all the night. To return to myself. About five in the morning, or a little after, I was broad awake, and attempted to get up and walk, but I could not move. I saw the shepherds and workmen at a distance and cried, but so faintly that it was impossible to hear me thirty yards off. And there I might have lain and died, for I was now almost given over, the ponds, and even the river (near which I was lying), having been dragged. But providentially Sir Stafford Northcote, who had been out all night, resolved to make one other trial, and came so near that he heard me crying. He carried me in his arms for nearly a quarter of a mile, when we met my father and Sir Stafford's servants. I remember, and never shall forget, my father's face as he looked upon me while I lay in the servant's arms—so calm, and the tears stealing down his face, for I was the child of his old age. My mother, as you may suppose, was outrageous with joy. Meantime in rushed a young lady, crying out, "*I hope you'll whip him, Mrs. Coleridge.*" This woman still lives at Ottery, and neither philosophy nor religion has been able to conquer the antipathy which I feel towards her whenever I see her.' So says Samuel. We ourselves have not yet seen this young lady, and now in 1849, considering that it is about eighty years from the date of her wickedness, it seems unlikely that we shall. But *our* antipathy we declare to be also, alas! quite unconquerable by the latest supplements to the Transcendental philosophy that we have yet received from Deutschland. Whip the Ancient Mariner, indeed! A likely thing *that*: and at the very moment when he was coming off such a hard night's duty, and supporting a character which a classical Roman has pronounced to be a spectacle for Olympus—viz., that of '*Puer bonus cum malâ-fortunâ compositus*' (a virtuous boy matched in duel with adversity)! The sequel of the adventure is thus reported: 'I was put to bed, and recovered in a day or so. But I was certainly injured; for I was weakly and subject to ague for many years after.' Yes; and to a worse thing than ague, as not so certainly to be cured, viz., rheumatism. More than twenty years after this cold night's rest, *à la belle étoile*, we can vouch that Coleridge found himself obliged to return suddenly from a tour amongst the Scottish Highlands solely in consequence of that painful rheumatic affection, which was perhaps traceable to this childish misadventure. Alas! Francis the beautiful scamp, that caused the misadventure, and probably the bad young lady that prescribed whipping as the orthodox medicine for curing it, and the poor Ancient Mariner himself—that had to fight his way through such enemies at the price of ague, rheumatism, and tears uncounted—are all asleep at present, but in graves how widely divided! One near London; one near Seringapatam; and the young lady, we suppose, in Ottery churchyard, but her offence, though beyond the power of Philosophy to pardon, is not remembered, we trust, in her epitaph!

We are sorry that S. T. C. having been so much of a darling with his father, and considering that he looked back to the brief connection between them as solemnized by its pathetic termination, had not reported some parts of their graver intercourse. One such fragment he does report; it is an elementary lesson upon astronomy, which his father gave him in the course of a walk upon a starry night. This is in keeping with the grandeur and responsibility of the paternal relation. But really, in the only other example (which immediately occurs) of Papa's attempt to bias the filial intellect, we recognise nothing but what is mystical; and involuntarily we think of him in the modern slang character of 'governor,' rather than as a 'guide, philosopher, and friend.' It seems that one Saturday, about the time when the Rev. Walker in Furness must have been sitting down to his *exegesis* of hard sayings in the *Town and Country Magazine*, the Rev. Coleridge thought fit to reward S. T. C. for the most singular act of virtue that we have ever heard imputed to man or boy—to 'saint, to savage, or to sage'—viz., the act of eating beans and bacon to a large amount. The stress must be laid on the word *large*; because simply to masticate beans and bacon, we do not recollect to have been regarded with special esteem by the learned vicar; it was the liberal consumption of them that entitled Samuel to reward. That reward was one penny, so that in degree of merit, after all, the service may not have ranked high. But what perplexes us is the *kind* of merit. Did it bear some mystical or symbolic sense? Was it held to argue a spirit of general rebellion against Philosophy, that S. T. C. should so early in life, by one and the same act, proclaim mutinous disposition towards two of the most memorable amongst earth's philosophers—Moses and Pythagoras; of whom the latter had set his face against beans, laying it down for his opinion that to eat beans and to cut one's father's throat were acts of about equal atrocity; whilst the other, who tolerated the beans, had expressly forbidden the bacon? We are really embarrassed; finding the mere fact recorded with no further declaration of the rev. governor's reasons, than that such an 'attachment' (an *attachment* to beans and bacon!) 'ought to be encouraged'; but upon what principle we no more understand than we do the principle of the *Quale-quare-quidditive* case.

The letters in which these early memorabilia of Coleridge's life are reported did not proceed beyond the fifth. We regret this greatly, for they would have become instructively interesting as they came more and more upon the higher ground of his London experience in a mighty world of seven hundred boys—insulated in a sort of monastic but troubled seclusion amongst the billowy world of London; a seclusion that in itself was a wilderness to a home-sick child, but yet looking verdant as an oasis amongst that other wilderness of the illimitable metropolis.

It is good to be mamma's darling; but not, reader, if you are to leave mamma's arms for a vast public school in childhood. It is good to be the darling of a kind, pious, and learned father—but not if that father is to be torn away from you for ever by a death without a moment's warning, whilst as yet you yourself are but nine years old, and he has not bestowed a thought on your future establishment in life. Upon poor S. T. C. the Benjamin of his family, descended first a golden dawn within the Paradise of his father's and his mother's smiles—descended secondly and suddenly an overcasting hurricane of separation from both father and mother for ever. How dreadful, if audibly declared, this sentence to a poor nerve-shattered child: Behold! thou art commanded, before thy first decennium is completed, to see father and mother no more, and to throw thyself into the wilderness of London. Yet *that* was the destiny of Coleridge. At nine years old he was precipitated into the stormy arena of Christ's Hospital. Amongst seven hundred boys he was to fight his way to distinction; and with no other advantages of favour or tenderness than would have belonged to the son of a footman. Sublime are these democratic institutions rising upon the bosom of aristocratic England. Great is the people amongst whom the foundations of kings *can* assume this popular character. But yet amidst the grandeur of a national triumph is heard, at intervals, the moaning of individuals; and from many a grave in London rises from time to time, in arches of sorrow audible to God, the lamentation of many a child seeking to throw itself round for comfort into some distant grave of the provinces, where rest the ear and the heart of its mother.

Concerning this chapter of Coleridge's childhood, we have therefore at present no vestige of any record beyond the exquisite sketches of his schoolfellow, Charles Lamb. The five letters, however, though going over so narrow a space, go far enough to throw a pathetic light upon Coleridge's frailties of temperament. They indicate the sort of nervous agitation arising from contradictory impulses, from love too tender, and scorn too fretful, by which already in childish days the inner peace had been broken up, and the nervous system shattered. This revelation, though so unpretending and simple in manner, of the drama substantially so fearful, that was constantly proceeding in a quiet and religious parsonage—the bare possibility that sufferings so durable in their effects should be sweeping with their eternal storms a heart so capacious and so passively unresisting—are calculated to startle and to oppress us with the sense of a fate long prepared, vested in the very seeds of constitution and character; temperament and the effects of early experience combining to thwart all the morning promise of greatness and splendour; the flower unfolding its silken leaves only to suffer canker and blight; and to hang withering on the stalk, with only enough of grace and colour left to tell pathetically to all that looked upon it what it might have been.

EDITOR'S NOTE TO THIS ESSAY.

Certainly this idea of De Quincey about the misfortune to Coleridge of the early loss of his father, separation from his mother, and removal from Devon to London, is fully borne out by the more personal utterances to be found in Coleridge's poems. Looking through them with this idea in view, we are surprised at the deposit left in them by this conscious experience on Coleridge's part. Not to dwell at all on what might be very legitimately regarded as *indirect* expressions of the sentiment, we shall present here, in order to add emphasis to De Quincey's position, some of the extracts which have most impressed us. From the poem in the Early Poems 'To an Infant,' are these lines:

'Man's breathing miniature! thou mak'st me sigh—A babe art thou—and such a thing am I,To anger rapid and as soon appeased,For trifles mourning and by trifles pleased,Break friendship's mirror with a tetchy blow,Yet snatch what coals of fire on pleasure's altar glow.'

Still more emphatic is this passage from the poem, 'Frost at Midnight':

'My babe so beautiful! it thrills my heartWith tender gladness thus to look at thee,And think that thou shalt learn far other lore,And in far other scenes! For I was rearedIn the great city, pent 'mid cloisters dim,And saw nought lovely but the sky and stars.But thou, my babe! shalt wander like a breezeBy lakes and sandy shores beneath the cragsOf ancient mountain, and beneath the clouds,Which image in their bulk both lakes and shoresAnd mountain crags; so shalt thou see and hearThe lovely shapes and sounds intelligibleOf that eternal language, which thy GodUtters, who from eternity doth teachHimself in all and all things in Himself.Great Universal Teacher! he shall mouldThy spirit, and by giving make it ask.'

In another place, when speaking of the love of mother for child and that of child for mother, awakened into life by the very impress of that love in voice and touch, he concludes with the line:

'Why was I made for Love and Love denied to me?'

And, most significant of all, is that Dedication in 1803 of his Early Poems to his brother, the Rev. George Coleridge of Ottery St. Mary, when he writes, after having dwelt on the bliss this brother had enjoyed in never having been really removed from the place of his early nurture:

'To me the Eternal Wisdom hath dispensedA different fortune, and more different mind—Me, from the spot where first I sprang to lightToo soon transplanted, ere my soul had fixedIts first domestic loves; and hence, through lifeChasing chance-started friendships. A brief whileSome have preserved me from life's pelting ills,But like a tree with leaves of feeble stem,If the clouds lasted, and a sudden breezeRuffled the boughs, they on my head at onceDropped the collected shower: and some most false,False and fair-foliaged as the manchineel,Have tempted me to slumber in their shadeE'en 'mid the storm; then breathing subtlest dampsMixed their own venom with the rain from Heaven,That I woke poisoned! But (all praise to HimWho gives us all things) more have yielded mePermanent shelter: and beside one friend,Beneath the impervious covert of one oakI've raised a lowly shed and know the nameOf husband and of father; not unhearingOf that divine and nightly-whispering voice,Which from my childhood to maturer yearsSpake to me of predestinated wreaths,Bright with no fading colours!Yet, at times,My soul is sad, that I have roamed through lifeStill most a stranger, most with naked heart,At mine own home and birthplace: chiefly thenWhen I remember thee, my earliest friend!Thee, who didst watch my boyhood and my youth;Did'st trace my wanderings with a father's eye;And, boding evil yet still hoping good,Rebuked each fault and over all my woesSorrowed in silence!'

And certainly all this only gains emphasis from the entry we have in the 'Table Talk' under date August 16, 1832, and under the heading, 'Christ's Hospital, Bowyer':

'The discipline of Christ's Hospital in my time was ultra-Spartan; all domestic ties were to be put aside. "Boy!" I remember Bowyer saying to me once when I was crying the first day of my return after the holidays. "Boy! the school is your father! Boy! the school is your mother! Boy! the school is your brother! the school is your sister! the school is your first cousin, and all the rest of your relations! Let's have no more crying!"'

FOOTNOTES:

[1] Really now I can't say that. No; I couldn't have stood Cruger's arguments. 'Ditto to Mr. Burke' is certainly not a very brilliant observation, but still it's supportable, whereas I must have found the pains of contradiction insupportable.

[2] This sublimest of all Greek poets did really die, as some biographers allege, by so extraordinary and, as one may say, so insulting a mistake on the part of an eagle.

[3] *Frankistan.*—There is no word, but perhaps Frankistan might come nearest to such a word, for expressing the territory of Christendom taken jointly with that of those Mahometan nations which have for a long period been connected with Christians in their hostilities, whether of arms or of policy. The Arabs and the Moors belong to these nations, for the circle of their political system has always been made up in part by a segment from Christendom, their relations of war being still more involved with such a segment.

[4] 'Merry Wives of Windsor,' Act I., Sc. 4. Mrs. Quickly: '... An honest, willing, kind fellow, as ever servant shall come in house withal; and I warrant you no tell-tale, nor no breed-hate; his worst fault is, that he is given to prayer; he is something peevish that way; but nobody but has his fault—but let that pass.'—ED.

[5] '*Pun them into shivers*': Troilus and Cressida, Act II., Sc. 1. We refer specially to the jolly boatswain, having already noticed the fact, that sailors as a class, from retaining more of the simplicity and quick susceptibility belonging to childhood, are unusually fond of waxen exhibitions. Too much worldly experience indisposes men to the playfulness and to the *toyfulness* (if we may invent that word) of childhood, not less through the ungenial churlishness which it gradually deposits, than through the expansion of understanding which it promotes.

[6] '*Science not always fathomable.*' Several distinguished Frenchmen have pursued a course of investigations into these fenestral phenomena, which one might call the *Fata Morgana of Frost*; and, amongst these investigators, some—not content with watching, observing, recording—have experimented on these floral prolusions of nature by arranging beforehand the circumstances and conditions into which and under which the Frost Fairy should be allowed to play. But what was the result? Did they catch the Fairy? Did they chase her into her secret cells and workshops? Did they throw over the freedom of her motions a harness of net-work of coercion as the Pagans over their pitiful Proteus? So far from it, that the more they studied the less they understood; and all the traps which they laid for the Fairy, did but multiply her evasions.

[7] The passage occurs at p. 354, vol. ii. of the *Lectures*; and we now find, on looking to the place, that the illustration is drawn from 'a dell of lazy Sicily.' The same remark has virtually been anticipated at p. 181 of the same volume in the rule about 'converting mere abstractions into persons.'

[8] It is true that Mr. De Quincey *did* make the mistake of supposing Coleridge to have 'calculated on' a remark which Mrs. Coleridge justly characterises as a blind one. It *was* blind as compared with the fact resulting from grounds not then known; else it was *not* blind as a reasonable inference under the same circumstances.

[9] If for the words 'more than fifteen years' we say sixteen or seventeen, as Coleridge died in 1834, this article would be written in 1850 or 1851.—ED.

[10] 'The Saintly Herbert,' the brother, oddly enough, of the brilliant but infidel Lord Herbert of Cherbury; which lord was a versatile man of talent, but not a man of genius like the humble rustic—his unpretending brother.

[11] In saying this, Coleridge unduly disparaged his own personal advantages. In youth, and before sorrow and the labour of thought had changed him, he must have been of very engaging appearance. The *godlike forehead*, which afterwards was ascribed to him, could not have been wanting at any age. That exquisite passage in Wordsworth's description of him,

'And a pale face, that seem'd undoubtedlyAs if a blooming face it ought to be,'

had its justification in those early days. If to be blooming was the natural tendency and right of his face, blooming it then was, as we have been assured by different women of education and taste, who saw him at twenty-four in Bristol and Clifton. Two of these were friends of Hannah More, and had seen all the world. They could judge: that is, they could judge in conformity to the highest standards of taste; and both said, with some enthusiasm, that he was a most attractive young man; one adding, with a smile at the old pastoral name, 'Oh, yes, he was a perfect Strephon.' Light he was in those days and agile as a feathered Mercury; whereas he afterwards grew heavy and at times bloated; and at that gay period of life his animal spirits ran up *naturally* to the highest point on the scale; whereas in later life, when most tempestuous, they seemed most artificial. That this, which was the ardent testimony of females, was also the true one, might have been gathered from the appearance of his children. Berkeley died an infant, and him only we never saw. The sole daughter of Coleridge, as she inherited so much of her father's intellectual power, inherited also the diviner part of his features. The upper part of her face, at seventeen, when last we saw her, seemed to us angelic, and pathetically angelic; for the whole countenance was suffused by a pensive nun-like beauty too charming and too affecting ever to be forgotten. Derwent, the youngest son, we have not seen since boyhood, but at that period he had a handsome cast of features, and (from all we can gather) the representative cast of the Coleridge family. But Hartley, the eldest son, how shall we describe *him*? He was most intellectual and he was most eccentric, and his features expressed all that in perfection. Southey, in his domestic playfulness, used to call him the *Knave of Spades*; and he certainly *had* a resemblance to that well-known young gentleman. But really we do not know that it would have been at all better to resemble the knave of hearts. And it must be remembered that the knave of spades may have a brother very like himself, and yet a hundred times handsomer. There *are* such things as handsome likenesses of very plain people. Some folks pronounced Hartley Coleridge too Jewish. But to be a Jew is to be an Arab. And our own feeling was, when we met Hartley at times in solitary or desolate places of Westmoreland and Cumberland, that here was a son of Ishmael walking in the wilderness of Edom. The coruscating *nimbus* of his curling and profuse black hair, black as erebus, strengthened the Saracen impression of his features and complexion. He wanted only a turban on his head, and a spear in his right hand, to be perfect as a Bedouin. But it affected us as all things are affecting which record great changes, to hear that for a long time before his death this black hair had become white as the hair of infancy. Much sorrow and much thought had been the worms that gnawed the roots of that raven hair; that, in Wordsworth's fine way of expressing the very same fact as to Mary Queen of Scots:

'Kill'd the bloom before its time, And blanch'd, without the owner's crime, The most resplendent hair.'

Ah, wrecks of once blooming nurseries, that from generation to generation, from John Coleridge the apostolic to S. T. C. the sunbright, and from S. T. C. the sunbright to Hartley the starry, lie scattered upon every shore!

II. MR. FINLAY'S HISTORY OF GREECE.

In attempting to appraise Mr. Finlay's work comprehensively, there is this difficulty. It comes before us in two characters; first, as a philosophic speculation upon history, to be valued against others speculating on other histories; secondly, as a guide, practical altogether and not speculative, to students who are navigating that great trackless ocean the *Eastern* Roman history. Now under either shape, this work traverses so much ground, that by mere multiplicity of details it denies to us the opportunity of reporting on its merits with that simplicity of judgment which would have been available in a case of severer unity. So many separate situations of history, so many critical continuations of political circumstances, sweep across the field of Mr. Finlay's telescope whilst sweeping the heavens of four centuries, that it is naturally impossible to effect any comprehensive abstractions, as to principles, from cases individual by their nature and separated by their period not less than by their relations in respect to things and persons. The mere necessity of the plan in such a work ensures a certain amount of dissent on the part of every reader; he that most frequently goes along with the author in his commentary, will repeatedly find himself diverging from it in one point or demurring to its inferences in another. Such, in fact, is the eternal disadvantage for an author upon a subject which recalls the remark of Juvenal:

'Vester porro labor fecundior, historiarumScriptores: petit hic plus temporis, atque olei plus:Sic *ingens rerum numerus* jubet, atque operum lex.'

It is this *ingens rerum numerus* that constitutes at once the attraction of these volumes, and the difficulty of dealing with them in any adequate or satisfactory manner.

Indeed, the vistas opened up by Mr. Finlay are infinite; in *that* sense it is that he ascribes inexhaustibility to the trackless savannahs of history. These vast hunting-grounds for the imaginative understanding are in fact but charts and surveyors' outlines meagre and arid for the timid or uninspired student. To a grander intellect these historical delineations are not maps but pictures: they compose a forest wilderness, veined and threaded by sylvan lawns, 'dark with horrid shades,' like Milton's haunted desert in the 'Paradise Regained,' at many a point looking back to the towers of vanishing Jerusalem, and like Milton's desert, crossed dimly at uncertain intervals by forms doubtful and (considering the character of such awful deserts) suspicious.

Perhaps the reader, being rather 'dense,' does not understand, but we understand ourselves, which is the root of the matter. Let us try again: these historical delineations are not lifeless facts, bearing no sense or moral value, but living realities organized into the unity of some great constructive idea.

Perhaps we are obscure; and possibly (though it is treason in a writer to hint such a thing, as tending to produce hatred or disaffection towards his liege lord who is and must be his reader), yet, perhaps, even the reader— that great character—may be 'dense.' 'Dense' is the word used by young ladies to indicate a slight shade—a *soupçon*—of stupidity; and by the way it stands in close relationship of sound to *Duns*, the schoolman, who (it is well known) shared with King Solomon the glory of furnishing a designation for men weak in the upper quarters. But, reader, whether the fault be in you or in ourselves, certain it is that the truth which we wish to communicate is not trivial; it is the noblest and most creative of truths, if only we are not a Duns Scholasticus for explanation, nor you (most excellent reader!) altogether a Solomon for apprehension. Therefore, again lend us your ears.

It is not, it has not been, perhaps it never will be, understood—how vast a thing is combination. We remember that Euler, and some other profound Prussians, such as Lambert, etc., tax this word *combination* with a fault: for, say they, it indicates that composition of things which proceeds two by two (viz., com-*bina*); whereas three by three, ten by ten, fifty by fifty, is combination. It is so. But, once for all, language is so difficult a structure, being like a mail-coach and four horses required to turn round Lackington's counter[12]—required in one syllable to do what oftentimes would require a sentence—that it must use the artifices of a short-hand. The word *bini-æ-a* is here but an exponential or representative word: it stands for any number, for *number* in short generally as opposed to unity. And the secret truth which some years ago we suggested, but which doubtless perished as pearls to swine, is, that com*bina*tion, or com*terna*tion, or com*quaterna*tion, or com*dena*tion, possesses a mysterious virtue quite unobserved by men. All knowledge is probably within its keeping. What we mean is, that where A is not capable simply of revealing a truth (*i.e.*, by way of direct inference), very possible it is that A viewed by the light of B (*i.e.*, in some mode of combination with B) shall be capable; but again, if A + B cannot unlock the case, these in combination with C shall do so. And if not A + B + C, then, perhaps, shall A + B + C combined with D; and so on *ad infinitum*; or in other words that pairs, or binaries, ternaries, quaternaries, and in that mode of progression will furnish keys intricate enough to meet and to decipher the wards of any lock in nature.

Now, in studying history, the difficulty is about the delicacy of the lock, and the mode of applying the key. We doubt not that many readers will view all this as false refinement. But hardly, if they had much considered the real experimental cases in history. For instance, suppose the condition of a people known as respects (1) civilization, as respects (2) relation to the sovereign, (3) the prevailing mode of its industry, (4) its special circumstances as to taxation, (5) its physical conformation and temperament, (6) its local circumstances as to neighbours warlike or not warlike, (7) the quality and depth of its religion, (8) the framework of its jurisprudence, (9) the machinery by which these laws are made to act, (10) the proportion of its towns to its rural labour, and the particular action of its police; these and many other items, elements, or secondary features of a people being known, it yet remains unknown which of these leads, which is inert, and of those which are not inert in what order they arrange their action. The *principium movendi*, the central force which organizes and assigns its place in the system to all the other forces, these are quite undetermined by any mere arithmetical recitation of the agencies concerned. Often these primary principles can be deduced only tentatively, or by a regress to the steps, historically speaking, through which they have arisen. Sometimes, for instance, the population, as to its principle of expansion, and as to its rate, together with the particular influence socially of the female sex, exercises the most prodigious influence on the fortunes of a nation, and its movement backwards or forwards. Sometimes again as in Greece (from the oriental seclusion of women) these causes limit their own action, until they become little more than names.

In such a case it is essential that the leading outlines at least should be definite; that the coast line and the capes and bays should be well-marked and clear, whatever may become of the inland waters, and the separate heights in a continuous chain of mountains.

But we are not always sure that we understand Mr. Finlay, even in the particular use which he makes of the words 'Greece' and 'Grecian.' Sometimes he means beyond a doubt the people of Hellas and the Ægean islands, as *opposed* to the mixed population of Constantinople. Sometimes he means the Grecian element as opposed to the Roman element *in* the composition of this mixed Byzantine population. In this case the Greek does not mean (as in the former case) the non-Byzantine, but the Byzantine. Sometimes he means by preference that vast and most diffusive race which throughout Asia Minor, Syria, Egypt, the Euxine and the Euphrates, represented the Græco-Macedonian blood from the time of Alexander downwards. But why should we limit the case to an origin from this great Alexandrian æra? Then doubtless (330 B.C.) it received a prodigious expansion. But already, in the time of Herodotus (450 B.C.), this Grecian race had begun to sow itself broadcast over Asia and Africa. The region called *Cyrenaica* (viz., the first region which you would traverse in passing from the banks of the Nile and the Pyramids to Carthage and to

Mount Atlas, *i.e.*, Tunis, Algiers, Fez and Morocco, or what we now call the Barbary States) had been occupied by Grecians nearly seven hundred years before Christ. In the time of Crœsus (say 560 B.C.) it is clear that Grecians were swarming over Lydia and the whole accessible part of Asia Minor. In the time of Cyrus the younger (say 404 B.C.) his Grecian allies found their fiercest opponents in Grecian soldiers of Artaxerxes. In the time of Alexander, just a septuagint of years from the epoch of this unfortunate Cyrus, the most considerable troops of Darius were Greeks. The truth is, that, though Greece was at no time very populous, the prosperity of so many little republics led to as ample a redundancy of Grecian population as was compatible with Grecian habits of life; for, deceive not yourself, the *harem*, what we are accustomed to think of as a Mahometan institution, existed more or less perfectly in Greece by seventeen centuries at least antecedently to Mahometanism. Already before Homer, before Troy, before the Argonauts, woman was an abject, dependent chattel in Greece, and living in nun-like seclusion. There is so much of *intellectual* resemblance between Greece and Rome, shown in the two literatures, the two religions, and the structure of the two languages, that we are apt to overlook radical repulsion between their *moral* systems. But such a repulsion did exist, and the results of its existence are 'writ large' in the records, if they are studied with philosophic closeness and insight, and could be illustrated in many ways had we only time and space for such an exercise. But we must hurry on to remark that Mr. Finlay's indefiniteness in the use of the terms 'Greece' and 'Grecian' is almost equalled by his looseness in dealing with institutions and the principles which determined their character. He dwells meditatively upon that tenacity of life which he finds to characterize them—a tenacity very much dependent upon physical[13] circumstances, and in that respect so memorably inferior to the social economy of Jewish existence, that we have been led to dwell with some interest upon the following distinctions as applicable to the political existence of all nations who are in any degree civilized. It seems to us that three forces, amongst those which influence the movement of nations, are practically paramount; viz., first, the *legislation* of a people; secondly, the *government* of a people; thirdly, the *administration* of a people. By the quality of its legislation a people is moulded to this or that character; by the quality of its government a people is applied to this or that great purpose; by the quality of its administration a people is made disposable readily and instantly and completely for every purpose lying within the field of public objects. *Legislation* it is which shapes or qualifies a people, endowing them with such qualities as are more or less fitted for the ends likely to be pursued by a national policy, and for the ends suggested by local relations when combined with the new aspects of the times. *Government* it is which turns these qualifications to account, guiding them upon the new line of tendencies opening spontaneously ahead, or (as sometimes we see) upon new tendencies created deliberately and by forethought. But *administration* it is which organizes between the capacities of the people on the one hand, and the enlightened wishes of the government on the other—that intermediate *nexus* of social machinery without which both the amplest powers in a nation and the noblest policy in a government must equally and continually fall to the ground. A general system of instruments, or if we may use the word, system of instrumentation and concerted arrangements—behold the one sole *conditio sine qua non* for giving a voice to the national interests, for giving a ratification to the national will, for giving mobility to the national resources. Amongst these three categories which we have here assigned as summing up the relations of the public will in great nations to the total system of national results, this last category of *administration* is that which (beyond the rest) postulates and presupposes vast developments of civilization. Instincts of nature, under favourable circumstances, as where the national mind is bold, the temper noble, veracity adorning the speech, and simplicity the manners, may create and *have* created good elementary laws; whilst it is certain that, where any popular freedom exists, the government must resemble and reflect the people. Hence it cannot be denied that, even in semi-barbarous times, good legislation and good government may arise. But good administration is not conceivable without the aids of high civilization. How often have piracy by sea, systematic robbery by land, tainted as with a curse the blessings of life and property in great nations! Witness the state of the Mediterranean under the Cilicians during the very sunset of Marius; or, again, of the Caribbean seas, in spite of a vast Spanish empire, of Buccaneers and Filibusters. Witness Bagandæ in Roman Spain, or the cloud of robbers gathering in France through twelve centuries after *every* period of war; witness the scourges of public peace in Italy, were it in papal Rome or amongst the Fra Diavolos of Naples.

We believe that, so far from possessing any stronger principle of vitality than the Roman institutions, those of Greece Proper (meaning those originally and authentically Greek) had any separate advantage only when applied locally. They were essentially *enchorial* institutions, and even *physically* local (*i.e.*, requiring the same place as well as the same people); just as the ordinances of Mahomet betray his unconscious frailty and ignorance by presuming and postulating a Southern climate as well as an Oriental temperament. The Greek usages and traditionary monuments of civilization had adapted themselves from the first to the singular physical conformation of Hellas—as a 'nook-shotten'[14] land, nautically accessible and laid down in seas that were studded with islands systematically adjusted to the continental circumstances, whilst internally her mountainous structure had split up almost the whole of her territory into separate chambers or wards, predetermining from the first that galaxy of little republics into which her splintered community threw itself by means of the strong mutual repulsion derived originally from battlements of hills, and, secondarily, from the existing state of the military art. Having these advantages to begin with, reposing upon these foundations, the Greek civil organization sustained itself undoubtedly through an astonishing tract of time; before the ship *Argo* it had commenced; under the Ottoman Turks it still survived: for even in the Trojan æra, and in the pre-Trojan or Argonautic æra, already (and perhaps for many centuries before) the nominal kingdoms were virtually republics, the princes being evidently limited in their authority by the 'sensus communis' of the body politic almost as much as the Kings of Sparta were from the time of Lycurgus to the extinction of the Peloponnesian independence.

Accidents, therefore, although accidents of a permanent order (being founded in external nature), gave to Greece a very peculiar advantage. On her own dunghill her own usages had a tenacity of life such as is seen in certain weeds (couch-grass, for instance). This natural advantage, by means of intense local adaptation, did certainly prove available for Greece, under the circumstances of a hostile invasion. Even had the Persian invasion succeeded, it is possible that Grecian civilization would still have survived the conquest, and would have predominated, as actually it did in Ionia, etc.

So far our views seem to flow in the channel of Mr. Finlay's. But these three considerations occur:

1st. That oftentimes Greece escaped the ravages of barbarians, not so much by any quality of her civil institutions, whether better or worse, as by her geographical position. It is 'a far cry to Loch Awe'; and had Timon of Athens together with Apemantus clubbed their misanthropies, joint and several, there would hardly have arisen an impetus strong enough to carry an enemy all the way from the Danube to the Ilyssus; yet so far, at least, every European enemy of Thebes and Athens had to march. Nay, unless Monsieur le Sauvage happened to possess the mouths of the Danube, so as to float down 'by the turn of tide' through the Euxine, Bosphorus, Propontis, Hellespont, etc., he would think twice before he would set off a-gallivanting to the regions of the South, where certainly much sunshine was to be had of undeniable quality, but not much of anything else. The Greeks were never absolute paupers, because, however slender their means, their social usages never led to any Irish expansion of population; but under no circumstances of government were they or could they have been rich. Plunder therefore, that could be worth packing and cording, there was little or none in Greece. People do not march seven hundred miles to steal old curious bedsteads, swarming, besides, with fleas. Sculptured plate was the thing. And, from the times of Sylla, *that* had a strange gravitation towards

Rome. It is, besides, worth noticing—as a general rule in the science of robbery—that it makes all the difference in the world which end of a cone is presented to the robber. Beginning at the apex of a sugar-loaf, and required to move rapidly onwards to the broad basis where first he is to halt and seek his booty, the robber locust advances with hope and cheerfulness. Invert this order, and from the vast base of the Danube send him on to the promontory of Sunium—a tract perpetually dwindling in its breadth through 500 miles—and his reversion of booty grows less valuable at every step. Yet even this feature was not the most comfortless in the case. That the zone of pillage should narrow with every step taken towards its proper ground, this surely was a bad look-out. But it was a worse, that even this poor vintage lay hid and sheltered under the Ægis of the empire. The whole breadth of the empire on that side of the Mediterranean was to be traversed before one cluster of grapes could be plucked from Greece; whereas, upon all the horns of the Western Empire, plunder commenced from the moment of crossing the frontier. Here, therefore, lies one objection to the supposed excellence of Grecian institutions: they are valued, upon Mr. Finlay's scale, by their quality of elastic rebound from violence and wrong; but, in order that this quality might be truly tested, they ought to have been equally and fairly tried: now, by comparison with the Western provinces, that was a condition not capable of being realized for Greece, having the position which she had.

2ndly. The reader will remark that the argument just used is but negative: it does not positively combat the superiority claimed for the Greek organization; that superiority may be all that it is described to be; but it is submitted that perhaps the manifestation of this advantage was not made on a sufficient breadth of experiment.

Now let us consider this. Upon the analogy of any possible precedent, under which Rome could be said to have taken seven centuries in unfolding her power, our Britain has taken almost fourteen. So long is the space between the first germination of Anglo-Saxon institutions and the present expansion of British power over the vast regions of Hindostan. Most true it is that a very small section of this time and a very small section of British energies has been applied separately to the Indian Empire. But precisely the same distinction holds good in the Roman case. The total expansion of Rome travelled, perhaps, through eight centuries; but five of these spent themselves upon the mere *domestic* growth of Rome; during five she did not so much as attempt any foreign appropriation. And in the latter three, during which she did, we must figure to ourselves the separate ramifications of her influence as each involving a very short cycle indeed of effort or attention, though collectively involving a long space, separately as involving a very brief one. If the eye is applied to each conquest itself, nothing can exhibit less of a slow or gradual expansion than the Roman system of conquest. It was a shadow which moved so rapidly on the dial as to be visible and alarming. Had newspapers existed in those days, or had such a sympathy bound nations together[15] as could have supported newspapers, a vast league would have been roused by the advance of Rome. Such a league *was* formed where something of this sympathy existed. The kingdoms formed out of the inheritance of Alexander being in a sense Grecian kingdoms—Grecian in their language, Grecian by their princes, Grecian by their armies (in their privileged sections)—*did* become alarming to the Greeks. And what followed? The Achæan league, which, in fact, produced the last heroes of Greece—Aratus, Philopœmen, Cleomenes. But as to Rome, she was too obscure, too little advertised as a danger, to be separately observed. But, partly, this arose from her rapidity. Macedonia was taken separately from Greece. Sicily, which was the advanced port of Greece to the West, had early fallen as a sort of appanage to the Punic struggle. And all the rest followed by insensible degrees. In Syria, and again in Pontus, and in Macedonia, three great kingdoms which to Greece seemed related rather as enemies than as friends, and which therefore roused no spirit of resistance in Greece, through Rome had already withdrawn all the contingent proper from Greece. Had these powers concerted with Egypt and with Greece a powerful league, Rome would have been thrown back upon her Western chambers.

The reason why the Piratic power arose, we suppose to have been this, and also the reason why such a power was not viewed as extra-national. The nautical profession as such flowed in a channel altogether distinct from the martial profession. It was altogether and exclusively commercial in its general process. Only, upon peculiar occasions arose a necessity for a nautical power as amongst the resources of empire. Carthage reared upon the basis of her navy, as had done Athens, Rhodes, Tyre, some part of her power: and Rome put forth so much of this power as sufficed to meet Carthage. But that done, we find no separate ambition growing up in Rome and directing itself to naval war. Accidentally, when the war arose between Cæsar and Pompey, it became evident that for rapidly transferring armies and for feeding these armies, a navy would be necessary. And Cicero, but for *this crisis*, and not as a *general* remark, said—that 'necesse est qui mare tenuit rerum potiri.'

Hence it happened—that as no permanent establishment could arise where no permanent antagonist could be supposed to exist—oftentimes, and indeed always, unless when some new crisis arose, the Roman navy went down. In one of these intervals arose the Cilician piracy. Mr. Finlay suggests that in part it arose out of the fragments from Alexander's kingdoms, recombining: partly out of the Isaurian land pirates already established, and furnished with such astonishing natural fortresses as existed nowhere else if we except those aërial caves—a sort of mountain nests on the side of declivities, which Josephus describes as harbouring Idumean enemies of Herod the Great, against whom he was obliged to fight by taking down warriors in complete panoply ensconced in baskets suspended by chains; and partly arising on the temptation of rich booties in the commerce of the Levant, or of rich temples on shore amidst unwarlike populations. These elements of a warlike form were required as the means of piracy, these fortresses and Isaurian caves as the resources of piracy, these notorious cargoes or temples stored with wealth as temptations to piracy, before a public nuisance could arise demanding a public chastisement. And yet, because this piracy had a local settlement and nursery, it seemed hardly consonant to the spirit of public (or international) law, that all civil rights should be denied them.

Not without reason, not without a profound purpose, did Providence ordain that our two great precedents upon earth should be Greece and Rome. In all planets, if you could look into them, doubt not (oh, reader of ours!) that something exists answering to Greece and Rome. Odd it would be—*curioes*! as the Germans say—if in Jupiter—or Venus—those precedents should exist under the same *names* of Greece and Rome. Yet, why not? Jovial—and Venereal—people may be better in some things than our people (which, however, we doubt), but certainly a better language than the Greek man cannot have invented in either planet. Falling back from cases so low and so lofty (Venus an inferior, Jupiter a far superior planet) to our own case, the case of poor mediocre Tellurians, perhaps the reader thinks that other nations might have served the purpose of Providentia. Other nations might have furnished those Providential models which the great drama of earth required. No. Haughtily and despotically we say it— No. Take France. *There* is a noble nation. We honour it exceedingly for that heroic courage which on a morning of battle does not measure the strength of the opposition; which, when an enemy issues from the darkness of a wood, does not stop to count noses, but like that noblest of animals, the British bull-dog, flies at his throat, careless whether a leopard, a buffalo, or a tiger of Bengal. This we vehemently admire. This we feel to be an echo, an iteration, of our own leonine courage, concerning which—take you note of this, oh, chicken-hearted man! (if any such is amongst *our* readers)—that God sees it with pleasure, blesses it, and calls it 'very good!' Next, when we come to think at odd times of that other courage, the courage of fidelity, which stands for hours under the storm of a cannonade—British courage, Russian courage—in mere sincerity we cannot ascribe this to the Gaul. All this is true: we feel that the French is an imperfect nation. But suppose it *not* imperfect, would the French therefore have fulfilled for us the mission of the Greek and the Roman? Undoubtedly they would not. Far enough are we from admiring either Greek or Roman in that degree to which the ignorance, but oftener the hypocrisy, of man has ascended.

We, reader, are misanthropical—intensely so. No luxury known amongst men—neither the paws of bears nor the tails of sheep—to us is so sweet and dear as that of hating (yet much oftener of despising) our excellent fellow-creatures. Oftentimes we exclaim in our dreams, where excuse us for expressing our multitude by unity, 'Homo sum; humani nihil mihi tolerandum puto.' We kick backwards at the human race, we spit upon them; we void our rheum upon their ugly gaberdines. Consequently we do not love either Greek or Roman; we regard them in some measure as humbugs. But although it is no cue of ours to admire them (viz., in any English sense of that word known to Entick's Dictionary), yet in a Grecian or Roman sense we may say that θαυμαζομεν, *admiramur*, both of these nations: we marvel, we wonder at them exceedingly. Greece we shall omit, because to talk of the arts, and Phidias, and Pericles, and '*all that*,' is the surest way yet discovered by man for tempting a vindictive succession of kicks. Exposed to the world, no author of such twaddle could long evade assassination. But Rome is entitled to some separate notice, even after all that has been written about her. And the more so in this case, because Mr. Finlay has scarcely done her justice. He says: 'The Romans were a tribe of warriors. All their institutions, even those relating to property, were formed with reference to war.' And he then goes on to this invidious theory of their history—that, as warriors, they overthrew the local institutions of all Western nations, these nations being found by the Romans in a state of civilization much inferior to their own. But eastwards, when conquering Greece, her institutions they did *not* overthrow. And what follows from that memorable difference? Why, that in after days, when hives of barbarians issued from central Europe, all the Western provinces (as not cemented by any native and home-bred institutions, but fighting under the harness of an exotic organization) sank before them; whereas Greece, falling back on the natural resources of a system self-evolved and *local*, or epichorial in its origin, not only defied these German barbarians for the moment, but actually after having her throat cut in a manner rose up magnificently (as did the Lancashire woman after being murdered by the M'Keans of Dumfries)[16], staggered along for a considerable distance, and then (as the Lancashire woman did not) mounted upon skates, and skated away into an azure infinite of distance (quite forgetting her throat), so as to—do what? It is really frightful to mention: so as to come safe and sound into the nineteenth century, leaping into the centre of us all like the ghost of a patriarch, setting her arms a-kimbo, and crying out: 'Here I come from a thousand years before Homer.' All this is really true and undeniable. It is past contradiction, what Mr. Finlay says, that Greece, having weathered the following peoples, to wit, the Romans; secondly, the vagabonds who persecuted the Romans for five centuries; thirdly, the Saracens; fourthly and fifthly, the Ottoman Turks and Venetians; sixthly, the Latin princes of Constantinople—not to speak seventhly and eighthly of Albanian or Egyptian Ali Pashas, or ninthly, of Joseph Humes and Greek loans, is now, viz., in March, 1844, alive and kicking. Think of a man, reader, at a *soirée* in the heavenly spring of '44 (for heavenly it *will* be), wearing white kid gloves, and descended from Deucalion or Ogyges!

Amongst the great changes wrought in every direction by Constantine, it is not to be supposed that Mr. Finlay could overlook those which applied a new organization to the army. Rome would not be Rome; even a product of Rome would not be legitimate; even an offshoot from Rome would be of suspicious derivation, which *could* find that great master-wheel of the state machinery a secondary force in its system. It is wonderful to mark the martial destiny of all which inherited, or upon any line descended from Rome in every age of that mighty evolution. War not barbaric, war exquisitely systematic, war according to the vigour of all science as yet published to man, was the talisman by which Rome and the children of Rome prospered: the S.P.Q.R. on the legionary banners was the sign set in the rubric of the heavens by which the almighty nation, looking upwards, read her commission from above: and if ever that sign shall grow pale, then look for the coming of the end, whispered the prophetic heart of Rome to herself even from the beginning. But are not all great kingdoms dependent on their armies? No. Some have always been protected by their remoteness, many by their adjacencies. Germany, in the first century from Augustus, retreated into her mighty forests when closely pressed, and in military phrase 'refused herself' to the pursuer. Persia sheltered herself under the same tactics for ages;[17] scarcely needed to fight, unless she pleased, and, when she did so, fought in alliance with famine—with thirst—and with the confusion of pathless deserts. Other empires, again, are protected by their infinity; America was found to have no local existence by ourselves: she was nowhere because she was everywhere. Russia had the same illimitable ubiquity for Napoleon. And Spain again is so singularly placed with regard to France, a chamber within a chamber, that she cannot be approached by any power not maritime except on French permission. Manifold are the defensive resources of nations beyond those of military systems. But for the Roman empire, a ring fence around the Mediterranean lake, and hemmed in upon every quarter of that vast circuit by an *indago* of martial hunters, nature and providence had made it the one sole available policy to stand for ever under arms, eternally 'in procinctu,' and watching from the specular altitude of her centre upon which radius she should slip her wolves to the endless circumference.

Mr. Finlay, in our judgment, not only allows a most disproportionate weight to vicious taxation, which is but one wheel amongst a vast system of wheels in the machinery of administration, and which, like many similar agencies, tends oftentimes to react by many corrections upon its own derangements; but subsequently he views as through a magnifying glass even these original exaggerations when measured upon the scale of moral obligations. Not only does false taxation ruin nations and defeat the possibility of self-defence—which is much—but it cancels the duties of allegiance. He tells us (p. 408) that 'amidst the ravages of the Goths, Huns, and Avars, the imperial tax-gatherers had never failed to enforce payment of the tribute as long as anything remained undestroyed; though according to the rules of justice, the Roman government had really forfeited its right to levy the taxes, as soon as it failed to perform its duty in defending the population.' We do not believe that the government succeeded in levying tribute vigorously under the circumstances supposed; the science and machinery of administration were far from having realized that degree of exquisite skill. But, if the government *had* succeeded, we cannot admit that this relation of the parties dissolved their connection. To have failed at any time in defending a province or an outwork against an overwhelming enemy, *that* for a prince or for a minister is a great misfortune. Shocking indeed it were if this misfortune could be lawfully interpreted as his crime, and made the parent of a second misfortune, ratifying the first by authorizing revolt of the people; and the more so, as that first calamity would encourage traitors everywhere to prepare the way for the second as a means of impunity for their own treason. In the prospect of escaping at once from the burdens of war, and from the penalties of broken vows to their sovereign, multitudes would from the first enter into compromise and collusion with an invader; and in this way they would create the calamity which they charged upon their rulers as a desertion; they would create the embarrassments for their government by which they hoped to profit, and they would do this with an eye to the reversionary benefit anticipated under the maxim here set up. True, they would often find their heavy disappointment in the more grievous yoke of that invader whom they had aided. But the temptation of a momentary gain would always exist for the improvident many, if such a maxim were received into the law of nations; and, if it would not always triumph, we should owe it in that case to the blessing that God has made nations proud. Even in the case where men had received a license from public law for deserting their sovereign, thanks be to the celestial pride which is in man, few and anomalous would be the instances in which they really *would* do so. In reality it must be evident that, under such a rule of Publicists, subjects must stand in perpetual doubt whether the case had emerged or not which law contemplated as the dissolution of their fealty. No man would say that a province was licensed to desert, because the central government had lost a battle. But a whole campaign, or ten campaigns, would stand in the same predicament as a solitary battle, so long as the struggle was not formally renounced by the sovereign. How many years of absolute abandonment might justify a provincial people in considering themselves surrendered to their own discretion, is a question standing on the separate circumstances of each separate case. But generally it may be said, that a ruler will be presumed justly *not* to have renounced the cause of resistance so long as he makes no treaty or compromise with the enemy, and so long as he desists from open resistance only through momentary exhaustion, or with a view to more elaborate preparation. Would ten battles, would a campaign, would ten campaigns lost, furnish the justifying motive? Certainly it would be a false casuistry that would say so.

Why did the Romans conquer the Greeks? By *why* we mean, Upon what principle did the children of Romulus overthrow the children of Ion, Dorus, Æolus? Why did not these overthrow those? We, speak *Latino more*—Vellem ostenderes quare *hi* non profligaverint *illos*? The answer is brief: the Romans were *one*, the Greeks were *many*. Whilst no weighty pressure from without had assaulted Greece, it was of particular service to that little rascally system that they were split into sections more than ever we *have* counted or mean to count. They throve by mutual repulsion, according to the ballad:

When Captain X. kick'd Miss Roe, Miss Roe kick'd Captain X. again.'

Internally, for pleasant little domestic quarrels, the principle of division was excellent; because, as often as the balance tended to degravitation (a word we learned, as Juliet tells her nurse, 'from one we danc'd withal'), *instanter* it was redressed and trimmed by some renegade going over to the suffering side. People talk of Athens being beaten by the Spartans in the person of Lysander; and the vulgar notion is, that the Peloponnesian war closed by an eclipse total and central for our poor friend Athens. Nonsense! she had life left in her to kick twenty such donkeys to death; and, if you look a very little ahead, gazettes tell you, that before the peace of Antalcidas, those villains, the Spartans (whom may heaven confound!) had been licked almost too cruelly by the Athenians. And there it is that we insist upon closing that one great intestine[18] war of the Greeks. So of other cases: absolute defeat, final overthrow, we hold to be impossible for a Grecian state, as against a Grecian state, under the conditions which existed from the year 500 B.C. But when a foreign enemy came on, the possibilities might alter. The foreigner, being one, and for the moment at least united, would surely have a great advantage over the crowd of little pestilent villains—right and left— that would be disputing the policy of the case. There lay the original advantage of the Romans; *one* they were, and *one* they were to the end of Roman time. Did you ever hear of a Roman, unless it were Sertorius, that fought against Romans? Whereas, scoundrel Greeks were always fighting against their countrymen. Xenophon, in Persia, Alexander, seventy years later, met with their chief enemies in Greeks. We may therefore pronounce with firmness, that unity was one cause of the Roman superiority. What was the other? Better military institutions. These, if we should go upon the plan of rehearsing them, are infinite. But let us confine our view to the separate mode in each people of combining their troops. In Greece, the *phalanx* was the ideal tactical arrangement; for Rome, the *legion*. Everybody knows that Polybius, a Greek, who fled from the Peloponnesus to Rome a little before the great Carthaginian war, terminated by Scipio Africanus, has left a most interesting comparison between the two forms of tactical arrangement: and, waiving the details, the upshot is this—that the phalanx was a holiday arrangement, a tournament arrangement, with respect to which you must suppose an excess of luck if it could be made available, unless by mutual consent, under a known possibility of transferring the field of battle to some smooth bowling-green in the neighbourhood. But, on the other hand, the legion was available everywhere. The *phalanx* was like the organ, an instrument almighty indeed where it can be carried; but it cost eight hundred years to transfer it from Asia Minor to the court of Charlemagne (*i.e.*, Western Europe), so that it travelled at the rate of two miles *per annum*; but the *legion* was like the violin, less terrifically tumultuous, but more infinite than the organ, whilst it is in a perfect sense portable. Pitch your camp in darkness, on the next morning everywhere you will find ground for the *legion*, but for the fastidious *phalanx* you need as much choice of ground as for the arena of an opera stage.

And the same influence that had tended to keep the Greeks in division, without a proper unity, operated also to infect the national character at last with some lack of what may be called self-sufficiency. They were in their later phases subtle, but compliant, more ready to adapt themselves to changes than to assert a position and risk all in the effort to hold it. Hence it came that even the most honourable and upright amongst a nation far nobler in a moral sense (nobler, for instance, on the scale of capacity for doing and suffering) never rose to a sentiment of respect for the ordinary Grecian. The Romans viewed him as essentially framed for ministerial offices. Am I sick? Come, Greek, and cure me. Am I weary? Amuse me. Am I diffident of power to succeed? Cheer me with flattery. Am I issuing from a bath? Shampoo me.

The point of view under which we contemplate the Romans is one which cannot be dispensed with in that higher or transcendental study of history now prompted by the vast ferment of the meditative mind. Oh, feeble appreciators of the public mind, who can imagine even in dreams that this generation—self-questioned, agitated, haunted beyond any other by the elementary problems of our human condition, by the awful *whence* and the more awful *whither*, by what the Germans call the 'riddle of the universe,' and oppressed into a rebellious impatience by

'The burthen of the mysteryOf all this unintelligible world,'

—that this, above all generations, is shallow, superficial, unfruitful? That was a crotchet of the late S. T. Coleridge's; that was a crotchet of the present W. Wordsworth's, but which we will venture to guess that he has now somewhat modified since this generation has become just to himself. No; as to the multitude, in no age can it be other than superficial. But we do contend, with intolerance and scorn of such opposition as usually we meet, that the tendencies of this generation are to the profound; that by all its natural leanings, and even by its infirmities, it travels upwards on the line of aspiration and downwards in the direction of the unfathomable. These tendencies had been awakened and quickened by the vast convulsions that marked the close of the last century. But war is a condition too restless for sustained meditation. Even the years *after* war, if that war had gathered too abundantly the vintages of tears and tragedy and change, still rock and undulate with the unsubsiding sympathies which wars such as we have known cannot but have evoked. Besides that war is by too many issues connected with the practical; the service of war, by the arts which it requires, and the burthen of war, by the discussions which it prompts, almost equally tend to alienate the public mind from the speculation which looks beyond the interests of social life. But when a new generation has grown up, when the forest trees of the elder generation amongst us begin to thicken with the intergrowth of a younger shrubbery that had been mere ground-plants in the æra of war, *then* it is, viz., under the heavenly lull and the silence of a long peace, which in its very uniformity and the solemnity of its silence has something analogous to the sublime tranquillity of a Zaarrah, that minds formed for the great inquests of meditation—feeling dimly the great strife which they did not witness, and feeling it the more deeply because for *them* an idealized retrospect, and a retrospect besides being potently contrasted so deeply with the existing atmosphere, peaceful as if it had never known a storm—are stimulated preternaturally to those obstinate questionings which belong of necessity to a complex state of society, turning up vast phases of human suffering under all varieties, phases which, having issued from a chaos of agitation, carry with them too certain a promise of sooner or later revolving into a chaos of equal sadness, universal strife. It is the relation of the immediate isthmus on which we stand ourselves to a past and (prophetically speaking) to a coming world of calamity, the relation of the smiling and halcyon calm which we have inherited to that darkness and anarchy out of which it arose, and towards which too gloomily we augur its return—this relation it is which enforces the other impulses, whether many or few, connecting our own transitional stage of society with objects always of the same interest for man, but not felt to be of the same interest. The sun, the moon, and still more the starry heavens alien to our own peculiar system—what a different importance in different ages have they had for man! To man armed with science and glasses, labyrinths of anxiety and study; to man ignorant or barbarous less interesting than glittering points of dew. At present those 'other impulses,' which the permanent condition of modern society, so multitudinous and feverish, adds to the meditative impulses of our particular and casual condition as respects a terrific revolutionary war, are *not* few, but many, and are all in one direction, all favouring, none thwarting, the solemn fascinations by which with spells and witchcraft the shadowy nature of man binds him down to look for ever into this dim abyss. The earth, whom with sublimity so awful the poet apostrophized after Waterloo, as 'perturbed' and restless exceedingly, whom with a harp so melodious and beseeching he adjured to rest—and again to rest from instincts of war so deep, haunting the very rivers with blood, and slumbering not through three-and-twenty years of woe—is again unsealed from slumber by the mere reaction of the mighty past working together with the too probable future and with the co-agencies from the unintelligible present. The fervour and the strife of human thought is but the more subtle for being less derived from immediate action, and more so from hieroglyphic mysteries or doubts concealed in the very shows of life. The centres of civilization seethe, as it were, and are ebullient with the agitation of the self-questioning heart.

The fervour is universal; the tumult of intellectual man, self-tormented with unfathomable questions, is contagious everywhere. And both from what we know, it might be perceived *à priori*, and from what we see, it may be known experimentally, that never was the mind of man roused into activity so intense and almost morbid as in this particular stage of our progress. And it has added enormously to this result—that it is redoubled by our own consciousness of our own state so powerfully enforced by modern inventions, whilst the consciousness again is reverberated from a secondary mode of consciousness. All studies prosper; all, with rare exceptions, are advancing only too impetuously. Talent of every order is almost become a weed amongst us.

But this would be a most unreasonable ground for charging it upon our time and country that they are unprogressive and commonplace. Nay, rather, it is a ground for regarding the soil as more prepared for the seed that is sown broadcast. And before our England lies an ample possibility—

to outstrip even Rome itself in the extent and the grandeur of an empire, based on principles of progress and cohesion such as Rome never knew.

FURTHER NOTES FOR ARTICLE ON MR. FINLAY'S HISTORY.

Civilization.—Now about prisoners, strange as this may seem, it really is not settled whether and how far it is the duty in point of honour and reasonable forbearance to make prisoners. At Quatre Bras very few were made by the French, and the bitterness, the frenzy of hatred which this marked, led of necessity to a reaction.

But the strangest thing of all is this, that in a matter of such a nature it should be open to doubt and mystery whether it is or is not contradictory, absurd, and cancellatory or obligatory to make prisoners. Look here, the Tartars in the Christian war, not from cruelty—at least, no such thing is proved—but from mere coercion of what they regarded as good sense the Tartars thought it all a blank contradiction to take and not kill enemies. It seemed equal to taking a tiger laboriously and at much risk in a net, then next day letting him go. Strange it is to say, but it really requires an express experience to show the true practical working of the case, and this demonstrates (inconceivable as that would have been to the Tartars) that the capture is quite equal (quoad damage to the enemy) to the killing.

(1.) As to durability, was it so? The Arabs were not strong except against those who were peculiarly weak; and even in Turkey the Christian Rajah predominates.

(2.) As to bigotry and principles of toleration Mr. Finlay says—and we do not deny that he is right in saying—they arose in the latter stages. This, however, was only from policy, because it was not safe to be so; and repressed only from caution.

(3) About the impetuosity of the Arab assaults. Not what people think.

(4.) About the permanence or continuance of this Mahometan system—we confound the religious system with the political. The religious movement engrafted itself on other nations, translated and inoculated itself upon other political systems, and thus, viz., as a principle travelling through or along new machineries, propagated itself. But here is a deep delusion. What should we Europeans think of an Oriental historian who should talk of the Christians amongst the Germans, English, French, Spaniards, as a separate and independent nation? My friend, we should say, you mistake that matter. The Christians are not a local tribe having an insulated local situation amongst Germans, French, etc. The Christians *are* the English, Germans, etc., or the English, Germans, French, *are* the Christians. So do many readers confer upon the Moslems or Mahometans of history a separate and independent unity.

(*a*) Greek administration had a vicarious support.

(*b*) Incapacity of Eastern nations to establish primogeniture.

(*c*) Incapacity of Eastern nations to be progressive.

FOOTNOTES:

[12] '*Lackington's counter*': Lackington, an extensive seller of old books and a Methodist (see his *Confessions*) in London, viz., at the corner of Finsbury Square, about the time of the French Revolution, feeling painfully that this event drew more attention than himself, resolved to turn the scale in his own favour by a *ruse* somewhat unfair. The French Revolution had no counter; he *had*, it was circular, and corresponded to a lighted dome above. Round the counter on a summer evening, like Phæton round the world, the Edinburgh, the Glasgow, the Holyhead, the Bristol, the Exeter, and the Salisbury Royal Mails, all their passengers on board, and canvas spread, swept in, swept round, and swept out at full gallop; the proximate object being to publish the grandeur of his premises, the ultimate object to publish himself.

[13] 'Dependent upon *physical* circumstances,' and, amongst those physical circumstances, intensely upon climate. The Jewish ordinances, multiplied and burthensome as they must have been found under any mitigations, have proved the awfulness (if we may so phrase it) of the original projectile force which launched them by continuing to revolve, and to propagate their controlling functions through forty centuries under all latitudes to which any mode of civilization has reached. But the *Greek* machineries of social life were absolutely and essentially limited by nature to a Grecian latitude. Already from the earliest stages of their infancy the Greek cities or rural settlements in the Tauric Chersonese, and along the shores (Northern and Eastern) of the Black Sea, had been obliged to unrobe themselves of their native Grecian costumes in a degree which materially disturbed the power of the Grecian literature as an influence for the popular mind. This effect of a new climate to modify the influence of a religion or the character of a literature is noticed by Mr. Finlay. Temples open to the heavens, theatres for noonday light and large enough for receiving 30,000 citizens—these could no longer be transplanted from sunny regions of Hymettus to the churlish atmospheres which overcast with gloom so perpetual poor Ovid's sketches of his exile. Cherson, it is true, in the Tauric Chersonese, survived down to the middle of the tenth century; so much is certain from the evidence of a Byzantine emperor; and Mr. Finlay is disposed to think that this famous little colonial state retained her Greek

'municipal organization.' If this could be proved, it would be a very interesting fact; it is, at any rate, interesting to see this saucy little outpost of Greek civilization mounting guard, as it were, at so great a distance from the bulwark of Christianity (the city of Constantine), under whose mighty shadow she had so long been sheltered, and maintaining *by whatever means* her own independence. But, if her municipal institutions were truly and permanently Greek, then it would be a fair inference that to a Grecian mechanism of society she had been indebted for her Grecian tenacity of life. And this is Mr. Finlay's inference. Otherwise, and for our own parts, we should be inclined to charge her long tenure of independence upon her strong situation, rendered for *her* a thousand times stronger by the two facts of her commerce in the first place, and secondly, of her commerce being maritime. Shipping and trade seem to us the two anchors by which she rode.

[14] 'Nook-shotten,' an epithet applied by Shakspeare to England.

[15] Christianity is a force of unity. But was Paganism such? No. To be idolatrous is no bond of union.

[16] See Murder as one of the Fine Arts. (Postscript in 1854.)

[17] '*Under the same tactics*'—the tactics of 'refusing' her columns to the enemy. On this subject we want an elaborate memoir historico-geographical revising every stage of the Roman warfare in Pers-Armenia, from Crassus and Ventidius down to Heraclius—a range of six and a half centuries; and specifically explaining why it was that almost always the Romans found it mere destruction to attempt a passage much beyond the Tigris or into central Persia, whilst so soon after Heraclius the immediate successors of Mahomet overflowed Persia like a deluge.

[18] 'Intestine war.' Many writers call the Peloponnesian war (by the way, a very false designation) the great *civil* war of Greece. 'Civil'!—it might have been such, had the Grecian states had a central organ which claimed a common obedience.

III. THE ASSASSINATION OF CÆSAR.

The assassination of Cæsar, we find characterized in one of his latter works (*Farbenlehre*, Theil 2, p. 126) by Goethe, as '*die abgeschmackteste That die jemals begangen worden*'—*the most outrageously absurd act that ever was committed*. Goethe is right, and more than right. For not only was it an atrocity so absolutely without a purpose as never to have been examined by one single conspirator with a view to its probable tendencies—in that sense therefore it was absurd as pointing to no result—but also in its immediate arrangements and precautions it had been framed so negligently, with a carelessness so total as to the natural rebounds and reflex effects of such a tragic act, that the conspirators had neither organized any resources for improving their act, nor for securing their own persons from the first blind motions of panic, nor even for establishing a common rendezvous. When they had executed their valiant exploit, the very possibility of which from the first step to the last they owed to the sublime magnanimity of their victim—well knowing his own continual danger, but refusing to evade it by any arts of tyranny or distrust—when they had gone through their little scenic mummery of swaggering with their daggers—cutting '5,' '6' and 'St. George,' and 'giving point'—they had come to the end of the play. *Exeunt omnes: vos plaudite*. Not a step further had they projected. And, staring wildly upon each other, they began to mutter, 'Well, what are you up to next?' We believe that no act so thoroughly womanish, that is, moving under a blind impulse without a thought of consequences, without a concerted succession of steps, and no *arrière pensée* as to its final improvement, ever yet had a place or rating in the books of Conspiracy, far less was attended (as by accident this was) with an equipage of earth-shattering changes. Even the poor deluded followers of the Old Mountain Assassin, though drugged with bewildering potions, such men as Sir Walter Scott describes in the person of that little wily fanatic gambolling before the tent of Richard *Coeur-de-lion*, had always settled which way they would run when the work was finished. And how peculiarly this reach of foresight was required for these anti-Julian conspirators—will appear from one fact. Is the reader aware, were these boyish men aware, that—besides, what we all know from Shakespeare, a mob won to Cæsar's side by his very last codicils of his will; besides a crowd of public magistrates and dependents charged upon the provinces, etc., for two years deep by Cæsar's act, though in requital of no services or attachment to himself; besides a distinct Cæsarian party; finally, besides Antony, the express representative and assignee of Cæsar, armed at this moment with the powers of Consul—there was over and above a great military officer of Cæsar's (Lentulus), then by accident in Rome, holding a most potent government through the mere favour of Cæsar, and pledged therefore by an instant interest of self-promotion, backed by a large number of Julian troops at that instant billeted on a suburb of Rome— veterans, and fierce fellows that would have cut their own fathers' throats 'as soon as say dumpling' (see Lucan's account of them in Cæsar's harangue before Pharsalia)? Every man of sense would have predicted ruin to the conspirators. '*You'll tickle it for your concupy*' (Thersites in 'Troil and Cress.') would have been the word of every rational creature to these wretches when trembling from their tremulous act, and reeking from their bloody ingratitude. For most remarkable it is that not one conspirator but was personally indebted to Cæsar for eminent favours; and many among them had even received that life from their victim which they employed in filching away *his*. Yet after that feature of the case, so notorious as it soon became, historians and biographers are all ready to notice of the centurion who amputated Cicero's head that, he had once been defended by Cicero. What if he had, which is more than we know—must *that* operate as a perpetual retaining fee on Cicero's behalf? Put the case that we found ourselves armed with a commission (no matter whence emanating) for abscinding the head of Mr. Adolphus who now pleads with so much lustre at the general jail delivery of London and Middlesex, or the head of Mr. Serjeant Wild, must it bar our claim that once Mr. Adolphus had defended us on a charge of sheep-stealing, or that the Serjeant had gone down 'special' in our cause to York? Very well, but doubtless they had their fees. 'Oh, but Cicero could not receive fees by law.' Certainly not by law; but by custom many *did* receive them at dusk through some postern gate in the shape of a huge cheese, or a guinea-pig. And, if the 'special retainer' from Popilius Lænas is somewhat of the doubtfullest, so is the 'pleading' on the part of Cicero.

However, it is not impossible but some will see in this desperate game of hazard a sort of courage on the part of the conspirators which may redeem their knavery. But the courage of desperation is seldom genuine, and least of all where the desperation itself was uncalled for. Yet even this sort of merit the conspirators wanted. The most urgent part of the danger was that which in all probability they had not heard of, viz., the casual presence at Rome of Julian soldiers. Pursuing no inquiries at all, they would hear not; practising no caution, they would keep no secret. The plot had often been betrayed, we will swear: but Cæsar and Cæsar's friends would look upon all such stories as the mere expressions of a permanent case, so much inevitable exposure on *their* part—so much possibility of advantage redounding to the other side. And out of these naked possibilities, as some temptation would continually arise to use them profitably, much more would arise to use them as delightful offsets to the sense of security and power.

[Mommsen is more at one with De Quincey here than Merivale, who, at p. 478, vol. ii., writes: 'We learn with pleasure that the conspirators did not venture even to sound Cicero'; but at vol. iii., p. 9, he has these significant words: 'Cicero, himself, we must believe, was not ashamed to lament the scruples which had denied him initiation into the plot.' Forsyth writes of Cicero's views: 'He was more than ever convinced of the want of foresight shown by the conspirators. Their deed, he said, was the deed of men, their counsels were the counsels of children,' 'Life of Cicero,' 3rd edition, pp. 435-6.—ED.]

IV. CICERO (SUPPLEMENTARY TO PUBLISHED ESSAY).

Some little official secrets we learn from the correspondence of Cicero as Proconsul of Cilicia.[19] And it surprises us greatly to find a man, so eminently wise in his own case, suddenly turning romantic on behalf of a friend. How came it—that he or any man of the world should fancy any substance or reality in the public enthusiasm for one whose character belonged to a past generation? Nine out of ten amongst the Campanians must have been children when Pompey's name was identified with national trophies. For many years Pompey had done nothing to sustain or to revive his obsolete reputation. Capua or other great towns knew him only as a great proprietor. And let us ask this one searching question—Was the poor spirit-broken insolvent, a character now so extensively prevailing in Italian society, likely to sympathize more heartily with the lordly oligarch fighting only for the exclusive privileges of his own narrow order, or with the great reformer who amongst a thousand plans for reinfusing vitality into Roman polity was well understood to be digesting a large measure of relief to the hopeless debtor? What lunacy to believe that the ordinary citizen, crouching under the insupportable load of his usurious obligations, could be at leisure to support a few scores of lordly senators panic-stricken for the interests of their own camarilla, when he beheld—taking the field on the opposite quarter—one, the greatest of men, who spoke authentically to all classes alike, authorizing all to hope and to draw their breath in freedom under that general recast of Roman society which had now become inevitable! As between such competitors, which way would the popularity be likely to flow? Naturally the mere merits of the competition were decisive of the public opinion, although the petty aristocracy of the provincial boroughs availed locally to stifle those tumultuous acclamations which would else have gathered about the name of Cæsar. But enough transpired to show which way the current was setting. Cicero does not dissemble that. He acknowledges that all men's hopes turned towards Cæsar. And Pompey, who was much more forced into towns and public scenes, had even less opportunity for deceiving himself. He, who had fancied all Campania streaming with incense to heaven on his own personal account, now made the misanthropical discovery—not only that all was hollow, and that his own name was held in no esteem—but absolutely that the barrier to any hope of popularity for himself was that very man whom, on other and previous grounds, he had for some time viewed as his own capital antagonist.

Here then, in this schism of the public affections, and in the mortifying discovery so abruptly made by Pompey, lay the bitter affront which he could not digest—the injury which he purposed to avenge. What barbed this injury to his feelings, what prepared him for exhausting its bitterness, was the profound delusion in which he had been previously laid asleep by flattering friends—the perfect faith in his own uniform popularity. And now, in the very teeth of all current representations, we advance this proposition: That the quality of his meditated revenge and its horrid extent were what originally unveiled to Cicero's eyes the true character of Pompey and his partisans.

The last letter of the sixth book is written from Athens, which city, after a voyage of about a fortnight, Cicero reached precisely in the middle of October, having sailed out of Ephesus on the 1st. He there found a letter from Atticus, dated from Rome on the 18th of September; and his answer, which was 'by return of post,' closes with these words: 'Mind that you keep your promise of writing to me fully about my darling Tullia,' which means of course about her new husband Dolabella; next about the Commonwealth, which by this time I calculate must be entering upon its agony; and then about the Censors, etc. Hearken: 'This letter is dated on the 16th of October; that day on which, by your account, Cæsar is to reach Placentia with four legions. What, I ask myself for ever, is to become of us? My own situation at this moment, which is in the Acropolis of Athens, best meets my idea of what is prudent under the circumstances.'

Well it would have been for Cicero's peace of mind if he could seriously have reconciled himself to abide by that specular station. Had he pleaded ill-health, he might have done so with decorum. As it was, thinking his dignity concerned in not absenting himself from the public councils at a season so critical, after a few weeks' repose he sailed forward to Italy, which he reached on the 23rd of November. And with what result? Simply to leave it again with difficulty and by stratagem, after a winter passed in one continued contest with the follies of his friends, nothing done to meet his own sense of the energy required, every advantage forfeited as it arose, ruined in the feeble execution, individual activity squandered for want of plan, and (as Cicero discovered in the end) a principle of despair, and *the secret reserve of a flight operating* upon the leaders *from the very beginning*. The key to all this is obvious for those who read with their eyes awake. Pompey and the other consular leaders were ruined for action by age and by the derangement of their digestive organs. Eating too much and too luxuriously is far more destructive to the energies of action than intemperance as to drink. Women everywhere alike are temperate as to eating; and the only females memorable for ill-health from luxurious eating have been

Frenchwomen or Belgians—witness the Duchess of Portsmouth, and many others of the two last centuries whom we could name. But men everywhere commit excesses in this respect, if they have it in their power. With the Roman nobles it was almost a necessity to do so. Could any popular man evade the necessity of keeping a splendid dinner-table? And is there one man in a thousand who can sit at a festal board laden with all the delicacies of remotest climates, and continue to practise an abstinence for which he is not sure of any reward? All his abstinence may be defeated by a premature fate, and in the meantime he is told, with some show of reason, that a life defrauded of its genial enjoyments is *not* life, is at all events a present loss, whilst the remuneration is doubtful, except where there happen to be powerful intellectual activities to reap an *instant* benefit from such sacrifices. Certainly it is the last extremity of impertinence to attack men's habits in this respect. No man, we may be assured, has ever yet practised any true self-denial in such a case, or ever will. Either he has been trained under a wholesome poverty to those habits which intercept the very development of a taste for luxuries, which evade the very possibility therefore of any; or if this taste has once formed itself, he would find it as impossible in this as in any other case to maintain a fight with a temptation recurring *daily*. Pompey certainly could not. He was of a slow, torpid nature through life; required a continual supply of animal stimulation, and, if he had *not* required it, was assuredly little framed by nature for standing out against an *artificial* battery of temptation. There is proof extant that his system was giving way under the action of daily dinners. Cicero mentions the fact of his suffering from an annual illness; what may be called the *etesian* counter-current from his intemperance. Probably the liver was enlarged, and the pylorus was certainly not healthy. Cicero himself was not free from dyspeptic symptoms. If he had survived the Triumvirate, he would have died within seven years from some disease of the intestinal canal. Atticus, we suspect, was troubled with worms. Locke, indeed, than whom no man ever less was acquainted with Greek or Roman life, pretends that the ancients seldom used a pocket-handkerchief; knew little of catarrhs, and even less of what the French consider indigenous to this rainy island—*le catch-cold*. Nothing can be more unfounded. Locke was bred a physician, but his practice had been none; himself and the cat were his chief patients. Else we, who are no physicians, would wish to ask him—what meant those continual *febriculæ* to which all Romans of rank were subject? What meant that *fluenter lippire*, a symptom so troublesome to Cicero's eyes, and always arguing a functional, if not even an organic, derangement of the stomach? Take this rule from us, that wherever the pure white of the eye is clouded, or is veined with red streaks, or wherever a continual weeping moistens the eyelashes, there the digestive organs are touched with some morbid affection, probably in it's early stages; as also that the inferior viscera, *not* the stomach, must be slightly disordered before toothache *can* be an obstinate affection. And as to *le catch-cold*, the-most dangerous shape in which it has ever been known, resembling the English *cholera morbus*, belongs to the modern city of Rome from situation; and probably therefore to the ancient city from the same cause. Pompey, beyond all doubt, was a wreck when he commenced the struggle.

Struggle, conflict, for a man who needed to be in his bed! And struggle with whom? With that man whom his very enemies viewed as a monster (τερας is Cicero's own word), as preternaturally endowed, in this quality of working power. But how then is it consistent with our view of Roman dinners, that Cæsar should have escaped the universal scourge? We reply, that one man is often stronger than another; every man is stronger in some one organ; and secondly, Cæsar had lived away from Rome through the major part of the last ten years; and thirdly, the fact that Cæsar *had* escaped the contagion of dinner luxury, however it may be accounted for, is attested in the way of an exception to the general order of experience, and with such a degree of astonishment, as at once to prove the general maxim we have asserted, and the special exemption in favour of Cæsar. He *only*, said Cato, he, as a contradiction to all precedents—to the Gracchi, to Marius, to Cinna, to Sylla, to Catiline—had come in a state of temperance (*sobrius*) to the destruction of the state; not meaning to indicate mere superiority to wine, but to *all* modes of voluptuous enjoyment. Cæsar practised, it is true, a refined epicureanism under the guidance of Greek physicians, as in the case of his emetics; but this was by way of evading any gross effects from a day of inevitable indulgence, not by way of aiding them. Besides, Pompey and Cicero were about seven years older than Cæsar. They stood upon the threshold of their sixtieth year at the *opening* of the struggle; Cæsar was a hale young man of fifty-two. And we all know that Napoleon at forty-two was incapacitated for Borodino by incipient disease of the stomach; so that from that day he, though junior by seventeen years to Pompey, yet from Pompey's self-indulgence (not certainly in splendid sensuality, but in the gross modes belonging to his obscure youth) was pronounced by all the judicious, superannuated as regarded the indispensable activity of martial habits. If he cannot face the toils of military command, said his officers, why does he not retire? Why does he not make room for others? Neither was the campaign of 1813 or 1814 any refutation of this. Infinite are the cases in which the interests of nations or of armies have suffered through the dyspepsy of those who administered them. And above all nations the Romans laid themselves open to this order of injuries from a dangerous oversight in their constitutional arrangements, which placed legal bars on the youthful side of all public offices, but none on the aged side. Of all nations the Romans had been most indebted to men emphatically young; of all nations they, by theory, most exclusively sanctioned the pretensions of old ones. Not before forty-three could a man stand for the consulship; and we have just noticed a case where a man of pestilent activity in our own times had already become dyspeptically incapable of command at forty-two. Besides, after laying down his civil office (which, by itself, was often in the van of martial perils), the consul had to pass into some province as military leader, with the prospect by possibility of many years' campaigning. It is true that some men far anticipated the legal age in assuming offices, honours, privileges. But this, being always by infraction of fundamental laws, was no subject of rejoicing to a patriotic Roman. And the Roman folly at this very crisis, in trusting one side of the quarrel to an elderly, lethargic invalid, subject to an annual struggle for his life, was appropriately punished by that catastrophe which six years after threw them into the hands of a schoolboy.

Yet on the other hand it may be asked, by those who carry the proper spirit of jealousy into their historical reading, was Cicero always right in these angry comments upon Pompey's strategies? Might it not be, that where Cicero saw nothing but groundless procrastination, in reality the obstacle lay in some overwhelming advantage of Cæsar's? That, where his reports to Atticus read the signs of the time into the mere panic of a Pompey, some more impartial report would see nothing to wonder at but the overcharged expectations of a Cicero? Sometimes undoubtedly this is the plain truth. Pompey's disadvantages were considerable; he had no troops upon which he could rely; that part which had seen service happened to be a detachment from Cæsar's army, sent home as a pledge for his civic intentions at an earlier period, and their affection was still lively to their original leader. The rest were raw levies. And it is a remarkable fact, that the insufficiency of such troops was only now becoming matter of notoriety. In foreign service, where the Roman recruits were incorporated with veterans, as the natives in our Eastern army, with a small proportion of British to steady them, they often behaved well, and especially because they seldom acted against an enemy that was not as raw as themselves. But now, in civil service against their own legions, it was found that the mere novice was worth nothing at all; a fact which had not been fully brought out in the strife of Marius and Sylla, where Pompey had himself played a conspicuous and cruel part, from the tumultuary nature of the contest; besides which the old legions were then by accident as much concentrated on Italian ground as now they were dispersed in transmarine provinces. Of the present Roman army, ten legions at least were scattered over Macedonia, Achaia, Cilicia, and Syria; five were in Spain; and six were with Cæsar, or coming up from the rear. To say nothing of the forces locked up in Sicily, Africa, Numidia, etc. It was held quite unadvisable by Pompey's party to strip the distant provinces of their troops, or the great provincial cities of their garrisons. All these were accounted as so many reversionary chances against

Cæsar. But certainly a bolder game was likely to have prospered better; had large drafts from all these distant armies been ordered home, even Cæsar's talents might have been perplexed, and his immediate policy must have been so far baffled as to force him back upon Transalpine Gaul. Yet if such a plan were eligible, it does not appear that Cicero had ever thought of it; and certainly it was not Pompey, amongst so many senatorial heads, who could be blamed for neglecting it. Neglect he did; but Pompey had the powers of a commander-in-chief for the immediate arrangements; but in the general scheme of the war he, whose game was to call himself the servant of the Senate, counted but for one amongst many concurrent authorities. Combining therefore his limited authority with his defective materials, we cannot go along with Cicero in the whole bitterness of his censure. The fact is, no cautious scheme whatever, no practicable scheme could have kept pace with Cicero's burning hatred to Cæsar. 'Forward, forward! crush the monster; stone him, stab him, hurl him into the sea!' This was the war-song of Cicero for ever; and men like Domitius, who shared in his hatreds, as well as in his unseasonable temerity, by precipitating upon Cæsar troops that were unqualified for the contest, lost the very *élite* of the Italian army at Corfinium; and such men were soon found to have been embarked upon the ludicrous enterprise of 'catching a Tartar;' following and seeking those

'Quos opimusFallere et effugere est triumphus.'

ADDITIONAL NOTES FOR CICERO.

I.

Bribery was it? which had been so organized as the sole means of succeeding at elections, and which, once rendered necessary as the organ of assertion for each man's birthright, became legitimate; in which Cicero himself declared privately that there was 'εξοχη in nullo,' no sort of pre-eminence, one as bad as another, *pecunia exaequet omnium dignitatem.* Money was the universal leveller. Was it gladiators bought for fighting with? These were bought by his friend Milo as well as his enemy Clodius, by Sextus Pompey on one side as much as by Cæsar on the other. Was it neglect of *obnunciatio?* And so far as regards treating, Cicero himself publicly justified it against the miserable theatrical Cato. How ridiculous to urge that against a popular man as a crime, when it was sometimes enjoined by the Senate with menaces as a duty! Was it the attacking all obnoxious citizens' houses? That was done by one side quite as much as by the other, and signifies little, for the attack always fell on some leading man in wealth; and such a man's house was a fortress. Was it accepting provinces from the people? Cicero would persuade us that this was an unheard of crime in Clodius. But how came it that so many others did the same thing? Nay, that the Senate abetted them in doing it; saying to such a person, 'Oh, X., we perceive that you have extorted from the people.'

II.

Then his being recalled; what if a man should say that his nephew was for it, and all his little nieces, not to mention his creditors? The Senate were for it. But why not? Had the Senate exiled him? And, besides, he was their agent.

III.

It was 'an impious bargain' are the words of Middleton, and Deiotarus who broke it was a prince of noble character. What was he noble for? We never heard of anything very noble that he did; and we doubt whether Dr. Conyers knew more about him than we. But we happen to know why he calls him noble. Cicero, who long afterwards came to know this king personally and gave him a good dinner, says now upon hearsay (for he had then never been near him, and could have no accounts of him but from the wretched Quintus) that *in eo multa regia fuerunt*. Why yes, amputating heads was in those parts a very regal act. But what he chiefly had in his eye, comes out immediately after. Speaking to Clodius, he says that the visit of this king was so bright, *maxime quod tibi nullum nummum dedit*.

IV.

Wicked Middleton says that Cicero followed his conscience in following Pompey and the cause approved by what in the odious slang of his own days he calls 'the honest men.' But be it known unto him that he tells a foul falsehood. He followed his personal gratitude. This he is careful to say over and over again. Some months before he had followed what he deemed the cause of the Commonwealth and of the *boni*. The *boni* were vanished, he sought them and found only a heap of selfish nobles, half crazy with fear and half crazy with pride. These were gone, but Pompey the man remained that he clung to. And in his heart of hearts was another feeling—hatred to Cæsar.

V.

403. 'Cicero had only stept aside' was the technical phrase for lurking from creditors. So Bishop Burnet of Sir Edmondbury Godfrey, it was thought he might have stept aside for debt.

FOOTNOTES:

[19] Cicero entered on the office of Proconsul of Cilicia on the last day of July, 703 A.U.C.; he resigned it on the last day but one of July, 704.—ED.

V. MEMORIAL CHRONOLOGY.

I. *The Main Subject Opened.* What is Chronology, and how am I to teach it? The *what* is poorly appreciated, and chiefly through the defects of the *how*. Because it is so ill-taught, therefore in part it is that Chronology is so unattractive and degraded. Chronology is represented to be the handmaid of history. But unless the machinery for exhibiting this is judicious, the functions, by being obscured, absolutely lose all their value, flexibility, and attraction. Chronology is not meant only to enable us to refer each event to its own particular era—that may be but trivial knowledge, of little value and of slight significance in its application; but chronology has higher functions. It teaches not only when A happened, but also with what other events, B, C, or D, it was associated. It may be little to know that B happened 500 years before Christ, but it may be a most important fact that A and B happened concurrently with D, that both B and D were prepared by X, and that through their concurrent operation arose the ultimate possibility of Z. The mere coincidences or consecutions, mere accidents of simultaneity or succession, of precession or succession, maybe less than nothing. But the co-operation towards a common result, or the relation backwards to a common cause, may be so important as to make the entire difference between a story book, on the one hand, and a philosophic history, on the other, of man as a creature.

History is not an anarchy; man is not an accident. The very motions of the heavenly bodies for many a century were thought blind and without law. Now we have advanced so far into the light as to perceive the elaborate principles of their order, the original reason of their appearing, the stupendous equipoise of their attraction and repulsion, the divine artifice of their compensations, the original ground of their apparent disorder, the enormous system of their reactions, the almost infinite intricacy of their movements. In these very anomalies lies the principle of their order. A curve is long in showing its elements of fluxion; we must watch long in order to compute them; we must wait in order to know the law of their relations and the music of the deep mathematical principles which they obey. A piece of music, again, from the great hand of Mozart or Beethoven, which seems a mere anarchy to the dull, material mind, to the ear which is instructed by a deep sensibility reveals a law of controlling power, determining its movements, its actions and reactions, such as cannot be altogether hidden, even when as yet it is but dimly perceived.

So it is in history, though the area of its interest is yet wider, and the depths to which it reaches more profound; all its contradictory phenomena move under one embracing law, and all its contraries shall finally be solved in the clear perception of this law.

Reading and study ill-conducted run to waste, and all reading and study are ill-conducted which do not plant the result as well as the fact or date in the memory. With no form of knowledge is this more frequently the case than with history. Such is the ill-arranged way of telling all stories, and so perfectly without organization is the record of history, that of what is of little significance there is much, and of what is of deep and permanent signification there is little or nothing.

The first step in breaking ground upon this almost impracticable subject, is—to show the student a true map of the field in which his labours are to lie. Most people have a vague preconception, peopling the fancy with innumerable shadows, of some vast wilderness or Bilidulgerid of trackless time, over which are strewed the wrecks of events without order, and persons without limit. *Omne ignotum*, says Tacitus, *pro magnifico*; that is, everything which lies amongst the shades and darkness of the indefinite, and everything which is in the last degree confused, seems infinite. But the gloom of uncertainty seems far greater than it really is.

One short distribution and circumscription of historical ages will soon place matters in a more hopeful aspect. Fabulous history ceases, and authentic history commences, just three-quarters of a millennium before Jesus Christ; that is, just 750 years. Let us call this space of time, viz., the whole interval from the year 750 B.C. up to the Incarnation of Christ, the first chamber of history. I do not mean that precisely 750 years before our Saviour's birth, fabulous and mythological history started like some guilty thing at the sound of a cock-crowing, and vanished as with the sound of harpies' wings. It vanished as the natural darkness of night vanishes. A stealthy twilight first began to divide and give shape to the formless shadows: what previously had been one blank mass of darkness began to break into separate forms: outlines became perceptible, groups of figures started forward into relief; chaos began to shape and organize its gloomy masses. Next, and by degrees, came on the earliest dawn. This ripened imperceptibly into a rosy aurora that gave notice of some mightier power approaching. And at length, but not until the age of Cyrus, five centuries and a half before Christ, precisely one century later, the golden daylight of authentic history sprang above the horizon and was finally established. Since that time, whatever want of light we may have to lament is due to the *loss* of records, not to their original *absence*; due to the victorious destructions of time, not[20] to the error of the human mind confounding the provinces of Fable and of History.

Let the first chamber of history therefore be that which stretches from the year 750 B.C. to the era of His Incarnation. I say 750 for the present, because it would be quite idle, in dealing with intervals of time so vast, to take notice of any little excess or defect by which the actual period differed from the ideal; strictly speaking, the period of authentic history commences sixteen or seventeen years earlier. But for the present let us say in round numbers that this period commenced 750 years B.C. And let the first chamber of history be of that duration.

B. Next let us take an equal space *after* Christ. This will be the second chamber of history. Starting from the birth of our Saviour, it will terminate in the middle of the eighth century, or in the early years of Charlemagne. These surely are most remarkable eras.

C. Then passing for the present without explanation to the year 1100 for the first Crusade, let us there fix one foot of our 'golden compasses,' and with the other mark off an equal period of 750 years. This carries us up nearly to the reign of George III, of England. And this will be the third great chamber of history.

D. Fourthly, there will now remain a period just equal to one-half of such a chamber, viz.: 350 years between Charlemagne's cradle and the first Crusade, the terminal era of the second chamber and the inaugural era of the third. This we will call the ante-chamber of No. 3.

Now, upon reviewing these chambers and antechambers, the first important remark for the student is, that the second chamber is nearly empty of all incidents. Take away the migrations and invasions of the several Northern nations who overran the Western Empire, broke it up, and laid the foundations of the great nations of Christendom—England, France, Spain—and take away the rise of Mahommedanism, and there would remain scarcely anything memorable.

From all this we draw the following inference: that memory is, in certain cases, connected with great effort, in others, with no effort at all. Of one class we may say, that the facts absolutely deposit themselves in the memory; they settle in our memories as a sediment or deposition from a liquor settles in a glass; of another we may say that the facts cannot maintain their place in the memory without continued exertion, and with something like violence to natural tendencies. Now, beyond all other facts, the facts of dates are the most severely of this latter class. Oftentimes the very actions or sufferings of a man, empire, army, are hard to be remembered because they are non-significant, non-characteristic: they belong by no more natural or intellectual right to that man, empire, army, than to any other man, empire, army. We remember, for instance, the simple diplomacy of Greece, when she summoned all States to the grand duty of exterminating the barbarian from her limits, and throwing back the tides of barbarism within its natural limits; for this appealed to what was noblest in human nature. We forget the elaborate intrigues which preceded the Peloponnesian war, for these appealed only to vulgar and ordinary motives of self-aggrandisement. We remember the trumpet voice which summoned Christendom to deliver Christ's sepulchre from Pagan insults, for that was the great romance of religious sentiment. But we forget the treaties by which this or that Crusading king delivered his army from Mahometan victors, because these proceeded on the common principles of fear and self-interest; principles having no peculiar relation to those from which the Crusades had arisen.

Now, if even actions themselves are easily dropped from the memory, because they stand in no logical relation to the central interest concerned, how much more and how universally must dates be liable to oblivion— dates which really have no more discoverable connection with any name of man or place or event, than the letters or syllables of that name have with the great cause or principles with which it may happen to have been associated. Why should Themistocles or Aristides have flourished 500 B.C., rather than 250, 120, or any other number of years? No conceivable relation—hardly so much as any fanciful relation—can be established between the man and his era. And in this one (to all appearance insuperable) difficulty, in this absolute defect of all connection between the two objects that are to be linked together in the memory, lies the startling task of Chronology. Chronology is required to chain together—and so that one shall inevitably recall the other—a name and an era which with regard to each other are like two clouds, aerial, insulated, mutually repulsive, and throwing out no points for grappling or locking on, neither offering any natural indications of interconnection, nor apparently by art, contrivance,[21] or fiction, susceptible of any.

II. *Jewish as compared with other records.*—Let us open our review with the annals of Judea; and for two reasons: first, because in the order of time it *was* the inaugural chapter, so that the order of our rehearsal does but conform to the order of the facts; secondly, because on another principle of arrangement, viz., its relation to the capital interests of human nature, it stands first in another sense by a degree which cannot be measured.

These are two advantages, in comparison with all other history whatever, which have crowned the Jewish History with mysterious glory, and of these the pupil should be warned in her introductory lesson. The first is: that the Jewish annals open by one whole millennium before all other human records. Full a thousand years had the chronicles of the Hebrew nation been in motion and unfolding that sublime story, fitter for the lyre and the tumultuous organ, than for unimpassioned recitation, before the earliest whispers of the historic muse began to stir in any other land. Amongst Pagan nations, Greece was the very foremost to attempt that almost impracticable object under an imperfect civilization—the art of fixing in forms not perishable, and of transmitting to distant generations, her social revolutions.[22] She wanted paper through her earlier periods, she wanted typographic art, she wanted, above all, other resources for such a purpose—the art of reading as a national accomplishment. How could people record freely and fervently, with Hebrew rapture, those events which must be painfully chiselled out in marble, or expensively ploughed and furrowed into brazen tablets? What freedom to the motions of human passion, where an *extra* word or two of description must be purchased by a day's labour? But, above all, what motive could exist for the accumulation or the adequate diffusion of records, howsoever inscribed, on slabs of marble or of bronze, on leather, or plates of wood, whilst as yet no general machinery of education had popularized the art of reading? Until the age of Pericles each separate Grecian city could hardly have furnished three citizens on an average able to read. Amongst a people so illiterate, how could manu*scripts* or manu*sculpts* excite the interest which is necessary to their conservation? Of what value would a shipload of harps prove to a people unacquainted with the science or the practical art of music? Too much or too little interest alike defeat this primary purpose of the record. Records must be *self*-conservative before they can be applied to the conservation of events. Amongst ourselves the *black-letter* records of English heroes by Grafton and Hollinshed, of English voyagers by Hakluyt, of English martyrs by Fox, perished in a very unusual proportion by excessive use through successive generations of readers: but amongst the Greeks they would have perished by neglect. The too much of the English usage and the too little of the Grecian would have tended to the same result. Books and the art of reading must ever be powerful re-agents—each upon the other: until books were multiplied, there could be no general accomplishment of reading. Until the accomplishment was taken up into the system of education, books insculptured by painful elaboration upon costly substances must be too much regarded as jewellery to obtain a domestic value for the mass.

The problem, therefore, was a hard one for Greece—to devise any art, power or machinery for fixing and propagating the great memorials of things and persons. Each generation as it succeeded would more and more furnish subjects for the recording pen of History, yet each in turn was compelled to see them slipping away like pearls from a fractured necklace. It seems easy, but in practice it must be nearly impossible, to take aim, as it were, at a remote generation—to send a sealed letter down to a posterity two centuries removed—or by any human resources, under the Grecian conditions of the case, to have a chance of clearing that vast bridgeless gulf which separates the present from the far-off ages of perfect civilization. Maddening it must have been to know by their own experience, derived from the far-off past, that no monuments had much chance of duration, except precisely those small ones of medals and sculptured gems, which, if durable by metallic substance and interesting by intrinsic value, were in the same degree more liable to loss by shipwreck, fire, or other accidents applying to portable things, but above all furnished no field for more than an intense abstractiveness. The Iliad arose, as we shall say, a thousand years before Christ, consequently it bisected precisely the Hebrew history which arose two thousand years before the same era. Now the Iliad was the very first historic record of the Greeks, and it was followed at intervals by many other such sections of history, in the shape of *Nostoi*, poems on the homeward adventures of the Greek heroes returning from Troy, or of Cyclical Poems taking a more comprehensive range of action from the same times, filling up the interspace of 555 years between this memorable record of the one great Pagan Crusade[23] at the one limit, and the first Greek prose history—that of Herodotus—at the lower limit. Even through a space of 555 years *subsequent* to the Iliad, which has the triple honour of being the earliest Greek book, the earliest Greek poem, the earliest Greek history, we see the Grecian annals but imperfectly sustained; legends treated with a legendary variety; romances embroidered with romantic embellishments; poems, which, if Greek narrative poetry allowed of but little fiction and sternly rejected all pure invention, yet originally rested upon semi-fabulous and mythological marvels, and were thus far poetic in the basis, that when they durst not invent they could still garble by poetical selection where they chose; and thus far lying—that if they were compelled to conform themselves to the popular traditions which must naturally rest upon a pedestal of fact, it was fact as seen through an atmosphere of superstition, and imperceptibly modified by priestly arts.

The sum, therefore, of our review is, that one thousand [1,000] years B.C. did the earliest Grecian record appear, being also the earliest Greek poem, and this poem being the earliest Greek book; secondly, that for the five-hundred-and-fifty-five [555] years subsequent to the earliest record, did the same legendary form of historic composition continue to subsist. On the other hand, as a striking antithesis to this Grecian condition of history, we find amongst the Hebrews a circumstantial deduction of their annals from the very nativity of their nation—that is, from the birth of the Patriarch Isaac, or, more strictly, of his son the Patriarch Jacob—down to the captivity of the two tribes, their restoration by Cyrus, and the dedication of the Second Temple. This Second Temple brings us abreast of Herodotus, the first Greek historian. Fable with the Greeks is not yet distinguished from fact, but a sense of the distinction is becoming clearer.

The privileged use of the word Crusade, which we have ventured to make with reference to the first great outburst of Greek enthusiasm, suggests a grand distinction, which may not unreasonably claim some illustration, so deep does it reach in exhibiting the contrast between the character of the early annals of the Hebrews and those of every other early nation.

Galilee and Joppa, and Nazareth, Jerusalem and the Mount of Olives— what a host of phantoms, what a resurrection from the graves of twelve and thirteen centuries for the least reflecting of the army, had his mission connected him no further with these objects than as a traveller passing amongst them. But when the nature of his service was considered, the purposes with which he allied himself, and the vindicating which he supported, many times as a volunteer—the dullest natures must have been penetrated, the lowest exalted.[24]

To this grand passion of religious enthusiasm stands opposed, according to the general persuasion, the passion, equally exalted, or equally open to exaltation, of love. 'So the whole ear of Denmark is abused.' Love, chivalrous love, love in its noblest forms, was a passion unknown to the Greeks; as we may well suppose in a country where woman was not honoured, not esteemed, not treated with the confidence which is the basis of all female dignity. However, this subject I shall leave untouched: simply reminding the reader that even conceding for a moment so monstrous an impossibility as that pure chivalrous love, as it exists under Christian institutions, could have had an existence in the Greece of 1000 B.C.; the more elevated, the more tender it was, the less fitted it could be for the coarse air of a camp. The holy sepulchre would command reverence, and the expression of reverence, from the lowest sutler of the camp; but we may easily imagine what coarse jests would eternally surround the name of Helen amongst the Greek soldiery, and everything connected with the cause which drew them into the field.

Yet even this coarse travesty of a noble passion was a higher motive than the Greeks really obeyed in the war with Troy. England, it has been sometimes said, went to war with Spain, during George II.'s reign, on account of Capt. Jenkins's ears, which a brutal Spanish officer, in the cowardly abuse of his power, had nailed to the mast. And if she did, the cause was a noble one, however unsuitably expounded by its outward heraldry. There the cause was noble, though the outward sign was below its dignity. But in the Iliad, if we may give that name to the total expedition against Troy and the Troad, the relations were precisely inverted. Its outward sign, its ostensible purpose, was noble: for it was woman. *But the real and sincere motive which collected fifty thousand Grecians under one common banner, was* (I am well assured upon meditation) *money—money, and money's worth.* No less motive in that age was adequate to the effect. Helen was, assuredly, no such prize considering her damaged reputation and other circumstances. Revenge might intermingle in a very small proportion with the general principle of the war; as to the oath and its obligation, which is supposed to have bound over the princes of Greece: that I suppose to be mere cant; for how many princes were present in the field that never could have been suitors to Helen, nor parties to the oath? Do we suppose old Nestor to have been one? A young gentleman 'rising' 99, as the horse-jockeys say; or by some reckonings, 113! No, plunder was the object.

The truth was this—the plain historic truth for any man not wilfully blind—Greece was miserably poor; that we know by what we find five centuries after, when she must, like other people who find little else to do, have somewhat bettered her condition. Troy and the Troad were redundantly rich; it was their great crime to be so. Already the western coast of Asia Minor was probably studded with Greek colonies, standing in close connection with the great capitals on the Euphrates or the Tigris, and sharing in the luxurious wealth of the great capitals on the Euphrates or the Tigris. Mitford most justly explained the secret history of Cæsar's expedition to England out of his wish to find a new slave country.[25] And after all the romantic views of the Grecian expedition to the Troad, I am satisfied we should look for its true solution in the Greek poverty and the wealth—both *locally concentrated* and *portable*—of the Trojans. Land or cities were things too much diffused: and even the son of Peleus or of Telamon could not put them into his pocket. But golden tripods, purple hangings or robes, fine horses, and beautiful female slaves could be found over the Hellespont. Helen, the *materia litis*, the subject of quarrel on its earliest pretence, could not be much improved by a ten years' blockade. But thousands of more youthful Helens were doubtless carried back to Greece. And in this prospect of booty most assuredly lay the unromantic motive of the sole romantic expedition amongst the Greeks.

III. *Oriental History.*—We here set aside the earlier tangle of legend and fact which is called Oriental History, and for these reasons: (1) instead of promoting the solution of chronological problems, Oriental history is itself the most perplexing of those problems; (2) the perpetual straining after a high fabulous antiquity amongst the nations of the east, vitiates all the records; (3) the vast empires into which the plains of Asia moulded the eastern nations, allowed of no such rivalship as could serve to check their legends by collateral statements; and (4) were all this otherwise, still the great permanent schism of religion and manners has so effectually barred all coalition between Europe and Asia, from the oldest times, that of necessity their histories have flowed apart with little more reciprocal reference or relationship, than exists between the Rhine and the Danube—rivers, which almost meeting in their sources, ever after are continually widening their distance until they fall into different seas two thousand miles apart. Asia never, at any time, much acted upon Europe; and when later ages had forced them into artificial connections, it was always Europe that acted upon Asia; never Asia, upon any commensurate scale, that acted upon Europe.[26]

Not, therefore, in Asia can the first footsteps of chronology be sought; not in Africa, because, *first*, the records of Egypt, so far as any have survived, are intensely Asiatic; liable to the same charge of hieroglyphic ambiguity combined with the exaggerations of outrageous nationality; because, *secondly*, the separate records of the adjacent State of Cyrene have perished; because, *thirdly*, the separate records of the next State, Carthage, have perished; because, *fourthly*, the learned labours of Mauritania[27] have also perished.

Thus the pupil is satisfied that of mere necessity the chronologer must resort to Europe for his earliest monuments and his earliest authentications—for the facts to be attested, and for the evidences which are to attest them. But if to Europe, next, to what part of Europe? Two great nations—great in a different sense, the one by dazzling brilliancy of intellect, the other by weight and dignity of moral grandeur—divide between them the honours of history through the centuries immediately preceding the birth of Christ. To which of these, the pupil asks, am I to address myself? On the one hand, the greater refinement and earlier civilization of Greece would naturally converge all eyes upon her; but then, on the other hand, we cannot forget the '*levitas levissimæ gentis*'—the want of stability, the want of all that we call moral dignity, and by direct consequence, the puerile credulity of that clever, sparkling, but very foolish people, the Greeks. That quality which, beyond all others, the Romans imputed to the Grecian character; that quality which, in the very blaze of admiration, challenged by the Grecian intellect, still overhung with deep shadows their rational pretensions and degraded them to a Roman eye, was the essential *levitas*—the defect of any principle that could have given steadiness and gravity—which constituted the original sin of the Greek character. By *levitas* was meant the passive obedience to casual, random, or contradictory impulses, the absence of all determining principle. Now this *levitas* was the precise anti-pole of the Roman character; which was as massy, self-supported, and filled with resistance to chance impulses, as the Greek character was windy, vain, and servile to such impulses. Both nations, it is true, were superstitious, because all nations, in those ages were intensely superstitious; and each, after a fashion of its own, intensely credulous. But the Roman superstition was coloured by something of a noble pride; the Grecian by vanity. The Greek superstition was fickle and self-contradicting, and liable to sudden changes; the Roman, together with the gloom, had the unity and the perseverance of bigotry. No Christian, even, purified and enlightened by his sublime faith, could more utterly despise the base crawling adorations of Egypt, than did the Roman polytheist, out of mere dignity of mind, while to the frivolous Athenian they were simply objects of curiosity. In the Greek it was a vulgar sentiment of clannish vanity.[28] Even the national self-consequence of a Roman and a Greek were sentiments of different origin, and almost opposite quality; in the Roman it was a sublime and imaginative idea of Rome, of her self-desired grandeur, and, above all, of her divine *destiny*, over which last idea brooded a cloud of indefinite expectation, not so entirely unlike the exalting expectations of the Jews, looking for ever to some unknown 'Elias' that should come.

Thus perplexed by the very different claims upon his respect in these two exclusive authorities of the ancient world—carried to the Roman by his *moral* feelings, to the Grecian by his intellectual—the student is suddenly delivered from his doubts by the discovery that these two principal streams of history flow absolutely apart through the elder centuries of historical light.

IV. *777 and its Three Great Landmarks.*—In this perplexity, we say, the youthful pupil is suddenly delighted to hear that there is no call upon her to choose between Grecian and Roman guides. Fortunately, and as if expressly to save her from any of those fierce disputes which have risen up between the true Scriptural chronology and the chronology of the mendacious Septuagint, it is laid down that the Greek and Roman history, soon after both had formally commenced, flowed apart for centuries; nor did they so much as hear of each other (unless as we moderns heard of Prester John in Abyssinia, or of the Great Mogul in India), until the Greek colonies in Calabria, etc., began to have a personal meaning for a Roman ear, or until Sicily (as the common field for Greek, Roman, and Carthaginian) began to have a dangerous meaning for all three. As to the Romans, the very grandeur of their self-reliance and the sublime faith which they had in the destinies[29] of Rome, inclined them to carelessness about all but their nearest neighbours, and sustained for ages their illiterate propensities. Illiterate they were, because incurious; and incurious because too haughtily self-confident. The Greeks, on the other hand, amongst the other infirmities attached to their national levity, had curiosity in abundance. But it flowed in other channels. There was nothing to direct their curiosity upon the Romans. Generally speaking, there is good reason for thinking that as, at this day, the privilege of a man to present himself at any court of Christendom is recognised upon his producing a ticket signed by a Lord Chamberlain of some other court, to the effect that 'the Bearer is known at St. James's,' or 'known at the Tuileries,' etc.; so, after the final establishment of the Olympic games, the Greeks looked upon a man's appearance at that great national congress as the criterion and ratification of his being a known or knowable person. Unknown, unannounced personally or by proxy at the great periodic Congress of Greece, even a prince was a *homo ignorabilis*; one whose existence nobody was bound to take notice of. A Persian, indeed, was allowably absent; because, as a permanent public enemy, he could not safely be present. But as to all others, and therefore as to Romans, the rule of law held—that 'to those not coming forward and those not in existence, the same line of argument applies.' [*De non apparentibus et de non existentibus eadem est ratio.*]

Had this been otherwise—had the two nations met freely before the light of history had strengthened into broad daylight—it is certain that the controversies upon chronology would have been far more and more intricate than they are. This profound[30] separation, therefore, has been beneficial to the student in one direction. But in another it has increased his duties; or, if not increased, at all events it serves to remind him of a separate chapter in his chronological researches. Had Rome stood in as close a relation to Greece as Persia did, one single chronology would have sufficed for both. Hardly one event in Persian history has survived for our memory, which is not taken up by the looms of Greece and interwoven with the general arras and texture of Grecian history. And from the era of the Consul Paulus Emilius, something of the same sort takes place between Greece and Rome; and in a partial sense the same result is renewed as often as the successive assaults occur of the Roman-destroying power applied to the several members of the Græco-Macedonian Empire. But these did not commence until Rome had existed for half-a-thousand years. And through all that long period, two-thirds of the entire Roman history up to the Christian era, the two Chronologies flow absolutely apart.

Consequently, because all chronology is thrown back upon Europe, and because the pre-Christian Europe is split into two collateral bodies, and because each of these separate bodies must have a separate head—it follows that chronology, as a pre-Christian chronology, will, like the Imperial eagle, be two-headed. Now this accident of chronology, on a first glance, seems but too likely to confuse and perplex the young student.

How fortunate, then, it must be thought, and what a duty it imposes upon the teacher, not to defeat this bounty of accident by false and pedantic rigour of calculation, that these two heads of the eagle—that head which looks westward for Roman Chronology, that which looks eastward for Grecian Chronology—do absolutely coincide as to their nativity. The birthday of Grecian authentic history everybody agrees to look upon as fixed to the establishment [the *final* establishment] of the Olympic games. And when was *that*? Generally, chronologers have placed this event just 776 years before Christ. Now will any teacher be so 'peevish' [as hostess Quickly calls it]—so perversely unaccommodating—as not to lend herself to the very trivial alteration of one year, just putting the clock back to 7 instead of 6, even if the absolute certainty of the 6 were made out? But if she *will* break with her chronologer, 'her guide, philosopher and friend,' upon so slight a consideration as one year in three-quarters of a millennium, it then becomes my duty to tell her that there is no such certainty in the contested number as she chooses to suppose. Even the era of our Saviour's birth oscillates through an entire Olympiad, or period of four years; to that extent it is unsettled: and in fifty other ways I could easily make out a title to a much more considerable change. In reality, when the object is—not to secure an attorney-like[31] accuracy—but to promote the *liberal* pursuit of chronology, a teacher of good sense would at once direct her pupil to record the date in round terms as just reaching the three-quarters of a thousand years; she would freely sacrifice the entire twenty-six years' difference between 776 and 750, were it not that the same purpose, viz., the purpose of consulting the powers or convenience and capacity of the memory, in neglect and defiance of useless and superstitious arithmetic punctilios, may be much better attained by a more trifling sacrifice. Three-quarters of a millennium, that is three parts in four of a thousand years, is a period easily remembered; but a triple repetition of the number 7, simply saying '*Seven seven seven*' is remembered even *more* easily.[32]

Suppose this point then settled, for anything would be remarkable and highly rememberable which comes near to a common familiar fraction of so vast a period in human affairs as a millennium [a term consecrated to our Christian ears, (1) by its use in the Apocalypse; (2) by its symbolic use in representing the long Sabbath of rest from sin and misery, and finally (3) even to the profane ear by the fact of its being the largest period which we employ in our historical estimates]. But a triple iteration of the number 7, simply saying '*Seven seven seven*,' would be even more rememberable. And, lastly, were it still necessary to add anything by way of reconciling the teacher to the supposed inaccuracy (though, if a real[33] and demonstrated inaccuracy, yet, be it remembered, the very least which *can* occur, viz., an error of a single unit), I will—and once for all, as applying to many similar cases, as often as they present themselves—put this stringent question to every woman of good sense: is it not better, is it not more agreeable to your views for the service of your pupils, that they should find offered to their acceptance some close approximation to the truth which they can very easily remember, than an absolute conformity to the very letter of the truth which no human memory, though it were the memory of Mithridates, could retain? Good sense is shown, above all things, in seeking the practicable which is within our power, by preference to a more exquisite ideal which is unattainable. Not, I grant, in moral or religious things. Then I willingly allow, we are forbidden to sit down contented with imperfect attempts, or to make deliberate compromises with the slightest known evil in principle. To this doctrine I heartily subscribe. But surely in matters *not* moral, in questions of erudition or of antiquarian speculation, or of historical research, we are under a different rule. Here, and in similar cases, it is our business, I conceive with Solon legislating for the Athenians, to contemplate, not what is best in an abstract sense, but what is best under the circumstances of the case. Now the most important circumstances of this case are—that the memory of young ladies must be assumed as a faculty of average power, both as to its apprehensiveness and as to its tenacity; its power of mastering for the moment, and its power of retaining faithfully; that this faculty will not endure the oppression of mere blank facts having no organization or life of logical relation running through them; that by 'not enduring' I mean that it cannot support this harassing and persecution with impunity[34]; that the fine edge of the higher intellectual powers will be taken off by this laborious straining, which is not only dull, but the cause of dulness; that finally, the memory, supposing it in a given and rare case powerful enough to contend successfully with such tasks, must even as regards this time required, hold itself disposable for many other applications; and therefore, as the inference from the whole, that not any slight or hasty, but a most intense and determinate effort should be made to substitute some technical artifices for blank pulls against a dead weight of facts, to substitute fictions, or artificial imitations of logical arrangement, wherever that is possible, for blind arrangements of chance; and finally, in a process which requires every assistance from compromise and accommodation constantly to surrender the rigour of superstitious accuracy, (which, after all its magnificent pretensions, *must* fail in the performance), to humbler probability of a reasonable success.

I have dwelt upon this point longer than would else have been right, because in effect here lies the sole practical obstacle to the realization of a very beautiful framework of chronology, and because I consider myself as now speaking *once for all*. Let us now move forward. I now go on to the other head of the eagle—the head which looks westward.

Here it will be objected that the Foundation of Rome is usually laid down in the year 753 B.C.; and therefore that it differs from the foundation of the Olympiads by as much as 23 or 24 years; and can I have the conscience to ask my fair friends that they should *put the clock back* so far as that? Why, really there is no knowing; perhaps if I were hard pressed by some chronological enemy, I might ask as great a favour even as that. But at present it is not requisite; neither do I mean to play any jugglers' tricks, as perhaps lawfully I might, with the different computations of Varro, of the Capitoline Marbles, etc. All that need be said in this place is simply—that Rome is not Romulus. And let Rome have been founded when she pleases, and let her secret name have been what it might—though really, in default of a better, Rome itself is as decent and *'sponsible* a name as a man would wish—still I presume that Romulus must have been a little older than Rome, the builder a little anterior to what he built. Varro and the Capitoline Tables and Mr. Hook will all agree to that postulate. And whatever some of them may say as to the youth of Romulus, when he first began to wield the trowel, at least, I suppose, he was come to years of discretion; and, if we say twenty-three or twenty-four, which I am as much entitled to say as they to deny it, then we are all right. 'All right behind,' as the mail guards say, 'drive on.' And so I feel entitled to lay my hand upon my heart and assure my fair pupils that Romulus himself and the Olympiads did absolutely start together; and for anything known to the contrary, perhaps in the same identical moment or bisection of a moment. Possibly his first little wolfish howl (for it would be monstrous to think that he or even Remus condescended to a *vagitus* or cry such as a young tailor or rat-catcher might emit) may have symphonized with the ear-shattering trumpet that proclaimed the inauguration of the first Olympic contest, or which blew to the four winds the appellation of the first Olympic victor.

That point, therefore, is settled, and so far, at least, 'all's right behind.' And it is a great relief to my mind that so much is accomplished. Two great arrow-headed nails at least are driven 'home' to the great dome of Chronology from which my whole golden chain of historical dependencies is to swing. And even that will suffice. Careful navigators, indeed, like to ride by three anchors; but I am content with what I have achieved, even if my next attempt should be less satisfactory.

It is certainly a very striking fact to the imagination that great revolutions seldom come as solitary cases. It never rains but it pours. At times there *is* some dark sympathy, which runs underground, connecting remote events like a ground-swell in the ocean, or like the long careering[35] of an earthquake before it makes its explosion. *Abyssus abyssum invocat*—'One deep calleth to another.' And in some incomprehensible way, powers not having the slightest *apparent* interconnexion, no links through which any *casual* influence could rationally be transmitted, do, nevertheless, in fact, betray either a blind nexus—an undiscoverable web of dependency upon each other, or else a dependency upon some common cause equally undiscoverable. What possible, what remote connexion could the dissolution of the Assyrian empire have with the Olympiads or with the building of Rome? Certainly none at all that we can see; and yet these great events so nearly synchronize that even the latest of them seems but a more distant undulation of the same vast swell in the ocean, running along from west to east, from the Tiber to the Tigris. Some great ferment of revolution was then abroad. The overthrew of Nineveh as the capital of the Assyrian empire, the ruin of the dynasty ending in Sardanapalus, and the subsequent dismemberment of the Assyrian empire, took place, according to most chronologers, 747 years B.C., just 30 years, therefore, after the two great events which I have assigned to 777. These two events are in the strictest and most capital sense the inaugural events of history, the very pillars of Hercules which indicate a *ne plus ultra* in that direction; namely, that all beyond is no longer history but romance. I am exceedingly anxious to bring this Assyrian revolution also to the same great frontier line of columns. In a gross general way it might certainly be argued that in such a great period, thirty years, or one generation, can be viewed as nothing more than a trifling quantity. But it must also be considered that the exact time, and even the exact personality,[36] of Sardanapalus in all his relations are not known. All are vast phantoms in the Assyrian empire; I do not say fictions, but undefined, unmeasured, immeasurable realities; far gone down into the mighty gulf of shadows, and for us irrecoverable. All that is known about the Assyrian empire is its termination under Sardanapalus. It was then coming within Grecian twilight; and it will be best to say that, generally speaking, Sardanapalus coincided with Romulus and the Greek Olympiad. To affect any nearer accuracy than this would be the grossest reliance on the mere jingle of syllables. History would be made to rest on something less than a pun; for such as *Palus* and *Pul,* which is all that learned archbishops can plead as their vouchers in the matter of Assyria, there is not so much as the argument of a child or the wit of a punster.

Upon the whole, the teacher will make the following remarks to her pupils, after having read what precedes; remarks partly upon the new mode of delivering chronology, and partly upon the things delivered:

I. She will notice it—as some improvement—that the three great leading events, which compose the opening of history not fabulous, are here, for the first time, placed under the eye in their true relations of time, viz., as about contemporary. For without again touching on the question—do they, or do they not, vary from each other in point of time by twenty-three and by thirty years—it will be admitted by everybody that, at any rate, the three events stand equally upon the frontier line of authentic history. A frontier or debateable land is always of some breadth. They form its inauguration. And they would do so even if divided by a much wider interval. Now, it is very possible to know of A, B, and C, separately, that each happened in such a year, say 1800; and yet never to have noticed them consciously *as* contemporary. We read of many a man (L, M, N, suppose), that he was born in 1564, or that he died in 1616. And we may happen separately to know that these were the years in which Shakespeare was born and died. Yet, for all that, we may never happen consciously to notice with respect to any one of the men, L, M, N, that he was a contemporary of Shakespeare's. Now, this was the case with regard to the three great events, Greek, Roman, and Assyrian. No chronologer failed to observe of each in its separate place that it occurred somewhere about 750 years B.C. But every chronologer had failed to notice this coincident time of each *as* coincident. And, accordingly, all failed to converge these three events into one focus as the solemn and formal opening of history. It is good to have a beginning, a starting post, from which to date all possible historical events that are worthy to be regarded as such. But it is better still to find that by the rarest of accidents, by a good luck that could never have been looked for, the three separate starting posts—which historical truth obliges us to assume for the three great fields of history, Roman, Grecian, and Asiatic[37]—all closely coincide in point of time; or, to use the Greek technical term, all closely synchronize.

II. With respect to Greece and the Olympiad in particular, she will inform her pupil that the Olympic games, celebrated near the town of Olympia, recurred every fifth year; that is to say, there was a clear interval of four years between each revolution of the games. Each Olympiad, therefore, containing four years, it is usual in citing the particular Olympiad in which an event happened, to cite also the year, should that be known, or, being known, should that be of importance. Thus Olymp. CX. 3 would mean that such a thing, say X, occurred in the third year of the 110th Olympiad; that is, four times 110 will be 440; and this, deducted from 777 (the era of the Olympiads), leaves 337 years B.C. as the era when X occurred. Only that, upon reviewing the case, we find that the 110th Olympiad was not absolutely completed, not by one year; which, subtracted from the 337, leaves 336 B.C. as the true date. If her pupil should say, 'But were there no great events in Greece before the Olympiads?' the teacher will answer, 'Yes, a few, but not many of a rank sufficient to be called Grecian.' They are merely local events; events of Thessaly, suppose; events of Argos; but much too obscure, both as to the facts, as to the meaning of the facts, and as to the dates, to be worth any student's serious attention. There were, however, three events worthy to be called *Grecian*; partly because they interested more States than one of Greece; and partly because they have since occupied the Athenian stage, and received a sort of consecration from the great masters of Grecian tragedy. These three events were the fatal story of the house of Œdipus; a story stretching through three generations; and in which the war against the Seven Gates of Thebes was but an episode. Secondly, the Argonautic expedition (voyage of the ship *Argo*, and of the sailors in that ship, *i.e.*, the Argonauts), which is consecrated as the first voyage of any extent undertaken by Greeks. Both these events are as full of heroic marvels, and of supernatural marvels, as the legends of King Arthur, Merlin, and the Fairy Morgana. Later than these absolute romances comes the semi-romance of the Iliad, or expedition against Troy. This, the most famous of all Pagan romances, we know by two separate criteria to be later in date than either of the two others; first, because the actors in the Iliad are the descendants of those who figured as actors in the others; secondly, from the subdued tone of the romantic[38] which prevails throughout the Iliad. Now, with respect to these three events in Grecian history, anterior to the Olympiads, which are all that a young student ought to notice, it is sufficient if generally she is made aware of the order in which they stand to each other, or, at least, that the Iliad comes last in the series, and if as to this last and greatest of the series, she fixes its era precisely to one thousand years before Christ. Chronologers, indeed, sometimes bring it down to something lower. But one millennium, the clear unembarrassed cyphers of 1,000, whether in counting guineas or years, is a far simpler and a far more rememberable era than any qualifications of this round number; which qualifications, let it not for a moment be forgotten, are not at all better warranted than the simpler expression. One only amongst all chronologers has anything to stand upon that is not as unsubstantial as a cloud; and this is Sir Isaac Newton. And the way in which he proceeded it may be well to explain, in order that the young pupil may see what sort of evidences we have *prior to the Olympiads* for any chronological fact. Sir Isaac endeavoured by calculating backwards to ascertain the exact time of some celestial phenomenon—as, suppose, an eclipse of the sun, or such and such positions of the heavenly bodies with regard to each other. This phenomenon, whatever it were, call X. Then if (upon looking into the Argonautic Expedition or any other romance of those elder times) he finds X actually noticed as co-existing with any part of the adventures, in that case he has fixed by absolute observation, as it were, what we may call the latitude and longitude of that one historical event; and then using this, as we use our modern meridian of Greenwich, as a point of starting, he can deduce the distances of all subsequent events by tracing them through the sons, grandsons, and great-grandsons of the several actors concerned. The great question which will then remain to be settled is, how many years to allow for a generation; and, secondly, in monarchies, how much to allow for a reign, since often two successive reigns will not be two successive generations, because whilst the two reigns are distinct quantities, the two lives are coincident through a great part of their duration. Now, of course, Sir Isaac is very often open to serious criticism, or to overpowering doubts. That is inevitable. But on the whole he treads upon something like a firm footing. Others, as regards that era, tread upon mere clouds, and their authority goes for nothing at all.

Such being the state of the case, let the pupil never trouble her memory for one moment with so idle an effort as that of minutely fixing or retaining dates that, after all, are more doubtful, and for us irrecoverable, than the path of some obscure trading ship in some past generation through the Atlantic Ocean. Generally, it will be quite near enough to the truth if she places upon the meridian of 1000 years B.C. the three Romances—Argonautic, Theban, Trojan; and she will then have the satisfaction of finding that, as at the opening of authentic history, she found the Roman, the Greek, and the Asiatic inaugural events coinciding in the same exact focus, so in these semi-fabulous or ante-Olympian events, she finds that one and the same effort of memory serves to register *them*, and also the most splendid of the Jewish eras—that of David and Solomon. The round sum of 1000 years B.C., so easily remembered, without distinction, without modification, '*sans phrase*' (to quote a brutal regicide), serves alike for the Seven-gated Thebes,[39] for Troy, and for Jerusalem in its most palmy days.

V. *A Perplexity Cleared Up.*—Before passing onward here, it is highly important to notice a sort of episode in history, which fills up the interval between 777 and 555, but which is constantly confounded and perplexed with what took place before 777.

The word *Assyria* is that by which the perplexity is maintained. The Assyrian empire, as the pupil is told, was destroyed in the person of Sardanapalus. Yet, in her Bible, she reads of Sennacherib, King of Assyria. 'Was Sennacherib, then, before Sardanapalus?' she will ask; and her teacher will inform her that he was not.

Such things puzzle her. They seem palpable contradictions. But now let her understand that out of the Assyrian empire split off three separate kingdoms, of which one was called the Assyrian, not empire, but kingdom; there lurks the secret of the error. And to this kingdom of Assyria it was that Sennacherib belonged. Or, in order to represent by a sensible image this derivation of kingdoms from the stock of the old superannuated Assyrian empire (to which belonged Nimrod, Ninus, and Semiramis—those mighty phantoms, with their incredible armies); let her figure to herself some vast river, like the Nile or the Ganges, with the form assumed by its mouths. Often it will happen, where such a river is not hemmed in between rocks, or confined to the bed of a particular valley, that, perhaps, a hundred or two of miles before reaching the sea, upon coming into a soft, alluvial soil, it will force several different channels for itself. As these must make angles to each other, in order to form different roads, the land towards the disemboguing of the river will take the arrangement of a triangle. And as that happens to be the form of a Greek capital D (in the Greek alphabet called Delta), it has been usual to call such an arrangement of a great river's mouth a Delta.

Now, then, let her think of the Assyrian empire under the notion of the Nile, descending from far distant regions, and from fountains that were concealed for ages, if even now discovered. Then, when it approaches the sea, and splits up its streams, so as to form a Delta, let her regard that Delta as the final state of the Assyrian power, the kingdom state lasting for about two centuries until swallowed up altogether, and remoulded into unity by the Persian empire.

The Delta, therefore, or the Nile dividing into three streams, will represent the three kingdoms formed out of the ruins of the Assyrian empire, when falling to pieces by the death of Sardanapalus. One of these three kingdoms is often called the Median; one the Chaldæan; and the third is called the Assyrian kingdom. But the most rememberable shape in which they can be recalled is, perhaps, by the names of their capitals. The capital cities were as follows: of the first, *Ecbatana*, which is the modern *Hamadan*; of the second, *Babylon*, on the Euphrates, of which the ruins have been fully ascertained in our own times; at present, nothing remains *but* ruins, and these ruins are dangerous to visit, both from human marauders prowling in that neighbourhood, and from wild beasts of the most formidable class, which are so little disturbed in their awful lairs, that they bask at noon-day amongst the huge hills of half-vitrified bricks. Finally, of the third kingdom, which still retained the name of Assyria, the metropolis was *Nineveh*, on the Tigris, revealed by Layard.

These three kingdoms had some internal wars and revolutions during the two centuries which elapsed from the great period 777 (the period of Sardanapalus), until the days of Cyrus, the Persian. By that time the three had become two, the kingdom of Nineveh had been swallowed up, and Cyrus, who was destined to form the Persian empire upon their ruins, found one change less to be effected than might have been looked for. Of the two which remained, he conquered one, and the other came to him by maternal descent. Thus he gained all three, and moulded them into one, called Persia.

VI. *Five and Five and Five.*—The crowning action in which Cyrus figures is, therefore, that of conqueror of Babylon, and all the details of his career point forward, like markings on the dial, towards that great event, as full of interest for the imagination as any of the events of pre-Christian history. I would fain for once by the aid of metre, fix more firmly in the mind of the reader the grandeur and imposing significance of this event:

Thus in Five and Five and Five did Cyrus the Great of Elam,[40]On a festal night break in with roar of the fierce alalagmos.[41]Over Babylonian walls, over tower and turret of entrance,Over helmèd heads, and over the carnage of armies.Idle the spearsman's spear, Assyrian scymitar idle;Broken the bow-string lay of the Mesopotamian archer;'Ride to the halls of Belshazzar, ride through the murderous uproar;Ride to the halls of Belshazzar!' commanded Cyrus of Elam.They rode to the halls of Belshazzar. Oh, merciful, merciful angels!That prompt sweet tears to men, hang veils, hang drapery darkest,—If any may hide or may pall this night's tempestuous horror.Like a deluge the army poured in on their snorting Bactrian horses,Rattled the Parthian quivers, rang the Parthian harness of iron,High upon spears rode the torches, and from them in showery blazesRained splendour lurid and fierce on the dreamlike ruinous uproar,Such as delusions often from fever's fierce vertical ardourShow through the long-chambered halls and corridors endless,Blazing with cruel light—show to the brain of the stricken man;Such as the angel of dreams sometimes sends to the guilty.Such light lay in open front, but palpable ebony blackness,Sealed every far-off street in deep and awful abysses,Out of which rose like phantoms, rose and sank as a sea-birdRises and sinks on the waves of a dim, tumultuous ocean,Faces dabbled in blood, phantasmagory direful and scenic.

   *   *   *   *

But where is Belshazzar the Lord? Has he fled? Has he found an asylum?Or still does he pace in his palace, blind-seeming or moonstruck?Still does he tread proudly the palace, fancy-deluded,Prophets of falsehood trusting, or false Babylonian idols,Defying the odious truth from the summit of empire!Lo! at his palace gates the fierce Apollyon's great army,With maces uplifted, stand to make way for great Cyrus of Elam.Watching for signal from him whose truncheon this way or that bids:'Strike!' said Cyrus the King. 'Strike!' said the princes of Elam;And the brazen gates at the word, like flax that is broken asunderBy fire from earth or from heaven, snapped as a bulrush,Snapped as a reed, as a wand, as the tiny toy of an infant.Marvellous the sight that followed! Oh, most august revelation!Mile-long were the halls that appeared, and open spaces enormous;Areas fit to hold armies on the day of muster for battle;Hosts upon either side, for amplest castrametation.Depth behind depth, and dim labyrinthine apartments.Golden galleries above running high into darkening vistas,Staircases soaring and climbing, till sight grew dizzy with effortOf chasing the corridors up to their whispering gloomy recesses.Nations were ranged in the halls, nations ranged at a banquet,Even then lightly proceeding with timbrel, dulcimer, hautboy,Gong and loud kettledrum and fierce-blown tempestuous organ.Banners floated in air, colossal embroidery tissuesOf Tyrian looms, scarlet, black, violet and amber,Or the perfectest cunning of trained Babylonian artist,Or massy embossed, from the volant shuttle of Phrygian.Banners suspended in shade, or in the full glare of the lamplight,Mid cressets and chandeliers by jewelly chains swinging pendant.

* * * * *

Draw a veil o'er the rout when advances great Cyrus of Elam,Dusky-browed archers behind him, and spearmen before,When he cries 'Strike!' and the gorgeously inlaid pavementsRun ruddy with blood of the festive Assyrians there.

VII.—*Greece and Rome.*—My female readers, whom only I contemplate in every line of this little work, and who would have a right to consider it disrespectful if I were to leave a single word of Latin or Greek unexplained, must understand that the Greeks, according to that universal habit of viewing remote objects in a relation of ascent or descent with respect to the observer, whence the 'going up to Jerusalem,' and our own 'going up to London,' always figured a journey eastwards, that is, directed towards the Euphrates or Tigris, or to any part of Asia from Greece as tending *upwards*. In this mode of conceiving their relations to the East, they were governed semi-consciously by the sense of a vast presence beyond the Tigris—glorified by grandeur and by distance—the golden city of Susa, and the throne of the great king. Accordingly, the expedition therefore of Cyrus the younger against his brother Artaxerxes was called by Xenophon, when recording it, the Anabasis, or going up of Cyrus; and, from the accident of its celebrity, this title has adhered to that expedition; and to that book—as if either could claim it by some exclusive title; whereas, on the contrary, the Katabasis, or going down, furnishes by much the larger and the more interesting part of the work. And, in any case, the title is open to all Asiatic expeditions whatsoever; to the Trojan that just crossed the water, to the Macedonian that went beyond the Indus. The word Anàbăsis must have its accent on the syllable *ab*, not on the penultimate syllable *as*.

In coming to the history of Imperial Rome, one is fortunately made sensible at once of a vast advantage, which is this—that one is not throwing away one's labour. Sad it is, after ploughing a stiff and difficult clay, to find all at once that the whole is a task of so little promise that perhaps, on the whole, one might as well have left it untouched.

X. Yes, I remember that my cousin, Cecilia Dinbury, took the pains to master—or perhaps one ought to say to *mistress*—the history.

L. No, to *miss* it, is what one ought to say.

X. Fie, my dear second cousin—Fie, fie, if you please. To *miss* it, indeed! Ah, how we wished that we *had* missed it. But we had no such luck. There were we broiling through a hot, hot August, broiling away at this intolerable stew of Iskis and Fuskis, and all to no end or use. Granted that too often it is, or it may be so. But here we are safe. Who can fancy or feel so much as the shadow of a demur, when peregrinating Rome, that we might be losing our toil?

Now, then, in the highest spirits, let us open our studies. And first let us map out a chart of the *personnel* for pretty nearly a century. Twelve Cæsars—the twelve first—should clearly of themselves make more than a century. For I am sure all of you, except our two new friends, know so much of arithmetic as that multiplication and division are a great menace upon addition and subtraction. It is, therefore, a thing most desirable to set up compound modes—short devices for abridging these. Now 10 is the earliest number written with two digits: and the higher the multiplier, so much harder, apparently, the process. Yet here at least a great simplification offers. To multiply by 10, all you have to do is to put a cipher after the multiplicand. Twenty-seven soldiers are to have 10 guineas each, how much is required to pay all twenty-seven? Why, 27 into 10 is 27 with a cipher at the end—27 : 0, *i.e.*, 270. *Ergo*, twelve Cæsars, supposing each to reign ten years, would make, no, *should* make, with anything like great lives—12 : 0, *i.e.*, 120 years. And when you consider that one of the twelve, viz., Augustus, singly, for *his* share, contributed fifty and odd years, if the other eleven had given ten each that would be 11 : 0; this would make a total of about 170.

VIII.—*Beginning of Modern Era.*—From the period of Justinian commences a new era—an era of unusual transition. This is the broad principle of change. Old things are decaying, new things are forming and gathering. The lines of decay and of resurrection are moving visibly and palpably to every eye in counteracting agency for one result—life and a new truth for humanity. All the great armies of generous barbarians, showing, by contrast with Rome and Greece, the opulence of teeming nature as against the powers of form in utter superannuation, were now, therefore, no longer moving, roaming, seeking—they had taken up their ground; they were in a general process of castrametation, marking out their alignments and deploying into open order upon ground now permanently taken up for their settlement. The early trumpets, the morning *réveillé* of the great Christian nations—England, France, Spain, Lombardy—were sounding to quarters. Franks had knit into one the rudiments of a great kingdom upon the soil of France; the Saxons and Angles, with some Vandals, had, through a whole century, been defiling by vast trains into the great island which they were called by Providence to occupy and to ennoble; the Vandals had seated themselves, though in this case only with no definite hopes, along the extreme region of the Barbary States. Vandals might and did survive for a considerable period in ineffective fragments, but not as a power. The Visigoths had quartered themselves on Spain, there soon to begin a conflict for the Cross, and to maintain it for eight hundred years, and finally to prevail. And lastly, the Lombards had thrown a network of colonization over Italy, which, as much by the cohesions which it shook loose and broke asunder as by the new one which it bred, exhibited a power like that of the coral insects, and gave promise of a new empire built out of floating dust and fragments.

The movements which formerly had resembled those gigantic pillars of sand that mould themselves continually under the action of sun and wind in the great deserts—suddenly showing themselves upon the remote horizon, rear themselves silently and swiftly, then stalking forward towards the affected caravan like a phantom phantasmagoria, approach, manœuvre, overshadow, and then as suddenly recede, collapse, fluctuate, again to remould into other combinations and to alarm other travellers—have passed. This vast structure of Central Europe had been abandoned by all the greater tribes; they had crossed the vast barriers of Western Europe— the Alps, the Vosges, the Pyrenees, the ocean—these were now the wards within which they had committed their hopes and the graves of their fathers. Social developments tended to the same, and no longer either wishing or finding it possible to roam, they were all now, through an entire century, taking up their ground and making good their tumultuous irruptions; with the power of moving had been conjoined a propensity to move. Rustic life, which must essentially have been maintained on the great area of German vagrancy, was more and more confirmed.

With this physical impossibility of roaming, and with the reciprocal compression of each exercised on the other, coincided the new instincts of civilization. They were no longer barbarous by a brutal and animal barbarism. The deep soil of their powerful natures had long been budding into nobler capacities, and had expanded into nobler perceptions. Reverence for female dignity, a sentiment never found before in any nation, gave a vernal promise of some higher humanity, on a wider scale than had yet been exhibited. Strong sympathies, magnetic affinities, prepared this great encampment of nations for Christianity. Their nobility needed such a field for its expansion; Christianity needed such a human nature for its evolution. The strong and deep nature of the Teutonic tribes could not have been evolved, completed, without Christianity. Christianity in a soil so shallow and unracy as the Græco-Latin, could not have struck those roots which are immovable. The ultimate conditions of the soil and the capacities of the culture must have corresponded. The motions of Barbaria had hitherto indicated only change; change without hope; confusion without tendencies; strife without principle of advance; new births in each successive age without principle of regeneration; momentary gain balanced by momentary loss; the tumult of a tossing ocean which tends to none but momentary rest. But now the currents are united, enclosed, and run in one direction, and that is definite and combined.

Now truly began that modern era, of which we happily reap the harvest: then were laid the first foundations of social order and the first effective hint of that sense of mutual aid and dependence which has, century by century, been creating such a balance and harmony of adjusted operations—of agencies working night and day, which no man sees, for services which no man creates: the agencies are like Ezekiel's wheels—self-sustained; the services in which they labour have grown up imperceptibly as the growth of a yew, and from a period as far removed from cognizance. One man dies every hour out of myriads, his place is silently supplied, and the mysterious economy thus propagates itself in silence, like the motion of the planets, from age to age. Hands innumerable are every moment writing summonses, returns, reports, figures—records that would stretch out to the crack of doom, as yet every year accumulated, written by professional men, corrected by correctors, checked by controllers, and afterwards read by corresponding men, re-read by corresponding controllers, passed and ratified by corresponding ratifiers; and through this almighty pomp of wheels, whose very whirling would be heard into other planets, did not the very velocity of their motion seem to sleep on their soft axle, is the business of this great nation, judicial, fixed, penal, deliberative, statistical, commercial, all carried on without confusion, never distracting one man by its might, nor molesting one man by its noise.

Now, in the semi-fabulous times of Egypt and Assyria, things were not so managed. Ours are the ages of intellectual powers, of working by equivalents and substitutions; but theirs were done by efforts of brute power, possible only in the lowest condition of animal man, when all wills converged absolutely in one, and when human life, cheap as dog's, had left man in no higher a state of requirement, and had given up human power to be applied at will—without art or skill.

Then the armies of a Semiramis even were in this canine state. It was her curse to have subjects that had no elevation, swarming by myriads like flies; mere animal life, the mere animal armies which she needed; what she wanted was exactly what they would yield. To such cattle all cares beyond that of mere provender were thrown away. Surgical care and the ambulance, such as the elevation of man's condition, and the solemnity of his rights, seen by the awful eye of Christianity, will always require, were simply ridiculous. As well raise hospitals for decayed butterflies. Provender was all: not *panem et circenses*—bread and theatrical shows—but simply bread, and that wretched of its kind. Drink was an ideal luxury. Was there not the Euphrates, was there not the Tigris, the Aranes? The Roman armies carried *posca* by way of such luxury, a drink composed of vinegar and water. But as to Semiramis—what need of the vinegar? And why carry the water? Could it not be found in the Euphrates, etc.? Let the dogs lap at the Euphrates, and stay for their next draught till they come to the Tigris or the Aranes. Or, if they drank a river or so dry, and a million or two should die, what of that? Let them go on to the Tigris, and thence to the Aranes, the Oxus, or Indus. Clothes were dispensable from the climate, food only of the lowest quality, and finally the whole were summoned only for one campaign, and usually this was merely a sort of partisan camisade upon a colossal scale, in which the superfluous population of one vast nation threw themselves upon another. Mere momentum turned the scale; one nuisance of superfluous humanity was discharged upon such another nuisance, the one exterminating the other, or, if both by accident should be exterminated, what mattered it? The major part of the two nuisances, like algebraical quantities of plus and minus, extinguished each other. And, in any case, the result, whatever it might be, of that one campaign, which was rather a journey terminating in a bad battle of mobs, than anything artificial enough to deserve the title of camp, terminated the whole war. Here, at least, we see the determining impulse of political economy intervening, coming round upon them, if it had not been perceived before. If the two nations began their warfare, and planned it in defiance of all common laws and exchequers, at any rate the time it lasted was governed by that only. The same thing recurred in the policy of the feudal ages; the bumpkins, the vassals, were compelled to follow the standard, but their service was limited to a certain number of weeks. Afterwards, by law, as well as by custom, they dissolved for the autumnal labour of the harvest. And thus it was, until the princes would allow of mercenary armies, no system of connecting politics grew up in Europe, or could grow up; having no means of fighting each other, they were like leopards in Africa gnawing at a leopard in Asia; they fumed apart like planets that could not cross; a vast revolution, which Robertson ascribes to the reign of Francis I., but which I, upon far better grounds and on speculations much more exclusively pursued, date from the age of Louis XI. Differing in everything, and by infinite degrees for the worse from these early centuries, the age of Semiramis agreed in this—that if the non-culture of the human race allowed them to break out into war with little or no preparation but what each man personally could make, and if thus far political economy did not greatly control the policy of nations, yet in the reaction these same violated laws vindicated their force by sad retributions. Famines, at all events dire exhaustion, invariably put an end to such tumultuary wars, if they did not much control their beginnings,[42] and periodically expressed their long retributory convulsions.

Not, therefore, because political economy was of little avail, but because the details are lost in the wilderness of years, must we disregard the political economy in the early Assyrian combinations of the human race. The details are lost for political economy as a cause, and the details are equally lost of the wars and the revolutions which were its effects. But in coming more within the light of authentic history, I contend that political economy is better known, and that in that proportion it explains much of what ought to be known. For example, I contend that the condition of Athens, for herself and for the rest of the Greek confederacy, nay, the entire course of the Athenian wars, of all that Athens did or forbore to do, her actions alike, and her omissions, are to be accounted for, and lie involved in the statistics of her fiscal condition.

IX.—*Geography.*—Look next at geography. The consideration of this alone throws a new light on history. Every country that is now or will be, has had some of its primary determinations impressed upon its policy and institutions; nay, upon its feeling and character, which is the well of its policy, by its geographical position: that is, by its position as respects climate in the first place, secondly, as respects neighbours (*i.e.*, enemies), whether divided by mountains, rivers, deserts, or the great desert of the sea—or divided only by great belts of land—a passable solitude. Thirdly, as respects its own facilities and conveniences for raising food, clothing, luxuries. Indeed, not only is it so moulded and determined as to its character and aspects, but oftentimes even as to its very existence.

Many have noticed wisely and truly in the physical aspect of Asia and the South of Caucasus, that very destiny of slavery and of partition into great empires, which has always hung over them. The great plains of Asia fit it for the action of cavalry and vast armies—by which the fate of generations is decided in a day; and at the same time fit it for the support of those infinite myriads without object, which make human life cheap and degraded. That this was so is evident from what Xenophon tells.

On the other hand, many have seen in the conformation of Greece revolving round a nucleus able to protect in case of invasion, yet cut up into so many little chambers, of which each was sacred from the intrusion of the rest during the infancy of growth, the solution of all the marvels which Grecian history unfolds.

FOOTNOTES:

[20] This distinction is of some consequence. Else the student would be puzzled at finding [which is really the truth] that, after the Twelve Cæsars and the five patriotic emperors who succeeded them, we know less of the Roman princes through centuries after the Christian era, than of the Roman Consuls through a space of three centuries preceding the Christian

era. In fact, except for a few gossiping and merely *personal* anecdotes communicated by the Augustan History and a few other authorities, we really know little of the most illustrious amongst the Roman emperors of the West, beyond the fact (all but invariable) that they perished by assassination. But still this darkness is not of the same nature, nor owing to the same causes, as the Grecian darkness prior to the Olympiads.

[21] Except, indeed, by the barbarous contrivance of cutting away some letters from a name, and then filling up their place with other letters which, by previous agreement, have been rendered significant of arithmetic numbers. This is the idea on which the *Memoria Technica* of Dr. Grey proceeds. More appropriately it might have been named *Memoria Barbarica*, for the dreadful violence done to the most beautiful, rhythmical, and melodious names would, at any rate, have remained as a repulsive expression of barbarism to all musical ears, had the practical benefits of this machinery been all that they profess to be. Meantime these benefits are really none at all. They offer us a mere mockery, defeating with one hand what they accomplish with the other.

[22] It is all but an impossible problem for a nation in the situation of Greece to send down a record to a posterity distant by five centuries, to overlap the gulf of years between the point of starting—the absolute now of commencement and the remote generation at which you take aim. Trust to tradition, not to the counsel of one man. But tradition is buoyant.

[23] *Crusade.*—There seems a contradiction in the very terms of Pagan— that is, non-Christian, and Crusade—that is, warfare symbolically Christian. But, by a license not greater than is often practised in corresponding circumstances, the word Crusade may be used to express any martial expedition amongst a large body of confederate nations having or representing an imaginative (not imaginary) interest or purpose with no direct profession of separate or mercenary object for each nation apart.

[24] The truths of Scripture are of too vast a compass, too much like the Author of those truths—illimitable and incapable of verbal circumscription, and, besides, are too much diffused through many collateral truths, too deeply echoed and reverberated by trains of correspondences and affinities laid deep in nature, and above all, too affectingly transcribed in the human heart, ever to come within the compass or material influence of a few words this way or that; any more than all eternity can be really and locally confined within a little golden ring which is assumed for its symbol. The same thing, I repeat, may be said of chronology and its accidents. The chronologies of Scripture, its prophetic weeks of Daniel, and its mysterious æons of the Apocalypse, are too awful in their realities, too vast in their sweep and range of application, to be

controlled or affected by the very utmost errors that could arise from lapse of time or transcription unrevised. And the more so, because errors that by the supposition are errors of accident, cannot all point in one direction: one would be likely in many cases to compensate another. But, finally, I would make this frank acknowledgment to a young pupil without fear that it could affect her reverence for Scripture. It is of the very grandeur of Scripture that she can afford to be negligent of her chronology. Suppose this case: suppose the Scriptures protected by no special care or providence; suppose no security, no barrier to further errors, to have arisen from the discovery of printing—suppose the Scriptures to be in consequence transcribed for thousands of years—even in that case the final result would be this: it would be (and in part perhaps it really is) true or not true as to its minor or petty chronology—not true, as having been altered insensibly like any human composition where the internal sense was not of a nature to maintain its integrity. True, even as to trifles, in that sense which the majestic simplicity and self-conformity of truth in a tale originally true would guarantee, it might yet be, because of the grandeur of the main aim, and the sense of deeper relations and the perception of verisimilitude.

[25] '*A New Slave Country*'—and this for more reasons than one. Slaves were growing dearer in Rome; secondly, a practice had been for some time increasing amongst the richest of the noble families in Rome, of growing household bodies of gladiators, by whose aid they fought the civic battles of ambition; and thirdly, as to Cæsar in particular, he had raised and equipped a whole legion out of his own private funds, and, of course, for his own private service; so that he probably looked to Britain as a new quarry from which he might obtain the human materials of his future armies, and also as an arena or pocket theatre, in which he could organize and discipline these armies secure from jealous observation.

[26] Here the pupil will naturally object—was not Judæa an Asiatic land? And did not Judæa act upon Europe? Doubtless; and in the sublimest way by which it is possible for man to act upon man; not only through the highest and noblest part of man's nature, but (as most truly it may be affirmed) literally creating, in a practical sense, that nature. For, to say nothing of the sublime idea of Redemption as mystically involved in the types and prophecies of Jewish prophets, and in the very ceremonies of the Jewish religion, what was the very highest ideal of God which man— philosophic man even—had attained, compared with that of the very meanest Jew? It is false to say that amongst the philosophers of Greece or Rome the Polytheistic creed was rejected. No Pagan philosopher ever adopted, ever even conceived, the sublime of the Jewish God—as a being not merely of essential unity, but as deriving from that unity the moral relations of a governor and a retributive judge towards human creatures. So

that Judæa bore an office for the human race of a most awful and mysterious sanctity. But (and partly for that reason) the civil and social relations of Judæa to the human race were less than nothing. And thence arose the intolerant scorn of such writers as Tacitus for the Christians, whom, of course, they viewed as Jews, and nothing *but* Jews. Thus far they were right—that, as a nation, valued upon the only scale known to politicians, the Jews brought nothing at all to the common fund of knowledge or civilization. One element of knowledge, however, the Jews did bring, though at that time unknown, and long after, for want of historic criticism in the history of chronologic researches, viz., a chronology far superior to that of the Septuagint, as will be shown farther on, and far superior to the main guides of Paganism. But the reason why this superiority of chronology will, after all, but little avail the general student is, that it relates merely to the Assyrian or Persian princes in their intercourse with the courts of Jerusalem or of Samaria.

[27] Juba, King of Mauritania, during the struggle of Cæsar and Pompey.

[28] Which clannish feeling, be it observed, always depends for its life and intensity upon the comparison with others; as they are despised, in that ratio rises the clannish self-estimation. Whereas the nobler pride of a Roman patriotism is αυταρκης and independent of external relations. Nothing is more essentially opposed, though often confounded under the common name of patriotism, than the love of country in a Roman or English sense, and the spirit of clannish jealousy.

[29] This it was (a circumstance overlooked by many who have written on the Roman literature), this destiny announced and protected by early auguries, which made the idea of Rome a great and imaginative idea. The patriotism of the Grecian was, as indicated in an earlier note, a mean, clannish feeling, always courting support to itself, and needing support from imaginary 'barbarism' in its enemies, and raising itself into greatness by means of *their* littleness. But with the nobler Roman patriotism was a very different thing. The august destiny of his own eternal city [observe—*'eternal,'* not in virtue of history, but of prophecy, not upon the retrospect and the analogies of any possible experience, but by the necessity of an aboriginal doom], a city that was to be the centre of an empire whose circumference is everywhere, did not depend for any part of its majesty upon the meanness of its enemies; on the contrary, in the very grandeur of those enemies lay, by a rebound of the feelings inevitable to a Roman mind, the paramount grandeur of that awful Republic which had swallowed them all up.

[30] I do not mean to deny the casual intercourse between Rome and particular cities of Greece, which sometimes flash upon us for a moment in

the earliest parts of the Roman annals: what I am insisting upon, is the absence of all national or effectual intercourse.

[31] Even an attorney, however [according to an old story, which I much fear is a Joe Miller, but which ought to be fact], is not so rigorous as to allow of no latitude, for, having occasion to send a challenge with the stipulation of fighting at twelve paces, upon 'engrossing' this challenge the attorney directed his clerk to add—'Twelve paces, be the same more or less.' And so I say of the Olympiad—'777 years, be the same more or less.'

[32] And finally, were it necessary to add one word by way of reconciling the student to the substitution of 777 for 776, it might be sufficient to remind him that, even in the rigour of the minutest calculus, when the 776 years are fully accomplished—to prove which accomplishment we must suppose some little time over and above the 776 to have elapsed—then this surplus, were it but a single hour, throws us at once into the 777th year. This was, in fact, the oversight which misled a class of disputants, whom I hope the reader is too young to remember, but whom I, alas! remember too well in the year 1800. They imagined and argued that the eighteenth century closed upon the first day of the year 1800. New Year's Day of the year 1799, they understood as the birthday of the Christian Church, proclaiming it to be then 1799 years old, not as commencing its 1799th year. And so on. Pye, the Poet Laureate of that day, in an elaborate preface to a secular ode, argued the point very keenly. It is certain (though not evident at first sight) that in the year 1839 the Christian period of time is not, as children say, '*going of* 1840, but going of 1839: whereas the other party contend that it is in its 1840th year, tending in short to become that which it will actually be on its birthday, *i.e.*, on the calends of January, or *le Jour de l'an*, or New Year's Day of 1840.

[33] See note immediately preceding on previous page.

[34] '*With impunity.*'—There is no one point in which I have found a more absolute coincidence of opinion amongst all profound thinkers, English, German, and French, when discussing the philosophy of education, than this great maxim—*that the memory ought never to be exercised in a state of insulation*, that is, in those blank efforts of its strength which are accompanied by no law or logical reason for the thing to be remembered; by no such reason or principle of dependency as could serve to recall it in after years, when the burthen may have dropped out of the memory. The reader will perhaps think that I, the writer of this little work, have a pretty strong and faithful memory, when I tell him that every word of it, with all its details, has been written in a situation which sternly denied me the use of books bearing on my subject. A few volumes of rhetorical criticism and of polemic divinity, that have not, nor, to my knowledge, could have

furnished me with a solitary fact or date, are all the companions of my solitude. Other voice than the voice of the wind I have rarely heard. Even my quotations are usually from memory, though not always, as one out of three, perhaps, I had fortunately written down in a pocket-book; but no one date or fact has been drawn from any source but that of my unassisted memory. Now, this useful sanity of the memory I ascribe entirely to the accident of my having escaped in childhood all such mechanic exercises of the memory as I have condemned in the text—to this accident, combined with the constant and severe practice I have given to my memory, in working and sustaining immense loads of facts that had been previously brought under logical laws.

[35] '*The long careering of an earthquake.*'—It is remarkable, and was much noticed at the time by some German philosophers, that the earthquake which laid Lisbon in ruins about ninety-five years ago, could be as regularly traced through all its stages for some days previous to its grand *finale*, as any thief by a Bow Street officer. It passed through Ireland and parts of England; in particular it was dogged through a great part of Leicestershire; and its rate of travelling was not so great but that, by a series of telegraphs, timely notice might have been sent southwards that it was coming. [The Lisbon earthquake occurred in 1755; so that this paper must have been written about 1849 or 1850.—Ed.]

[36] '*The exact personality.*'—The historical personality, or complete identification of an individual, lies in the whole body of circumstances that would be sufficient to determine him as a responsible agent in a court of justice. Archbishop Usher and others fancy that Sardanapalus was the son of Pul; guided merely by the sound of a syllable. Tiglath-Pileser, some fancy to be the same person as Sardanapalus; others to be the very rebel who overthrew Sardanapalus. In short, all is confused and murky to the very last degree. And the reader who fancies that some accurate chronological characters are left, by which the era of Sardanapalus can be more nearly determined than it is determined above, viz., as generally coinciding with the era of Romulus and of the Greek Olympiad, is grossly imposed upon.

[37] '*And Asiatic.*'—*Asiatic*, let the pupil observe, and not merely Assyrian; for the Assyria of this era represents all that was afterwards Media, Persia, Chaldæa, Babylonia, and Syria. No matter for the exact limits of the Assyrian empire, which are as indistinct in space as in time. Enough that no Asiatic State is known as distinct from this empire.

[38] And this is so exceedingly striking, that I am much surprised at the learned disputants upon the era of Homer having failed to notice this argument; especially when we see how pitiably poor they are in probabilities or presumptions of any kind. The miserable shred of an

argument with those who wish to carry up Homer as high as any colourable pretext will warrant, is this, that he must have lived pretty near to the war which he celebrates, inasmuch as he never once alludes to a great revolutionary event in the Peloponnesus. Consequently, it is argued, Homer did not live to witness that revolution. Yet he must have witnessed it, if he had lived at the distance of eighty years from the capture of Troy; for such was the era of that event, viz., the return of the Heraclidæ. Now, in answer to this, it is obvious to say that negations prove little. Homer has failed to notice, has omitted to notice, or found no occasion for noticing, scores of great facts contemporary with Troy, or contemporary with himself, which yet must have existed for all that. In particular, he has left us quite in the dark about the great empires, and the great capitals on the Euphrates and the Tigris, and the Nile; and yet it was of some importance to have noticed the relation in which the kingdom of Priam stood to the great potentates on those rivers. The argument, therefore, drawn from the non-notice of the Heraclidæ, is but trivial. On the other hand, an argument of some strength for a lower era as the true era of Homer, may be drawn from the much slighter colouring of the marvellous, which in Homer's treatment of the story attaches to the *Iliad*, than to the *Seven against Thebes*. In the Iliad we have the mythologic marvellous sometimes; the marvellous of necessity surrounding the gods and their intercourse with men; but we have no Amphiaraus swallowed up by the earth, no Œdipus descending into a mysterious gulf at the summons of an unseen power. And beyond all doubt the shield of Achilles, supposing it no interpolation of a later age, argues a much more advanced state of the arts of design, etc., than the shields, (described by Æschylus, as we may suppose, from ancient traditions preserved in the several families), of the seven chiefs who invaded Thebes.

[39] '*Seven-gated*,' both as an expression which recalls the subject of the Romance (the Seven Anti-Theban Chieftains), and as one which distinguishes this Grecian Thebes from the Egyptian Thebes; that being called *Hekatómpylos*, or *Hundred-gated*. Of course some little correction will always be silently applied to the general expression, so as to meet the difference between the two generations that served at Troy and in the Argonautic expedition, and again between David and his son. If the elder generation be fixed to the year 1000, then 1000 *minus* 30 will express the era of the younger; if the younger be fixed to the year 1000, then 1000 *plus* 30 will express the era of the elder. Or, better still, 1000 may be taken as the half-way era in which both generations met; that era in which the father was yet living and active, whilst the son was already entering upon manhood; that era, for instance, at which David was still reigning, though his son Solomon had been crowned. On this plan, no correction at all will be required; 15 years on each side of the 1000 will mark the two terms

within which the events and persons range; and the 1000 will be the central point of the period.

[40] Elam is the Scriptural name for Persia.

[41] 'Alala! Alala!' the war cry of Eastern armies.

[42] And for the very reason that political economy had but a small share in determining the war of the year A, it became not so much a great force as the sole force for putting an end to the war of the year D.

VI. CHRYSOMANIA; OR, THE GOLD-FRENZY IN ITS PRESENT STAGE.

Some time back I published in this journal a little paper on the Californian madness—for madness I presumed it to be, and upon two grounds. First, in so far as men were tempted into a lottery under the belief that it was *not* a lottery; or, if it really *were* such, that it was a lottery without blanks. Secondly, in so far as men were tempted into a transitory speculation under the delusion that it was not transitory, but rested on some principle of permanence. We have since seen the Californian case repeated, upon a scale even of exaggerated violence, in Australia. There also, if great prizes seemed to be won in a short time, it was rashly presumed that something like an equitable distribution of these prizes took place. Supposing ten persons to have obtained £300 in a fortnight, people failed to observe that, if divided amongst the entire party of which these ten persons formed a section, the £300 would barely have yielded average wages. In one instance a very broad illustration of this occurred in the early experience of Victoria. A band of seven thousand people had worked together; whether simply in the sense of working as neighbours in the same local district, or in the commercial sense of working as partners, I do not know, nor is it material to know. The result sounded enormous, when stated in a fragmentary way with reference to particular days, and possibly in reference also to particular persons, distinguished for luck, but on taking the trouble to sum up the whole amount of labourers, of days, and of golden ounces extracted, it did not appear that the wages to each individual could have averaged quite so much as twenty shillings a week, supposing the total product to have been on that principle of participation. Very possibly it was *not*; and in that case the gains of some individuals may have been enormous. But a prudent man, if he quits a certainty or migrates from a distance, will compute his prospects upon this scale of averages, and assuredly not upon the accidents of exceptional luck. The instant objection will be, that such luck is *not* exceptional, but represents the ordinary case. Let us consider. The reports are probably much exaggerated; and something of the same machinery for systematic exaggeration is already forming itself as operated so beneficially for California. As yet, however, it is not absolutely certain that the reports themselves, taken literally, would exactly countenance the romantic impressions drawn from those reports by the public.

Until the reader has checked the accounts, or, indeed, has been enabled to check them, by balancing the amount of gain against the amount of labour applied, he cannot know but that the reports themselves would show on examination a series of unusual successes set against a series of entire failures, so as to leave a *facit*, after all corrections and allowances, of moderately good wages upon an equal distribution of the whole. I would remind him to propose this question: has it been asserted, even by these wild reports, with respect to any thousand men (taken as an aggregate), I do not mean to say that all have succeeded, or even that a majority have not failed decisively—that is more than I demand—but has it been asserted that they have realized so much in any week or any month as would, if divided equally amongst losers and winners, have allowed to each man anything conspicuously above the rate of ordinary wages? Of lotteries in general it has been often remarked, that if you buy a single ticket you have but a poor chance of winning, if you buy twenty tickets your chance is very much worse, and if you buy all the tickets your chance is none at all, but is exchanged for a certainty of loss. So as to the gold lottery of Australia, I suspect (and, observe, not assuming the current reports to be false, but, on the contrary, to be strictly correct for each separate case, only needing to be combined and collated as a whole) that if each separate century[43] of men emigrating to the goldfield of Mount Alexander were to make a faithful return of their aggregate winnings, that return would not prove seductive at all to our people at home, supposing these winnings to be distributed equally as amongst an incorporation of adventurers; though it *has* proved seductive in the case of the extraordinary success being kept apart so as to fix and fascinate the gaze into an oblivion of the counterbalancing failures.

There is, however, notoriously, a natural propensity amongst men to confide in their luck; and, as this is a wholesome propensity in the main, it may seem too harsh to describe by the name of *mania* even a morbid excess of it, though it ought to strike the most sanguine man, that in order to account for the possibility of any failures at all, we must suppose the main harvest of favourable chances to decay with the first month or so of occupation by any commensurate body of settlers; so that in proportion to the strength and reality of the promises to the earliest settlers, will have been the rapid exhaustion of such promises. Exactly *because* the district was really a choice one for those who came first, it must often be ruined for *him* who succeeds him.

Here, then, is a world of disappointments prepared and preparing for future emigrants. The favourite sports and chief lands of promise will by the very excess of their attractiveness have converged upon themselves the great strength of the reapers; and in very many cases the main harvest will have been housed before the new race of adventurers from Great Britain can have reached the ground. In most cases, therefore, ruin would be the instant solution of the disappointment. But in a country so teeming with promise as Australia, ruin is hardly a possible event. A hope lost is but a hope transfigured. And one is reminded of a short colloquy that took place on the field of Marengo. 'Is this battle lost?' demanded Napoleon of Desaix. 'It is,' replied Desaix; 'but, before the sun sets, there is plenty of time to win it back.' In like manner the new comers, on reaching the appointed grounds, will often have cause to say, 'Are we ruined this morning?' To which the answer will not unfrequently be, 'Yes; but this is the best place for being ruined that has yet been discovered. You have trusted to the guidance of a *will-of-the-wisp*; but a *will-of-the-wisp* has been known to lead a man by accident to a better path than that which he had lost.' There is no use, therefore, in wasting our pity upon those who may happen to suffer by the first of the two delusions which I noticed, viz., the conceit that either Australia or California offers a lottery without blanks. Blanks too probably they will draw; but what matters it, when this disappointment cannot reach them until they find themselves amidst a wilderness of supplementary hopes? One prize has been lost, but twenty others have been laid open that had never been anticipated.

Far different, on the other hand, is the second delusion—the delusion of those who mistake a transitional for a permanent prosperity, and many of whom go so far in their frenzy as to see only matter of congratulation in the very extremity of changes, which (if realized) would carry desperate ruin into our social economy. For these people there is no indemnification. I begin with this proposition—that no material extension can be given to the use of gold after great national wants are provided for, without an enormous lowering of its price: which lowering, if once effected, and exactly in proportion as it is effected, takes away from the gold-diggers all motive for producing it. The dilemma is this, and seems to me inevitable: Given a certain depreciation of gold, as, for instance, by 80 per cent., then the profits of the miners falling in that same proportion[44] (viz., by four-fifths) will leave no temptation whatever to pursue the trade of digging. But, on the other hand, such a depreciation *not* being given—gold being supposed to range at anything approaching to its old price—in that case no considerable extension as to the uses of gold is possible. In either case alike the motive for producing gold rapidly decays. To keep up any steady encouragement to the miners, the market for gold must be prodigiously extended. That the market may be extended, new applications of gold must be devised: the old applications would not absorb more than a very limited increase. That new applications may be devised, a prodigious lowering of the price is required. But precisely as that result is approached the *extra* encouragement to the miners vanishes. *That* drooping, the production will droop, even if nature should continue the extra supplies; and the old state of prices must restore itself.

The whole turns upon the possibility of extending the market for gold. A child must see that, if the demand for gold cannot be materially increased, it is altogether nugatory that nature should indefinitely enlarge the supply. In articles that adapt themselves to a variable scale of uses, so as to be capable of substitution for others, according to the relations of price, it is often possible enough that, in the event of any change which may lower their price, the increased demand may go on without assignable limits. For instance, when iron rises immoderately in price, timber is substituted to an indefinite extent. But, on the other hand, where the application is severely circumscribed, no fall of price will avail to extend the demand. Certain herbs, for instance, or minerals, employed for medicinal purposes, and for those only, have their supply regulated by the demand of hospitals and of private medical practitioners. That demand being once exhausted, no cheapness whatever will extend the market. Suppose the European market for leeches to be saturated; every man, suppose, is supplied; in that case, even an *extra* thousand cannot be sold. The purpose which leeches answer has been met. And after *that* nobody will take them as a gift. But in the case of gold, it is imagined that, although the market is pretty stationary whilst the price is stationary, let that price materially lower itself, and immediately the substitutions of gold for other metals, or for other decorative materials (as ivory, etc.), would begin to extend; and commensurately with such extensions the regular gold market would widen. This is the prevailing conceit. Now let us consider it.

What are the known applications of gold in the old state of circumstances, which may be supposed capable of furnishing a basis for extension in the altered circumstances? I will rapidly review them. First, a very large amount of gold more than people would imagine is annually wasted in gilding. Much of what has been applied to other purposes is continually reverting to the market; but the gold used in gilding is absolutely lost. This already makes a drain upon the gold market; but will that drain be materially larger in the event of gold falling by 50 *per cent.*? Apparently not. Amongst ourselves the chief subjects of gilding are books, picture-frames, and some varieties of porcelain. But none of these would be bought more extensively in consequence of gold being cheap: a man does not buy a book, for instance, simply with a view to its being gilt; the gilding follows as a contingency depending upon a previous act not modified in any degree by the price of gold. In the decoration of houses it is true that hitherto our English expenditure of gilding has been very trifling compared with that of France and Italy, and to a great extent therefore would allow of an increased use. Cornices, for instance, in rooms, and sections of panels, are rarely gilt with us; and apart from any reference to the depreciation of gold, I believe that this particular application of it is sensibly increasing at present. Of course an improvement, which has already begun, would extend itself further under a reduced price of gold; yet still, as the class of houses so decorated is somewhat aristocratic, the effect could not be very important. On the Continent it is probable that at any rate gilding will be more extensively applied to out-of-doors decoration, as for example, of domes, cupolas, balustrades, etc. But all architectural innovations are slow in travelling! And I am of opinion that five to seven thousand pounds' worth of gold would cover all the augmented expenditure of this class. It is doubtful, indeed, whether all the increase of gilding will do more than balance the total abolition of it on the panels of carriages. In the time of Louis XIV. an immense expenditure occurred in this way, and the disuse of it is owing to the superior chastity of taste amongst our English carriage-builders, who, in this particular art, have shot far ahead of continental Europe. But the main consumption of gold occurs, first, I should imagine, in watches and watch chains; secondly, in personal ornaments; and thirdly, in gold plate. Now we must remember, at starting, that what is called jewellers' gold, even when manufactured by honourable tradesmen, avowedly contains a very much smaller proportion of the pure metal than our gold coinage. Consequently an increase in the use of watches and personal ornaments, or of such trinkets as snuff-boxes, supposing it in the first year of cheapened gold to go the length of 20 per cent., would not even in that department of the gold demand enhance it by one-fifth, but perhaps by one-fourth the part of one-fifth—that is to say, by one-twentieth. The reader, I hope, understands me, for upon *that* depends a pretty strong presumption of the small real change that would be worked in the effective demand for gold by a great apparent change in our chief demand for gold manufactures. There can be no doubt that in watches and personal ornaments is involved our main demand upon the gold market; through these it is that we chiefly act upon the market. Now three corrections are applicable to the *primâ facie* view of this subject.

The first of these is—that gold chains, etc., and a pompous display of rings have long ago been degraded in public estimation by the practice and opinions prevailing in aristocratic quarters. This tendency of public feeling at once amounts to a large deduction from what would otherwise be our demand.

The second of these corrections is—that, since our main action upon the gold market lies through the jewellers, and, consequently, through jewellers' gold, therefore, on allowing for the way in which jewellers alloy their gold, our real means of operating upon the gold market may be estimated perhaps at not more than one-fourth part of our apparent means.

A third important correction is this—at first sight it might seem as though the purchaser of gold articles would benefit by the whole depreciation of gold, and that the depreciation might be taken to represent exactly the amount of stimulation applied to the sale, for instance, of gold plate. But this is not so. Taking the depreciation of gold at one-half, then upon any gold article, as suppose a salver, each ounce would have sunk from 77s. to 38s. 6d. Next, rate the workmanship at 40s. the ounce, and then the total cost upon each ounce will not be (77s. + 40)/2, or in other words 58s. 6d., as a hasty calculation might have fancied, but (77s./2) + 40, that is to say, 78s. 6d. Paying heretofore £5 17s., under the new price of gold you would pay £4 within a trifle. Consequently, when those who argue for the vast extension of the gold market, rely for its possibility upon a vast preliminary depreciation of gold, they are deceiving themselves as to the nature and compass of that depreciation. The main action of the public upon the gold market must always lie through *wrought* and not through unwrought gold, and in this there must always be two elements of price, viz., X, the metal, and Y, the workmanship; so that the depreciation will never be $= (x + y)/2$ but only $x/2 + y$; and y, which is a very costly element, will never be bound at all, not by the smallest fraction, through any possible change in the cost of x.

This is a most important consideration; for if the price of gold could fall to nothing at all, not the less the high price of the workmanship—this separately for itself—would for ever prevent the great bulk of society from purchasing gold plate. Yet, through what other channel than this of plate is it possible for any nation to reach the gold market by any effectual action upon the price? M. Chevalier, the most influential of French practical economists, supposes the case that California might reduce the price of gold by one-half. Let us say, by way of evading fractions, that gold may settle finally at the price of forty shillings the ounce. But to what purpose would the diggers raise enormous depôts of gold for which they can have no commensurate demand? As yet the true difficulty has not reached them. The tendency was frightful; but, within the short period through which the new power has yet worked, there was not range enough to bring this tendency into full play. Now, however, when new powers of the same quality, viz., in Australia, in Queen Charlotte's Island, in Owhyhee, and, lastly, on Lord Poltimore's estate in South Moulton, are in working, it seems sensibly nearer. It is a literal fact that we have yet to ascertain whether this vaunted gold will even pay for the costs of working it. Coals lying at the very mouth of a pit will be thankfully carried off by the poor man, but dig a little deeper, and it requires the capital of a rich man to raise them; and after *that* it requires a good deal of experience, and the trial of much mechanic artifice, to ascertain whether after all it will be worth while to raise them. To leap from the conclusion—that, because a solitary prize of 25 lb. weight may largely remunerate an emigrant to California, therefore a whole generation of emigrants will find the average profits of gold-washing, golddigging, etc., beyond those of Russia or of Borneo, is an insanity quite on a level with all the other insanities of the case. But, says the writer in the *Times*, the fact has justified the speculation; the result is equal to the anticipation; in practice nobody has been disappointed; everybody has succeeded; nobody complains of any delusion. We beg his pardon. There have been very distinct complaints of that nature. These have proceeded not from individuals merely, but from associations of ten or twelve, who, after working for some time, have not reaped the ordinary profits on their expenses; whereas, they were also entitled to expect high wages for their labour, in addition to extravagant profits on their outlay. Yet, suppose this to have been otherwise, what shadow of an argument can be drawn from the case of those privileged few, who entered upon a virgin harvest, applicable to the multitudes who will succeed to an inheritance of ordinary labour, tried in all quarters of the globe, and seldom indeed found to *terminate* in any extra advantages?

FOOTNOTES:

[43] '*Century of Men*,'—It may be necessary to remind some readers that this expression, to which I resort for want of any better or briefer, is strictly correct. The original Latin word *centuria* is a collection of one hundred separate items, no matter what, whether men, horses, ideas, etc. 'A Century of Sonnets' was properly taken as the title of a book. 'A Century of Inventions' was adopted by Lord Worcester as the title of *his* book. And when we use the word century (as generally we do) to indicate a certain duration of time, it is allowable only on the understanding that it is an elliptical expression; the full expression is *a century of years*.

[44] 'In that same proportion,' but in reality the profits would fall in a much greater proportion. To illustrate this, suppose the existing price of gold in Australia to be sixty shillings an oz. I assume the price at random, as being a matter of no importance; but, in fact, I understand that at Melbourne, and other places in the province of Victoria, this really *is* the ruling price at present. For some little time the price was steady at fifty-seven shillings; that is, assuming the mint price in England to be seventy-seven shillings (neglecting the fraction of 10-1/2d.), and the Australian price sank by twenty shillings; which sinking, however, we are not to understand as any depreciation that had the character of permanence; it arose out of local circumstances. Subsequently the price fell as low even as forty-five shillings, where it halted, and soon ascended again to sixty shillings. Sixty shillings therefore let us postulate as the present price. Upon this sum descended the expenses of the miner. Let these, including tools, machinery, etc., be assumed at three half-crowns for each ounce of gold. Then, at a price of sixty shillings, this discount descends upon each sovereign to the amount of one half-crown, or one-eighth. But at a reduced price of thirty shillings, this discount of three half-crowns amounts to one-fourth. And, at

a price of twelve shillings, it amounts to five-eighths. So that, as the gross profits descend, the *nett* profits descend in a still heavier proportion.

VII. DEFENCE OF THE ENGLISH PEERAGE.

It is by a continued *secretion* (so to speak) of all which forces itself to the surface of national importance in the way of patriotic services that the English peerage keeps itself alive. Stop the laurelled trophies of the noble sailor or soldier pouring out his heart's blood for his country, stop the intellectual movement of the lawyer or the senatorial counsellor, and immediately the sources are suffocated through which *our* peerage is self-restorative. The simple truth is, how humiliating soever it may prove I care not, that whether positively by cutting off the honourable sources of addition, or negatively by cutting off the ordinary source of subtraction, the other peerages of Europe are peerages of *Fainéans*. Pretend not to crucify for ignominy the sensual and torpid princes of the Franks; in the same boat row all the peerages that *can* have preserved their regular hereditary descent amongst civil feuds which *ought* to have wrecked them. The Spanish, the Scotch, the Walloon nobility are all of them nobilities from which their several countries would do well to cut themselves loose, so far as *that* is possible. How came *you*, my lord, we justly say to this and that man, proud of his ancient descent, to have brought down your wretched carcase to this generation, except by having shrunk from all your bloody duties, and from all the chances that beset a gallant participation in the dreadful enmities of your country? Would you make it a reproach to the Roman Fabii that 299 of that house perished in fighting for their dear motherland? And that, if a solitary Fabius survived for the rekindling of the house, it was because the restorer of his house had been an infant at the æra of his household catastrophe. And if, through such burning examples of patriotism, far remote collateral descendants entered upon the succession, was this a reproach? Was this held to vitiate or to impair the heraldic honours? A disturbance, a convulsion, that shook the house back into its primitive simplicities of standing, was that a shock to its hereditary grandeur? If it *had* been, there perished the efficient fountain of nobility as any *national* or *patriotic* honour; that being extinguished, it became a vile, *personal* distinction. For instance, like the Roman Fabii, the major part of the English nobility was destroyed in the contest (though so short a contest) of the two Roses. To restore it at all, recourse was had to every mode of healing family wounds through distant marriage connections, etc. But in the meantime, to a Spanish or a Scottish nobleman, who should have insisted upon the *directness* of his descent, the proper answer would have been: 'Dog! in what kennel were you lurking when such and such civil feuds were being agitated? As an honest man, as a gallant man, ten times over you ought to have died, had you felt, which the English nobility of the fifteenth century *did* feel, that your peerage was your summons to the field of battle and the scaffold.' For, again in later years than the fifteenth century, the English nobility—those even who, like the Scotch, had gained their family wealth by plundering the Church—in some measure washed out this original taint by standing forward as champions of what they considered (falsely or truly) national interests. The Russells, the Cavendishes, the Sidneys, even in times of universal profligacy, have held aloft the standard of their order; and no one can forget the many peers in Charles I.'s time, such as Falkland, or the Spencers (Sunderland), or the Comptons (Northampton), who felt and owned their paramount duty to lie in public self-dedication, and died therefore, and oftentimes left their inheritances a desolation. 'Thus far'—oh heavens! with what bitterness I said this, knowing it a thing undeniable by W. W. or by Sir George—you, the peerages that pretend to try conclusions with the English, you—French, German, Walloon, Spanish, Scottish—are able to do so simply because you are *fainéans*, because in time of public danger you hid yourselves under your mammas' petticoats, whilst the glorious work of reaping a bloody harvest was being done by others.

But the English peerage also celebrates services in the Senate as well as in the field. Look for a moment at the house of Cecil. The interest in this house was national, and at the same time romantic. Two families started off—one might say *simultaneously*—from the same radix, for the difference in point of years was but that which naturally divided the father and the son. Both were Prime Ministers of England, rehearsing by anticipation the relations between the two William Pitts—the statesmen who guided, first, the *Seven Years' War*, from 1757 to 1763; and, secondly, the French Revolutionary War, from the murder of Louis XVI. in 1793 to the battle of Trafalgar in October, 1805. Sir William Cecil, the father, had founded the barony of Burleigh, which subsequently was raised into the earldom of Exeter. Sir Robert Cecil, the son, whose personal merits towards James I. were more conspicuous than those of his father towards Queen Elizabeth, had leaped at once into the earldom of Salisbury. Through two centuries these distinguished houses—Exeter the elder and Salisbury the junior—had run against each other. At length the junior house ran ahead of its elder, being raised to a marquisate. But in this century the elder righted itself, rising also to a marquisate. In an ordinary case this would not have won any notice, but the historic cradle of the two houses, amongst burning feuds of Reformation and anti-Reformation policy, fiery beyond all that has ever raged amongst men, fixed the historic eye upon them. Neck and neck they ran together. Hatfield House for the family of Salisbury, Burleigh House (founded by the original Lord Burleigh) for the family of Exeter, expressed in the nineteenth century that fraternal conflict which had commenced in the sixteenth. Personal merits, if any such had varied and coloured the pretensions of this or that generation, had, in the midst of wealth and ease and dignity, withdrawn themselves from notice, except that about the splendid decennium of the Regency and the second decennium of George IV.'s reign, no lady of the Court had been so generally acceptable to the world of fashion and elegance, domestic or foreign, as the Marchioness of Salisbury, whose tragical death by fire at Hatfield House, in spite of her son's heroic exertions, was as memorable for the last generation as the similar tragedy at the Austrian Ambassador's continued to be for the Court and generation of Napoleon.[45] It is not often that two kindred houses, belonging in the Roman sense to the same *gens* or clan, run against each other with parity of honour and public consideration through nearly three centuries. The present representative of the Exeter house of the Cecils[46] was not individually considered a very interesting person. Or, at least, any interest that might distinguish him did not adapt itself to conversational display. His personal story was more remarkable than he was himself.

FOOTNOTES:

[45] Napoleon attached a superstitious importance to this event. In 1813, upon the sudden death of Moreau, whilst as yet the circumstances were entirely unknown, he fancied strangely enough that the ambassador (Prince Schwartzenberg) whose fête had given birth to the tragedy, must himself have been prefigured.

[46] 'The present representative of the Exeter Cecils' was the father of the present peer, Brownlow, 2nd Marquis; born 2nd July, 1785; succeeded 1st May, 1804, and died 16th Jan., 1867.—ED.

VIII. THE ANTI-PAPAL MOVEMENT.

The sincerity of an author sometimes borrows an advantageous illustration from the repulsiveness of his theme. That a subject is dull, however unfortunately it may operate for the impression which he seeks to produce, must at least acquit him of seeking any aid to that impression from alien and meretricious attractions. Is a subject hatefully associated with recollections of bigotry, of ignorance, of ferocious stupidity, of rancour, and of all uncharitableness? In that case, the reader ought to be persuaded that nothing less than absolute consciousness—in that case he ought to know that nothing short of TRUTH (not necessarily as it *is*, but at least as it *appears* to the writer) can have availed to draw within an arena of violence and tiger-like *acharnement* one who, by temperament and by pressure of bodily disease, seeks only for repose. Most unwillingly I enter the ring. Mere disgust at the wicked injustice, which I have witnessed silently through the last three months, forces me into the ranks of the combatants. Mere sympathy with the ill-used gives me any motive for stirring. People have turned Christian from witnessing the torments suffered with divine heroism by Christian martyrs. And I think it not impossible that many hearts may be turned favourably towards Popery by the mere recoil of disgust from the savage insolence with which for three weeks back it has in this country been tied to a stake, and baited. The actors, or at least the leaders, in such scenes seem to forget that Popery has peculiar fascinations of her own; her errors, supposing even all to be errors which Protestantism denounces for such, lie in doctrinal points; but her merit, and her prodigious advantage over Protestantism, lies in the devotional spirit which she is able to kindle and to sustain amongst simple, docile, and confiding hearts. In mere prudence it ought to be remembered, that to love, to trust, to adore, is a far more contagious tendency amongst the poor, the wretched, and the despised, than to question, investigate, and reflect.

How, then, did this movement begin? By *that*, perhaps, we may learn something of its quality. Who was it that first roused this movement? The greater half of the nation, viz., all the lower classes, cannot be said to have shared in the passions of the occasion; but the educated classes, either upon a sincere impulse, or in a spirit of excessive imitation, have come forward with a perseverance, which (in a case of perils confessedly so vague) is more like a moonstruck infatuation than any other recorded in history. Until Parliament met on the 4th of February, when a Roman Catholic member of the House of Commons first attempted to give some specific account of the legal effects incident to a substitution of bishops for vicars apostolic, no man has made the very cloudiest sketch of the evils that were apprehended, or that *could* be apprehended, or that were in the remotest way possible. Sir Edward Sugden, indeed, came forward with a most unsatisfactory effort to show how Cardinal Wiseman might be punished, or might be restrained, supposing that he had done wrong; but not at all to show that the Cardinal *had* done wrong, and far less to show that, if wrong could be alleged, any evils would follow from it. Sir Edward most undoubtedly did not satisfy himself, and so little did he satisfy anybody else, that already his letter is forgotten; nor was it urged or relied upon by any one of the great meetings which succeeded it. Too painful it would be to think that Sir Edward had in this instance stepped forward sycophantically, as so many prominent people undoubtedly did, to meet and to aid a hue and cry of fanaticism simply because it had emanated from a high quarter. But *what* quarter? Again I ask, *who* was it that originated this fierce outbreak of bigotry? Much depends upon *that*. It was Lord John Russell, it was the First Minister of the Crown, that abused the power of his place for a purpose of desperate fanaticism; yes, and for a purpose which his whole life had been dedicated to opposing, to stigmatizing, to overthrowing. Right or wrong, he has to begin life anew. Bigotry may *not* be bigotry, change of position may show it under a new aspect. But still upon that, which once was *called* bigotry, Lord John must now take his stand. Neither will *ratting* a second time avail to set him right. These things do not stand under algebraical laws, as though ratting to the right hand could balance a ratting to the left, and leave the guilt $= 0$. On the contrary, five rattings, of which each is valued at ten, amount to fifty degrees of crime; or, perhaps, if moral computations were better understood, amount to a crime that swells by some secret geometrical progression unintelligible to man.

But now, reader, pause. Suppose that Lord John Russell, aware of some evil, some calamity or disease, impending over the established Church of England—sure of this evil, but absolutely unable to describe it by rational remarks or premonitory symptom, had cast about for a channel by which he might draw attention to the evil, and, by exposing, make an end of it. But who could have dreamed that he would have chosen the means he has chosen? What propriety was there in Lord John's addressing himself upon such a subject to the Bishop of Durham? Who is that Bishop? And what are his pretensions to public authority? He is a respectable Greek scholar; and has re-edited the Prosodiacal Lexicon of Morell—a service to Greek literature not easily overestimated, and beyond a doubt not easily executed. But in relation to the Church he is not any official organ; nor was there either decorum or good sense in addressing a letter essentially official from the moment that it was published with consent of the writer, to a person clothed with no sort of official powers or official relation to the Church of England. If Lord John should have occasion to communicate with the

Bank of England, what levity, and in the proper sense of the word what impertinence, it would be to invoke the attention—not of the Governor—but of some clerk in a special department of that establishment whom Lord John might happen to know. Which of us, that wishes to bring a grievance before the authorities of the Post-Office, would address himself to his private friend that might happen to hold a respectable situation in the Money Order or in the Dead Letter Office? Of mere necessity, that he might gain for his own application an official privilege, he would address it to the Postmaster-General through the Secretary. Not being so addressed, his communication would take rank as gossip; neither meriting nor obtaining any serviceable notice. Two points are still in suspense: whether the people of England as a nation have taken any interest in the uproar caused by Lord John's letter; and secondly, whether the writer of that letter took much interest in it himself. Spite of all the noise and tumult kept up for three months by the Low-Church party, clerks and laymen, it is still a question with many vigilant lookers-on—whether the great neutral majority in the lower strata of society (five-sixths in short of what we mean by the nation) have taken any real interest in the agitation. Any real share in it, beyond all doubt, they have *not* taken: the movers in these meetings from first to last would not make fifteen thousand; and the inert subscribers of Petitions would not make seventy thousand. Secondly, in spite of the hysterical violence manifested by the letter of the Premier, and partly in consequence of that violence (so theatrical and foreign to Lord John's temperament), many doubt whether he himself carried any sincerity with the movement. And this doubt is strengthened by the singular indecorum of his having addressed himself to Dr. Maltby.

Counterfeit zeal is likely enough to have recoiled from its own act in the very moment of its execution. The purpose of Lord John was sufficiently answered, if he succeeded in diverting public attention from quarters in which it might prove troublesome: and to that extent was sure of succeeding by an extra-official note addressed to any bishop whatever—whether zoological like the late Bishop of Norwich, or Prosodiacal like Dr. Maltby. A storm in a slop-basin was desirable for the moment. But had the desire been profoundly sincere, and had it soared to that height which *real* fears for religious interests are apt to attain, then beyond all doubt the Minister would not have addressed himself to a Provincial bishop, but to the two Metropolitan bishops of Canterbury and York. They, but not an inferior prelate, represent the Church of England.

The letter therefore, had it been solemn and austere in the degree suitable to an *unsimulated* panic, would have taken a different direction. Gossip may be addressed to anybody. He that will listen is sought for; and not he that can co-operate. But earnest business, soaring into national buoyancy on the wings of panic, turns by instinct to the proper organs for giving it effect and instant mobility. Yet, on the other hand, if the letter really *had* been addressed to the Primate (as in all reason it would have been, if thoroughly in earnest), that change must have consummated the false step, diplomatically valued, which Lord John Russell has taken. Mark, reader! We are told, and so often that the very echoes of Killarney and Windermere will be permanently diseased by this endless iteration of lies, that His Holiness has been insulting us. Ancient Father of Christendom, under whose sheltering shadow once slept in peace for near a thousand years the now storm-tossed nations of Western and Central Christendom, couldst thou indeed, when turned out a houseless[47] fugitive like Lear upon a night of tempest, still retain aught of thy ancient prestige, and through the might of belief rule over those who have exiled thee?

EDITOR'S NOTE.

The famous Durham Letter which excited so much controversy, and re-opened what can only be called so many old sores, was addressed by Lord John Russell, the Prime Minister, to Dr. Maltby, in November, 1850. At first it was received with great approbation, as presenting a decisive front against Papal assumption; the Pope having recently issued a Bull, dividing England into twelve Sees, and appointing Dr. Wiseman, who was made a Cardinal, Archbishop of Westminster. But some expressions in Lord John's letter, especially the expression 'unworthy sons,' applied to High Churchmen, aroused the active opposition of a class, with whom, he never had much sympathy, looking on the attitude and spirit of Drs. Pusey and Newman with unaffected dislike. Catholics, of course, and with them many moderate Roman Catholics, set up an agitation, and soon the Durham Letter was in everybody's mouth. De Quincey, of course, writes from his own peculiar philosophic point of view; and when he somewhat sarcastically alludes to the informality of addressing such a letter to the Bishop of Durham, and not to one or other of the Archbishops, he was either ignorant of, or of set purpose ignored, the exceptionally intimate relations in which Lord John had for many years stood to Dr. Maltby, such relations as might well have been accepted as explaining, if not justifying, such a departure from strict formal propriety. Lord Russell's biographer writes:

'Dr. Maltby, who in 1850 held the See of Durham, to which he had been promoted on Lord John's own recommendation in 1836, was one of Lord John's oldest and closest friends. He had been his constant correspondent for more than twenty years; he had supplied him with much information for the religious chapters of the "Affairs of Europe," and he had been his frequent counsellor on questions affecting the Church, and on the qualifications and characters of the men who were candidates for promotion in it. It was natural, therefore, to Lord John, to open his mind freely to the Bishop' (ii. 119, 120).

Lord John had added in a postscript: 'If you think it will be of any use, you have my full permission to publish this letter.'

FOOTNOTES:

[47] 'A houseless fugitive.' No one expression of petty malice has struck the generous as more unworthy, amongst the many insolences levelled at the Pope, than the ridicule so falsely fastened upon the mode of his escape from Rome, and upon the apparently tottering tenure of his temporal throne. His throne rocked with subterraneous heavings. True, and was *his* the only throne that rocked? Or which was it amongst continental thrones that did *not* rock? But he escaped in the disguise of a livery servant. What odious folly! In such emergencies, no disguise can be a degradation. Do we remember our own Charles II. assuming as many varieties of servile disguise as might have glorified a pantomime? Do we remember Napoleon reduced to the abject resource of entreating one of the Commissioners to *whistle*, by way of misleading the infuriated mob into the belief that *l'empereur* could not be supposed present in that carriage when such an indecency was attempted? As to the insecurity of his throne, we must consider that other thrones, and amongst them some of the first rank (as those of Turkey and Persia) redress their own weakness by means of alien strength. In the jealousies of England and France is found a bulwark against the overshadowing ambition of Russia.

IX. THEORY AND PRACTICE:

Review of Kant's Essay on the Common Saying, that such and such a thing may be true in theory, but does not hold good in practice.

What was the value of Kant's essay upon this popular saying? Did it do much to clear up the confusion? Did it exterminate the vice in the language by substituting a better *formula?* Not at all. Immanuel Kant was, we admit, the most potent amongst all known intellects for functions of pure abstraction. But also, viewed in two separate relations: first, in relation to all *practical* interests (manners, legislation, government, spiritual religion); secondly, in relation to the arts of teaching, of explaining, of communicating any man's meaning where it happened to be dark or perplexed (above all, if that meaning were his own)—this same Kant was merely impotent; absolutely, and 'no mistake,' a child of darkness. Were it not that veneration and gratitude cause us to suspend harsh words with regard to such a man, who has upon the greatest question affecting our human reason almost, we might say, *revealed* the truth (viz., in his theory of the categories), we should describe him, and continually we are tempted to describe him as the most superhuman of recorded blockheads. Would it be credited, that at this time of day, actually in the very closing years of the eighteenth century, a man armed with some reading, but not too much study—and sixty years' profound meditation should treat it as a matter of obvious good sense that crowns and the succession to mighty empires ought to travel along the line of 'merit'; not exactly on the ground of personal beauty, or because the pretender was taller by the head than most of his subjects—no, *that* would be the idea of a barbarous nation. Thank God! a royal professor of Koenigsberg was above *that*. But on the assumption of an *appropriate* merit, as if, for instance, he were wiser, if he were well grounded in Transcendentalism, if he had gained a prize for 'virtue,' surely, surely, such graces ought to ensure a sceptre to their honoured professor. Especially when we consider how *readily* these personal qualities *prove* themselves to the general understanding, and how cheerfully they are always *allowed* by jealous and abominating competitors! Now turn from this haughty philosopher to a plain but most sensible and reflecting scholar—Isaac Casaubon. This man pretended to no philosophy, but a sincere, docile heart, much good sense, and patient observation of his own country's annals, which in the midst of belligerent papists, and very much against his own interest, had made him a good Church of England Protestant, made him also intensely attached to the doctrine of fixed succession under closer and clearer limitations than exist even in England.

For a thousand years this one plain rule had been the amulet for liberating France (else so constitutionally disposed to war) from the bloodiest of intestine contests. The man's career was pretty nearly concurrent as to its two limits with that of our own Shakespeare. Both he and Shakespeare were patronized, or, at least, countenanced by James the First, and both died many years before their patron. More than two centuries by a good deal have therefore passed away since he spoke, but this is the emphatic testimony which even at that time, wanting the political experience superadded, he bore to the peace and consequently to the civilization won for his country by this divine maxim, this *lex trabalis* (as so powerfully Casaubon calls it) of hereditary succession, the cornerstone, the main beam, in the framework of Gallic polity. These are the words: '*Occidebant et occidebantur*' (*i.e.*, in those days of Roman Cæsars) '*immanitate pari; cum in armis esset jus omne regnandi*'—in the sword lay the arbitration of the title. He speaks of the horrid murderous uniformity by which the Western Empire moved through five centuries (for it commenced in murder 42 years B.C. and lasted for 477 after Christ). But why? Simply by default of any conventional rule, and the consequent necessity that men should fall back upon the title of the strongest. For that ridiculous plausibility of Kant's superscribed with *Detur meliori*, it should never be forgotten, is so far from having any pacific tendencies, that originally, according to the eldest of Greek fables, it was Ἔρις, Eris, the goddess of dissension, no peace-making divinity, who threw upon a wedding-table the fatal apple thus ominously labelled. *Meliori*! in that one word went to wreck the harmony of the company. But for France, for the famous kingdom of the Fleur-de-lys, for the first-born child of Christianity, always so prone by her gentry to this sword-right, Nature herself had been silenced through a long millennium by this one almighty amulet. 'Inde' (that is, from this standing appeal made to personal vanity or to ambition amongst Roman nobles)—'*inde* haec tam spissa principatuum mutatio: quâ re nulla alia miseris populis ne dici quidem aut fingi queat perniciosior.' So often, he goes on to say, as this dreadful curse entailed upon Rome Imperial comes into my mind, so often 'Franciæ patriæ meæ felicitatem non possim non prædicare; quæ sub imperio Regum sexaginta trium (LXIII)—non dicam CLX annos' (which had been the upshot of time, the 'tottle,' upon sixty-three Imperatores) sed paullo minus CIↃ (one clear thousand, observe) 'et CC—rem omnibus seculis inauditam!—egit beata; fared prosperously; et egisset beatior, si sua semper bona intellexisset. Tanti est, jura regiæ successionis trabali lege semel fixisse.' Aye, faithful and sagacious Casaubon! there lies the secret. In that word '*fixisse*'—the having settled once and for ever, the having laid down as beams and main timbers those adamantine rules of polity which leave no opening to doubt, no licence to caprice, and no temptation to individual ambition. We are all interested, Christendom to her very depths is interested, in the well-being and progress of this glorious realm—the kingdom of the lilies, the kingdom of Charlemagne and his paladins; from the very fierceness and angry vigilance of whose constant hostility to ourselves has arisen one chief re-agent in sustaining our own concurrent advancement. Under the torpor of a German patriotism, under the languor of a *sensus communis* which is hardly at all developed, our own unrivalled energy would partially have gone to sleep. We are, therefore, deeply indebted to the rancorous animosity of France. And in this one article of a sound political creed we must be sensible that France, so dreadfully in arrear as to all other political wisdom, has run ahead of ourselves. For to what else was owing our ruinous war of the Two Roses than to an original demur in our courts of law whether the descendant of an elder son through the female line had a title preferable or inferior to that of a descendant in the male line from a son confessedly *junior*? Whether the element to the right hand of uncontested superiority balanced or did *not* balance that element to the left hand of undenied inferiority? How well for us English, and for the interests of our literature so cruelly barbarized within fifty years from the death of Chaucer (A.D. 1400), had we been able to intercept the murderous conflicts of Barnet, Towcester, Tewkesbury, St. Albans! How happy for Spain, had no modern line of French coxcombs (not succeeding by any claim of blood, but under the arbitrary testament of a paralytic dotard) interfered to tamper with the old Castilian rules, so that no man knew whether the Spanish custom or the French innovation really governed. The Salic law or the interested abrogation of that law were the governing principle in strict constitutional practice. To this point had the French dynasty brought matters, that no lawyer even could say on which side the line of separation lay the *onus* of treason. We have ultimately so far improved our law of succession by continued limitations, that now even the religion of a prince has become one amongst his indispensable qualifications. But how matters once stood, we see written in letters of blood. And yet to this state of perilous uncertainty would Kant have reduced every nation under the conceit of mending their politics. 'Orbis terrarum dominatio'—*that*, says Casaubon, was the prize at stake. And how was it awarded? '*In parricidii præmium cedebat.*' By tendency, by usage, by natural gravitation, this Imperial dignity passed into a bounty upon murder, upon treasonable murder, upon parricidal murder. For the oath of fealty to the *sacra Cæsaria majestas* was of awful obligation, although the previous title of the particular Cæsar had been worth nothing at all. And the consequent condition of insecurity, the shadowy tenure of all social blessings, is described by Casaubon in language truly forcible.

Kant's purpose, as elsewhere we shall show, was not primarily with the maxim: that was but a secondary purpose. His direct and real object lay in one or two of the illustrative cases under the maxim. With this particular obliquity impressed upon the movement of his own essay, we can have no right to quarrel. Kant had an author's right to deal with the question as best suited his own views. But with one feature of his treatment we quarrel determinately. He speaks of this most popular (and, we venture to add, most wise and beneficial) maxim, which arms men's suspicions against all that is merely speculative, on the ground that it is continually at war with the truth of practical results, as though it were merely and blankly a vulgar error, as though *sans phrase* it might be dismissed for nonsense. But, because there is a casual inaccuracy in the wording of a great truth, we are not at liberty to deny that truth, to evade it, to 'ignore' it, or to confound a faulty expression with a meaning originally untenable. Professor Kant, of all men, was least entitled to plead blindness as to the substance in virtue of any vice affecting the form. No man knew better the art of translating so wise and beneficial a sentiment, though slightly disfigured by popular usage, into the appropriate philosophic terms. To this very sentiment it is, this eternal *protest* against the plausible and the speculative, not as a flash sentiment for a gala dinner, but as a principle of action operative from age to age in all parts of the national conduct, that England is indebted more than she is to any other known influence for her stupendous prosperity on two separate lines of progress: first, on that of commercial enterprise; secondly, on that of political improvement. At this moment there are two forces acting upon Christendom which constitute the principles of movement all over Europe: these are, the questions incident to representative government, and the mighty interests combined by commercial enterprise. Both have radiated from England as their centre. There only did the early models of either activity prosper. Through North America, as the daughter of England, these two forces have transplanted themselves to every principal region (except one) of the vast Southern American continent. Thus, to push our view no further, we behold one-half of the habitable globe henceforth yoked to the two sole forces of *permanent* movement for nations, since war and religious contests are but intermitting forces; and these two principles, we repeat, have grown to what we now behold chiefly through the protection of this one great maxim which throws the hopes of the world, not upon what the scheming understanding can suggest, but upon what the most faithful experiment can prove.

X. POPE AND DIDACTIC POETRY.

The 'Essay on Criticism' illustrates the same profound misconception of the principle working at the root of Didactic Poetry as operated originally to disturb the conduct of the 'Essay on Man' by its author, and to disturb the judgments upon it by its critics. This 'Essay on Criticism' no more aims at unfolding the grounds and theory of critical rules applied to poetic composition, than does the *Epistola ad Pisones* of Horace. But what if Horace and Pope both believed themselves the professional expounders *ex cathedrá* of these very grounds and this very theory? No matter if they did. Nobody was less likely to understand their own purposes than themselves. Their real purposes were *immanent*, hidden in their poems; and from the poems they must be sought, not from the poets; who, generally, in proportion as the problem is one of analysis and evolution, for which, simply as the authors of the work, Horace and Pope were no better qualified than other people, and, as authors having that particular constitution of intellect which notoriously they had, were much worse qualified than other people. We cannot possibly allow a man to argue upon the meaning or tendency of his own book, as against the evidence of the book itself. The book is unexceptionable authority: and, as against *that*, the author has no *locus standi*. Both Horace and Pope, however little they might be aware of it, were secretly governed by the same moving principle—viz., not to teach (which was impossible for two reasons)—but to use this very impossibility, this very want of flexibility in the subject to the ostensible purpose of the writers, as the resistance of the atmosphere from which they would derive the motion of their wings. That it was impossible in a poem seriously to teach the principles of criticism, we venture to affirm on a double argument: 1st, that the teaching, if in earnest, must be *polemic*: and how alien from the spirit of poetry to move eternally through controversial discussions! 2ndly, that the teaching, from the very necessities of metre, must be *eclectic*; innumerable things must be suppressed; and how alien from the spirit of science to move by discontinuous links according to the capricious bidding of poetic decorum! Divinity itself is not more entangled in the necessities of fighting for every step in advance, and maintaining the ground by eternal preparation for hostility, than is philosophic criticism; a discipline so little matured, that at this day we possess in any language nothing but fragments and hints towards its construction. To dispute in verse has been celebrated as the accomplishment of Lucretius, of Sir John Davies, of Dryden: but then this very disputation has always been eclectic; not exhausting even the *essential* arguments; but playing gracefully with those only which could promise a brilliant effect. Such a mimic disputation is like a histrionic fencing match, where the object of the actor is not in good earnest to put his antagonist to the sword, but to exhibit a few elegant passes in *carte* and *tierce*, not forgetting the secondary object of displaying to advantage any diamonds and rubies that may chance to scintillate upon his sword-hand.

Had Pope, or had Horace, been requested to explain the *rationale* of his own poem on Criticism, it is pretty certain that each (and from the same causes) would have talked nonsense. The very gifts so rare and so exquisite by which these extraordinary men were adorned—the graceful negligence, the delicacy of tact, the impassioned *abandon*[48] upon subjects suited to their *modes* of geniality, though not absolutely or irreversibly incompatible with the sterner gifts of energetic attention and powerful abstraction, were undoubtedly not in alliance with them. The two sets of gifts did not exert a reciprocal stimulation. As well might one expect from a man, because he was a capital shot, that he should write the best essay on the theory of projectiles. Horace and Pope, therefore, would have talked so absurdly in justifying or explaining their own works, that we—naturally impatient of nonsense on the subject of criticism, as our own *métier*—should have said, 'Oh, dear gentlemen, stand aside for a moment, and we will right you in the eyes of posterity: at which bar, if either of you should undertake to be his own advocate, he will have a fool for his client.'

We do and must concede consideration even to the one-sided pleadings of an advocate. But it is under the secret assumption of the concurrent pleadings equally exaggerated on the adverse side. Without this counterweight, how false would be our final summation of the evidence upon most of the great state trials! Nay, even with both sides of the equation before us, how perplexing would be that summation generally, unless under the moderating guidance of a neutral and indifferent eye; the eye of the judge in the first instance, and subsequently of the upright historian—whether watching the case from the station of a contemporary, or reviewing it from his place in some later generation.

Now what we wish to observe about Criticism is, that with just the same temptation to personal partiality and even injustice in extremity, it offers a much wider latitude to the distortion of things, facts, grounds, and inferences. In fact, with the very same motives to a personal bias swerving from the equatorial truth, it makes a much wider opening for giving effect to those motives. Insincerity in short, and every mode of contradicting the truth, is far more possible under a professed devotion to a general principle than any personal expression could possibly be.

If the logic of the case be steadily examined, a definition of didactic poetry will emerge the very opposite to that popularly held: it will appear that in didactic poetry the teaching is not the *power*, but the *resistance*. It is difficult to teach even playfully or mimically in reconciliation with poetic effect: and the object is to wrestle with this difficulty. It is as when a man selects an absurd or nearly impracticable subject, his own chin,[49] suppose, for the organ of a new music: he does not select it as being naturally allied to music, but for the very opposite reason—as being eminently alien from music, that his own art will have the greater triumph in taming this reluctancy into any sort of obedience to a musical purpose. It is a wrestle with all but physical impossibility. Many arts and mechanic processes in human life present intermitting aspects of beauty, scattered amongst others that are utterly without interest of that sort. For instance, in husbandry, where many essential processes are too mean to allow of any poetic treatment or transfiguration, others are picturesque, and recommended by remembrances of childhood to most hearts. How beautiful, for instance, taken in all its variety of circumstances, the gorgeous summer, the gay noontide repast, the hiding of children in the hay, the little toy of a rake in the hands of infancy, is the hay-harvest from first to last! Such cases wear a Janus aspect, one face connecting them with gross uses of necessity, another connecting them with the gay or tender sentiments that accidents of association, or some purpose of Providence, may have thrown about them as a robe of beauty. Selecting therefore what meets his own purpose, the poet proceeds by *resisting* and rejecting all those parts of the subject which would tend to defeat it. But at least, it will be said, he does not resist those parts of the subject which he selects. Yes, he *does*; even those parts he resists utterly in their real and primary character, viz., as uses indispensable to the machinery of man's animal life; and adopts them only for a collateral beauty attached to the accidents of their evolution; a beauty oftentimes not even guessed by those who are most familiar with them as practical operations. It is as if a man, having a learned eye, should follow the track of armies—careless of the political changes which they created, or of the interests (all neutral as regarded any opinion of *his*) which they disturbed— but alive to every form of beauty connected with these else unmeaning hostilities—alive to the beauty of their battle-array, to the pomp of their manœuvres, to the awning of smoke-wreaths surging above the artilleries, to the gleaming of sabres and bayonets at intervals through loopholes in these gathering smoky masses. This man would abstract from the politics and doctrines of the hostile armies, as much as the didactic poet from the doctrinal part of his theme.

From this attempt to rectify the idea of didactic poetry, it will be seen at once why Pope failed utterly and inevitably in the 'Essay on Man.' The subject was too directly and commandingly interesting to furnish any opening to that secondary and playful interest which arises from the management by art and the subjugation of an intractable theme. The ordinary interest of didactic poetry is derived from the *repellent* qualities of the subject, and consequently from the dexterities of the conflict with what is doubtful, indifferent, unpromising. Not only was there no *resistance* in the subject to the grandeur of poetry, but, on the contrary, this subject offered so much grandeur, was so pathetic and the amplitude of range so vast as to overwhelm the powers of any poet and any audience, by its exactions. That was a fault in one direction. But a different fault was—that the subject allowed no power of selection. In ordinary didactic poetry, as we have just been insisting, you sustain the interest by ignoring all the parts which will not bear a steady gaze. Whatever fascinates the eye, or agitates the heart by mimicry of life is selected and emphasized, and what is felt to be intractable or repellent is authoritatively set aside. The poet has an unlimited discretion. But on a theme so great as man he has no discretion at all. This resource is denied. You *can* give the truth only by giving the whole truth. In treating a common didactic theme you may neglect merely transitional parts with as much ease as benefit, because they are familiar enough to be pre-supposed, and are besides essential only in the real process, but not at all in the mimic process of description; since A and C, that in the *reality* could reach one another only through B, may yet be intelligible as regards their beauty without any intermediation of B. The ellipsis withdraws a deformity, and does not generally create an obscurity: either the obscurity is none at all, or is irrelevant to the real purpose of beauty, or may be treated sufficiently by a line or two of adroit explanation. But in a poem treating so vast a theme as man's relations to his own race, to his habitation the world, to God his maker, and to all the commands of the conscience, to the hopes of the believing heart, and to the eternal self-conflicts of the intellect, it is clear that the purely transitional parts, essential to the understanding of the whole, cannot be omitted or dispensed with at the beck of the fancy or the necessities of the metre and rhyme.

There is also an objection to Man (or any other theme of that grandeur) as the subject of a didactic poem, which is more subtle, and which for that reason we have reserved to the last. In the ordinary specimens of didactic poetry, the theme and its sub-divisions wear (as we have already observed) a double-faced or Janus aspect; one derived from the direct experience of life, the other from the reflex experience of it. And the very reason why one face *does* affect you is because the other does *not*. Thus a Morland farmyard, a Flemish tavern, or a clean kitchen in an unpretending house seen by ruddy firelight reflected from pewter ware, scarcely interests the eye at all in the reality; but for that very reason it *does* interest us all in the mimicry. The very fact of seeing an object framed as it were, insulated, suddenly *relieved* to the steady consciousness, which all one's life has been seen *un*framed, *not* called into relief, but depressed into the universal level of subconsciousness, awakens a pleasurable sense of surprise. But now Man is too great a subject to allow of any unrelieved aspects. What the reader sees he must see directly and without insulation, else falseness and partiality are immediately apparent.

XI. SHAKSPEARE AND WORDSWORTH.

I take the opportunity of referring to the work of a very eloquent Frenchman, who has brought the names of Wordsworth and Shakspeare into connection, partly for the sake of pointing out an important error in the particular criticism on Wordsworth, but still more as an occasion for expressing the gratitude due to the French author for the able, anxious, and oftentimes generous justice which he has rendered to English literature. It is most gratifying to a thoughtful Englishman—that precisely from that period when the mighty drama of the French Revolution, like the Deluge, or like the early growth of Christianity, or like the Reformation, had been in operation long enough to form a new and more thoughtful generation in France, has the English literature been first studied in France, and first appreciated. Since 1810, when the generation moulded by the Revolution was beginning to come forward on the stage of national action, a continued series of able writers amongst the French—ardent, noble, profound—have laid aside their nationality in the most generous spirit for the express purpose of investigating the great English models of intellectual power, locally so near to their own native models, and virtually in such polar remoteness. Chateaubriand's intense enthusiasm for Milton, almost monomaniac in the opinion of some people, is notorious. This, however, was less astonishing: the pure marble grandeur of Milton, and his classical severity, naturally recommended themselves to the French taste, which can always understand the beauty of proportion and regular or teleologic tendencies. It was with regard to the anomalous, and to that sort of vaster harmonies which from moving upon a wider scale are apt at first sight to pass for discords, that a new taste needed to be created in France. Here Chateaubriand showed himself a Frenchman of the old leaven. Milton would always have been estimated in France. He needed only to be better known. Shakspeare was the *natural* stone of offence: and with regard to *him* Chateaubriand has shown himself eminently blind. His reference to Shakspeare's *female* gallery, so divine as that Pantheon really is, by way of most forcibly expressing his supposed inferiority to Racine (who strictly speaking has no female pictures at all, but merely *umrisse* or outlines in pencil) is the very perfection of human blindness. But many years ago the writers in *Le Globe*, either by direct papers on the drama or indirectly by way of references to the acting of Kean, etc., showed that even as to Shakspeare a new heart was arising in France. M. Raymond de Véricour, though necessarily called off to a more special consideration of the Miltonic poetry by the very promise of his title (*Milton, et la Poésie Epique*: Paris et Londres, 1838), has in various places shown a far more comprehensive sense of poetic truth than Chateaubriand. His sensibility, being originally deeper and trained to move upon a larger compass, vibrates equally under the chords of the Shakspearian music. Even he, however, has made a serious mistake as to Wordsworth in his relation to Shakspeare. At p. 420 he says: 'Wordsworth qui (de même que Byron) sympathise pen cordialement avec Shakspeare, se prosterne cependant comme Byron devant le *Paradis perdu*; Milton est la grande idole de Wordsworth; il ne craint pas quelquefois de se comparer lui-même à son géant;' (never unless in the single accident of praying for a similar audience—'fit audience let me find though few'); 'et en vérité ses sonnets ont souvent le même esprit prophétique, la même élévation sacrée que ceux de l'Homère anglais.' There cannot be graver mistakes than are here brought into one focus. Lord Byron cared little for the 'Paradise Lost,' and had studied it not at all. On the other hand, Lord Byron's pretended disparagement of Shakspeare by comparison with the meagre, hungry and bloodless Alfieri was a pure stage trick, a momentary device for expressing his Apemantus misanthropy towards the English people. It happened at the time he had made himself unpopular by the circumstances of his private life: these, with a morbid appetite for engaging public attention, he had done his best to publish and to keep before the public eye; whilst at the same time he was very angry at the particular style of comments which they provoked. There was no fixed temper of anger towards him in the public mind of England: but he believed that there was. And he took his revenge through every channel by which he fancied himself to have a chance for reaching and stinging the national pride; 1st, by ridiculing the English pretensions to higher principle and national morality; but *that* failing, 2ndly, by disparaging Shakspeare; 3rdly, on the same principle which led Dean Swift to found the first lunatic hospital in Ireland, viz.:

'To shew by one satiric touchNo nation wanted it so much.'

Lord Byron, without any *sincere* opinion or care upon the subject one way or other, directed in his will—that his daughter should not marry an Englishman: this bullet, he fancied, would take effect, even though the Shakspeare bullet had failed. Now, as to Wordsworth, he values both in the highest degree. In a philosophic poem, like the 'Excursion,' he is naturally led to speak more pointedly of Milton: but his own affinities are every way more numerous and striking to Shakspeare. For this reason I have myself been led to group him with Shakspeare. In those two poets alike is seen the infinite of Painting: in Æschylus and Milton alike are seen the simplicities and stern sublimiities of Sculpture.

XII. CRITICISM ON SOME OF COLERIDGE'S CRITICISMS OF WORDSWORTH.

One fault in Wordsworth's 'Excursion' suggested by Coleridge, but luckily quite beyond all the resources of tinkering open to William Wordsworth, is—in the choice of a Pedlar as the presiding character who connects the shifting scenes and persons in the 'Excursion.' Why should not some man of more authentic station have been complimented with that place, seeing that the appointment lay altogether in Wordsworth's gift? But really now who could this have been? Garter King-at-Arms would have been a great deal too showy for a working hero. A railway-director, liable at any moment to abscond with the funds of the company, would have been viewed by all readers with far too much suspicion for the tranquillity desirable in a philosophic poem. A colonel of Horse Marines seems quite out of the question: what his proper functions may be, is still a question for the learned; but no man has supposed them to be philosophic. Yet on the other hand, argues Coleridge, would not '*any* wise and beneficent old man,' without specifying his rank, have met the necessities of the case? Why, certainly, if it is *our* opinion that Coleridge wishes to have, we conceive that such an old gentleman, advertising in the *Times* as 'willing to make himself generally useful,' might have had a chance of dropping a line to William Wordsworth. But still we don't know. Beneficent old gentlemen are sometimes great scamps. Men, who give themselves the best of characters in morning papers, are watched occasionally in a disagreeable manner by the police. Itinerant philosophers are absolutely not understood in England. Intruders into private premises, even for grand missionary purposes, are constantly served with summary notices to quit. Mrs. Quickly gave a first-rate character to Simple; but for all *that*, Dr. Caius with too much show of reason demanded, 'Vat shall de honest young man do in my closet?' And we fear that Coleridge's beneficent old man, lecturing *gratis* upon things in general, would be regarded with illiberal jealousy by the female servants of any establishment, if he chose to lecture amongst the family linen. 'What shall de wise beneficent old Monsieur do amongst our washing-tubs?' We are perfectly confounded by the excessive blindness of Coleridge and nearly all other critics on this matter. 'Need the rank,' says Coleridge, 'have been at all particularized, when nothing follows which the knowledge of that rank is to explain or illustrate?' Nothing to explain or illustrate! Why, good heavens! it is only by the most distinct and positive information lodged with the constable as to who and what the vagrant was, that the leading philosopher in the 'Excursion' could possibly have saved himself over and over again from passing the night in the village 'lock-up,' and generally speaking in handcuffs, as one having too probably a design upon the village hen-roosts. In the sixth and seventh books, where the scene lies in the churchyard amongst the mountains, it is evident that the philosopher would have been arrested as a resurrection-man, had he not been known to substantial farmers as a pedlar 'with some money.' To be clothed therefore with an intelligible character and a local calling was as indispensable to the free movements of the Wanderer when out upon a philosophical spree, as a passport is to each and every traveller in France. Dr. Franklin, who was a very indifferent philosopher, but very great as a pedlar, and as cunning as Niccolo Machiavelli (which means as cunning as old Nick), was quite aware of this necessity as a tax upon travellers; and at every stage, on halting, he used to stand upright in his stirrups, crying aloud, 'Gentlemen and Ladies, here I am at your service; Benjamin Franklin by name; once (but *that* was in boyhood) a devil; viz., in the service of a printer; next a compositor and reader to the press; at present a master-printer. My object in this journey is—to arrest a knave who will else be off to Europe with £200 of my money in his breeches-pocket: that is my final object: my immediate one is—dinner; which, if there is no just reason against it, I beg that you will no longer interrupt.' Yet still, though it is essential to the free circulation of a philosopher that he should be known for what he is, the reader thinks that at least the philosopher might be known advantageously as regards his social standing. No, he could not. And we speak seriously. How *could* Coleridge and so many other critics overlook the overruling necessities of the situation? They argue as though Wordsworth had selected a pedlar under some abstract regard for his office of buying and selling: in which case undoubtedly a wholesale man would have a better chance for doing a 'large stroke of business' in philosophy than this huckstering retailer. Wordsworth however fixed on a pedlar—not for his commercial relations—but in spite of them. It was not for the *essential* of his calling that a pedlar was promoted to the post of central philosopher in his philosophic poem, but for an accident indirectly arising out of it. This accident lay in the natural privilege which a pedlar once had through all rural districts of common access to rich and poor, and secondly, in the leisurely nature of his intercourse. Three conditions there were for fulfilling that ministry of philosophic intercourse which Wordsworth's plan supposed. First, the philosopher must be clothed with a *real* character, known to the actual usages of the land, and not imaginary: else this postulate of fiction at starting would have operated with an unrealizing effect upon all that followed. Next, it must be a character that was naturally fitted to carry the bearer through a large circuit of districts and villages; else the *arena* would be too narrow for the large survey of life and conflict demanded: lastly, the character must be one recommending itself alike to all ranks in tracts remote from towns, and procuring an admission ready and gracious to him who supports that character. Now this supreme advantage belonged in a degree absolutely unique to the character of pedlar, or (as Wordsworth euphemistically terms it) of 'wandering merchant.' In past generations the *materfamilias*, the young ladies, and the visitors within their gates, were as anxious for his periodic visit as the humblest of the domestics. They received him therefore with the condescending kindness of persons in a state of joyous expectation: young hearts beat with the anticipation of velvets and brocades from Genoa, lace veils from the Netherlands, jewels and jewelled trinkets; for you are not to think that, like Autolycus, he carried only one trinket. They were sincerely kind to him, being sincerely pleased. Besides, it was politic to assume a gracious manner, since else the pedlar might take out his revenge in the price of his wares; fifteen per cent. would be the least he could reasonably clap on as a premium and *solatium* to himself for any extra hauteur. This gracious style of intercourse, already favourable to a tone of conversation more liberal and unreserved than would else have been conceded to a vagrant huckster, was further improved by the fact that the pedlar was also the main retailer of news. Here it was that a real advantage offered itself to any mind having that philosophic interest in human characters, struggles, and calamities, which is likely enough to arise amongst a class of men contemplating long records of chance and change through their wanderings, and so often left to their own meditations upon them by long tracts of solitude. The gossip of the neighbouring districts, whether tragic or comic, would have a natural interest from its locality. And such records would lead to illustration from other cases more remote—losing the interest of neighbourhood, but compensating that loss by their deeper intrinsic hold upon the sensibilities. Ladies of the highest rank would suffer their reserve to thaw in such interviews; besides that, before unresisting humility and inferiority too apparent even haughtiness the most intractable usually abates its fervour.

Coleridge also allows himself, for the sake of argument, not merely to assume too hastily, but to magnify too inordinately. Daniel, the poet, really *was* called the 'well-languaged' (p. 83, vol. ii.), but by whom? Not, as Hooker was called the 'judicious,' or Bede the 'venerable,' by whole generations; but by an individual. And as to the epithet of 'prosaic,' we greatly doubt if so much as one individual ever connected it with Daniel's name.

But the whole dispute on Poetic Diction is too deep and too broad for an occasional or parenthetic notice. It is a dispute which renews itself in every cultivated language;[50] and even, in its application to different authors within the same language, as for instance, to Milton, to Shakspeare, or to Wordsworth, it takes a special and varied aspect. Declining this, as far too ample a theme, we wish to say one word, but an urgent word and full of clamorous complaint, upon the other branch. This dispute, however, is but one of two paths upon which the Biographical Literature approaches the subject of Wordsworth: the other lies in the direct critical examination of Wordsworth's poems. As to this, we wish to utter one word, but a word full of clamorous complaint. That the criticisms of Coleridge on William Wordsworth were often false, and that they betrayed fatally the temper of one who never *had* sympathized heartily with the most exquisite parts of the Lyrical Ballads, might have been a record injurious only to Coleridge himself. But unhappily these perverse criticisms have proved the occasions of ruin to some admirable poems; and, as if that were not enough, have memorialized a painful feature of weakness in Wordsworth's judgment. If ever on this earth there was a man that in his prime, when saluted with contumely from all quarters, manifested a stern deafness to criticism—it was William Wordsworth. And we thought the better of him by much for this haughty defiance to groundless judgments. But the cloak, which Boreas could not tear away from the traveller's resistance, oftentimes the too genial Phœbus has filched from his amiable spirit of compliance. These criticisms of Coleridge, generally so wayward and one-sided, but sometimes desperately opposed to every mode of truth, have been the means of exposing in William Wordsworth a weakness of resistance—almost a criminal facility in surrendering his own rights—which else would never have been suspected. We will take one of the worst cases. Readers acquainted with Wordsworth as a poet, are of course acquainted with his poem (originally so fine) upon Gipseys. To a poetic mind it is inevitable— that every spectacle, embodying any remarkable quality in a remarkable excess, should be unusually impressive, and should seem to justify a poetic record. For instance, the solitary life of one[51] who should tend a lighthouse could not fail to move a very deep sympathy with his situation. Here for instance we read the ground of Wordsworth's 'Glen Almain.' Did he care for torpor again, lethargic inertia? Such a spectacle as *that* in the midst of a nation so morbidly energetic as our own, was calculated to strike some few chords from the harp of a poet so vigilantly keeping watch over human life.

FOOTNOTES:

[50] Valckenaer, in his famous 'Dissertation on the Phœnissæ,' notices such a dispute as having arisen upon the diction of Euripides. The question is old and familiar as to the quality of the passion in Euripides, by comparison with that in Sophocles. But there was a separate dispute far less notorious as to the quality of the *lexis*.

[51] 'One,' but in the Eddystone or other principal lighthouses on our coast there are *two* men resident. True, but these two come upon duty by alternate watches, and generally are as profoundly separated as if living leagues apart.

XIII. WORDSWORTH AND SOUTHEY: AFFINITIES AND DIFFERENCES.

(*An Early Paper.*)

Of late the two names of Wordsworth and Southey have been coupled chiefly in the frantic philippics of Jacobins, out of revenge for that sublime crusade which, among the intellectual powers of Europe, these two eminent men were foremost (and for a time alone) in awakening against the brutalizing tyranny of France and its chief agent, Napoleon Bonaparte: a crusade which they, to their immortal honour, unceasingly advocated—not (as others did) at a time when the Peninsular victories, the Russian campaign, and the battle of Leipsic, had broken the charm by which France fascinated the world and had made Bonaparte mean even in the eyes of the mean—but (be it remembered!) when by far the major part of this nation looked upon the cause of liberty as hopeless upon the Continent, as committed for many ages to the guardianship of England, in which (or not at all) it was to be saved as in an Ark from the universal deluge. Painful such remembrances may be to those who are now ashamed of their idolatry, it must not be forgotten that, from the year 1803 to 1808, Bonaparte was an idol to the greater part of this nation; at no time, God be thanked! an idol of love, but, to most among us, an idol of fear. The war was looked upon as essentially a *defensive* war: many doubted whether Bonaparte could be successfully opposed: almost all would have treated it as lunacy to say that he could be conquered. Yet, even at that period, these two eminent patriots constantly treated it as a feasible project to march an English army triumphantly into Paris. Their conversations with various friends—the dates of their own works—and the dates of some composed under influences emanating from them (as, for example, the unfinished work of Colonel Pasley of the Engineers)—are all so many vouchers for this fact. We know not whether (with the exception of some few Germans such as Arndt, for whose book Palm was shot) there was at that time in Europe another man of any eminence who shared in that Machiavellian sagacity which revealed to them, as with the power and clear insight of the prophetic spirit, the craziness of the French military despotism when to vulgar politicians it seemed strongest. For this sagacity, and for the strength of patriotism to which in part they owed it (for in all cases the *moral* spirit is a great illuminator of the *intellect*), they have reaped the most enviable reward, in the hatred of traitors and Jacobins all over the world: and in the expressions of that hatred we find their names frequently coupled. There was a time, however, when these names were coupled for other purposes:

they were coupled as joint supporters of a supposed new creed in relation to their own art. Mr. Wordsworth, it is well known to men of letters, did advance a new theory upon two great questions of art: in some points it might perhaps be objected that his faith, in relation to that which he attacked, was as the Protestant faith to the Catholic—*i.e.*, not a new one, but a restoration of the primitive one purified from its modern corruptions. Be this as it may, however, Mr. Wordsworth's exposition of his theory is beyond all comparison the subtlest and (not excepting even the best of the German essays) the most finished and masterly specimen of reasoning which has in any age or nation been called forth by any one of the fine arts. No formal attack has yet been made upon it, except by Mr. Coleridge; of whose arguments we need not say that they furnish so many centres (as it were) to a great body of metaphysical acuteness; but to our judgment they fail altogether of overthrowing Mr. Wordsworth's theory. All the other critics have shown in their casual allusions to this theory that they have not yet come to understand what is its drift or main thesis. Such being the state of their acquaintance with the theory itself, we need not be surprised to find that the accidental connection between Mr. Wordsworth and the Laureate arising out of friendship and neighbourhood should have led these blundering critics into the belief that the two poets were joint supporters of the same theory: the fact being meanwhile that in all which is peculiar to Mr. Wordsworth's theory, Mr. Southey dissents perhaps as widely and as determinately as Mr. Coleridge; dissents, that is to say, not as the numerous blockheads among the male blue-stockings who dignify their ignorance with the name of dissent—but as one man of illustrious powers dissents from what he deems after long examination the errors of another; as Leibnitz on some occasions dissented from Plato, or as the great modern philosopher of Germany occasionally dissents from Leibnitz. That which Mr. Wordsworth has in common with all great poets, Mr. Southey cannot but reverence: he has told us that he does: and, if he had not, his own originality and splendour of genius would be sufficient pledges that he did. That which is peculiar to Mr. Wordsworth's theory, Mr. Southey may disapprove: he may think that it narrows the province of the poet too much in one part—that, in another part, it impairs the instrument with which he is to work. Thus far he may disapprove; and, after all, deduct no more from the merits of Mr. Wordsworth, than he will perhaps deduct from those of Milton, for having too often allowed a Latin or Hebraic structure of language to injure the purity of his diction. To whatsoever extent, however, the disapprobation of Mr. Southey goes, certain it is (for his own practice shows it) that he does disapprove the *innovations* of Mr. Wordsworth's theory—very laughably illustrates the sagacity of modern English critics: they were told that Mr. Southey held and practised a certain system of innovations: so far their error was an error of misinformation: but next they turn to Mr. Southey's works, and there they fancy that they find in every line an illustration of the erroneous tenets which their misinformation had led them to expect that they should find. A more unfortunate blunder, one more confounding to the most adventurous presumption, can hardly be imagined. A system, which no man could act upon unless deliberately and with great effort and labour of composition, is supposed to be exemplified in the works of a poet who uniformly rejects it: and this ludicrous blunder arises not from any over-refinements in criticism (such, for instance, as led Warburton to find in Shakspeare what the poet himself never dreamt of), but from no more creditable cause than a misreport of some blue-stocking miss either maliciously or ignorantly palmed upon a critic whose understanding passively surrendered itself to anything however gross.

Such are the two modes in which the names of these two eminent men have been coupled. As true patriots they are deservedly coupled: as poets their names cannot be justly connected by any stricter bond than that which connects all men of high creative genius. This distinction, as to the main grounds of affinity and difference between the two writers, was open and clear to any unprejudiced mind prepared for such investigations, and we should at any rate have pointed it out at one time or other for the sake of exposing the hollowness of those impostures which offer themselves in our days as criticisms.

XIV. PRONUNCIATION.

To *write* his own language with propriety is the ambition of here and there an individual; to speak it with propriety is the ambition of multitudes. Amongst the qualifications for a public writer—the preliminary one of *leisure* is granted to about one man in three thousand; and, this being indispensable, there at once, for most men, mercifully dies in the very instant of birth the most uneasy and bewildering of temptations. But *speak* a man must. Leisure or no leisure, to *talk* he is obliged by the necessities of life, or at least he thinks so; though my own private belief is, that the wisest rule upon which a man could act in this world (alas! I did not myself act upon it) would be to seal up his mouth from earliest youth, to simulate the infirmity of dumbness, and to answer only by signs. This would soon put an end to the impertinence of questions, to the intolerable labour of framing and uttering replies through a whole life, and, above all (oh, foretaste of Paradise!), to the hideous affliction of sustaining these replies and undertaking for all their possible consequences. That notion of the negroes in Senegal about monkeys, viz., that they *can* talk if they choose, and perhaps with classical elegance, but wisely dissemble their talent under the fear that the unjust whites would else make them work in Printing Houses, for instance, as 'readers' and correctors of the press, this idea, which I dare say is true, shows how much wiser, in his generation, is a monkey than a man. For, besides the wear and tear to a man's temper by the irritation of talking, and the corrosion of one's happiness by the disputes which talking entails, it is really frightful to think of the mischief caused, if one measures it only by the fruitless expense of words. Eleven hundred days make up about three years; consequently, eleven thousand days make up thirty years. But that day must be a very sulky one, and probably raining cats and dogs, on which a man throws away so few as two thousand words, not reckoning what he loses in sleep. A hundred and twenty-five words for every one of sixteen hours cannot be thought excessive. The result, therefore, is, that, in one generation of thirty years, he wastes irretrievably upon the impertinence of answering—of wrangling, and of prosing, not less than twice eleven thousand times a thousand words; the upshot of which comes to a matter of twenty-two million words. So that, if the English language contains (as some curious people say it does) forty thousand words, he will have used it up not less than five hundred and fifty times. Poor old battered language! One really pities it. Think of any language in its old age being forced to work at that rate; kneaded, as if it were so much dough, every hour of the day into millions of fantastic shapes by millions of capricious bakers! Being old, however, and superannuated, you will say that our English language must have got used to it: as the sea, that once (according to Camoens) was indignant at having his surface scratched, and his feelings harrowed, by keels, is now wrinkled and smiling.

Blessed is the man that is dumb, when speech would have betrayed his ignorance; and the man that has neither pens nor ink nor crayons, when a record of his thought would have delivered him over to the derision of posterity. This, however, the reader will say, is to embroider a large moral upon a trivial occasion. Possibly the moral may be disproportionately large; and yet, after all, the occasion may not be so trivial as it seems. One of the many revolutions worked by the railway system is, to force men into a much ampler publicity; to throw them at a distance from home amongst strangers; and at their own homes to throw strangers amongst *them*. Now, exactly in such situations it is, where all other gauges of appreciation are wanting, that the two great external indications of a man's rank, viz., the quality of his manners and the quality of his pronunciation, come into play for assigning his place and rating amongst strangers. Not merely pride, but a just and reasonable self-respect, irritates a man's aspiring sensibilities in such a case: not only he *is*, but always he *ought* to be, jealous of suffering in the estimation of strangers by defects which it is in his own choice to supply, or by mistakes which a little trouble might correct. And by the way we British act in this spirit, whether we ought to do or not, it is noticed as a broad characteristic of us Islanders, viz., both of the English and the Scotch, that we are morbidly alive to jealousy under such circumstances, and in a degree to which there is nothing amongst the two leading peoples of the Continent at all corresponding.[52] A Scotchman or an Englishman of low rank is anxious on a Sunday to dress in a style which may mislead the casual observer into the belief that perhaps he is a gentleman: whereas it is notorious that the Parisian artisan or labourer of the lower class is proud of connecting himself conspicuously with his own order, and ostentatiously acknowledging it, by adopting its usual costume. It is his way of expressing an *esprit de corps*. The same thing is true very extensively of Germans. And it sounds pretty, and reads into a sentimental expression of cheerful contentedness, that such customs should prevail on a great scale. Meantime I am not quite sure that the worthy Parisian is not an ass, and the amiable German another, for thus meekly resigning himself to the tyranny of his accidental situation. What they call the allotment of Providence is, often enough, the allotment of their own laziness or defective energy. At any rate, I feel much more inclined to respect the aspiring Englishman or Scotchman that kicks against these self-imposed restraints; that rebels in heart against whatever there may be of degradation in his own particular employment; and, therefore, though submitting to this degradation as the *sine quâ non* for earning his daily bread, and submitting also to the external badges and dress of his trade as frequently a matter of real convenience, yet doggedly refuses to abet or countersign any such arrangements as tend to lower him in other men's opinion. And exactly this is what he *would* be doing by assuming his professional costume on Sundays; the costume would then become an exponent of his choice, not of his convenience or his necessity; and he would thus be proclaiming that he glories in what he detests. To found a meek and docile nation, the German is the very architect wanted; but to found a go-ahead nation quite another race is called for, other blood and other training. And, again, when I hear a notable housewife exclaiming, 'Many are the poor servant girls that have been led into temptation and ruin by dressing above their station,' I feel that she says no more than the truth; and I grieve that it should be so. Out of tenderness, therefore, and pity towards the poor girls, if I personally had any power to bias their choice, my influence should be used in counteraction to their natural propensities. But this has nothing to do with the philosophic estimate of those propensities. Perilous they are; but *that* does not prevent their arising in fountains that contain elements of possible grandeur, such as would never be developed by a German Audrey (see 'As You Like It') content to be treated as a doll by her lover, and viewing it as profane to wear petticoats less voluminous, or a headdress less frightful than those inherited from her grandmother.

Excuse this digression, reader. What I wished to explain was that, if a man in a humble situation seeks to refine his pronunciation of English, and finds himself in consequence taxed with pride that will not brook the necessities of his rank, at all events, he is but *integrating* his manifestations of pride. Already in his Sunday's costume he has *begun* this manifestation, and, as I contend, rightfully. If a carpenter or a stonemason goes abroad on a railway excursion, there is no moral obligation upon him—great or small—to carry about any memento whatsoever of his calling. I contend that his right to pass himself off for a gentleman is co-extensive with his power to do so: the right is limited by the power, and by that only. The man may say justly: "What I am seeking is a holiday. This is what I pay for; and I pay for it with money earned painfully enough. I have a right therefore to expect that the article shall be genuine and complete. Now, a holiday means freedom from the pains of labour—not from some of those pains, but from all. Even from the memory of these pains, if *that* could be bought, and from the anticipation of their recurrence. Amongst the pains of labour, a leading one next after the necessity of unintermitting muscular effort, is the oppression of people's superciliousness or of their affected condescension in conversing with one whom they know to be a working mechanic. From this oppression it is, from this oppression whether open or poorly disguised, that I seek to be delivered. It taints my pleasure: it spoils my holiday. And if by being dressed handsomely, by courtesy in manners, and by accuracy in speaking English, I can succeed in obtaining this deliverance for myself, I have a right to it." Undoubtedly he has. His real object is not to disconnect himself from an honest calling, but from that burthen of contempt or of slight consideration which the world has affixed to his calling. He takes measures for gratifying his pride—not with a direct or primary view to that pride, but indirectly as the only means open to him for evading and defeating the unjust conventional scorn that would settle upon himself *through* his trade, if that should happen to become known or suspected. This is what I should be glad to assist him in; and amongst other points connected with his object, towards which my experience might furnish him with some hints, I shall here offer him the very shortest of lessons for his guidance in the matter of English pronunciation.

What can be attempted on so wide a field in a paper limited so severely in dimensions as all papers published by this journal *must* be limited in obedience to the transcendent law of variety? To make it possible that subjects *enough* should be treated, the Proprietor wisely insists on a treatment vigorously succinct for each in particular. I myself, it suddenly strikes me, must have been the chief offender against this reasonable law: but my offences were committed in pure ignorance and inattention, faults which henceforth I shall guard against with a penitential earnestness. Reformation meanwhile must begin, I fear, simultaneously with this confession of guilt. It would not be possible (would it?) that, beginning the penitence this month of November, I should postpone the amendment till the next? No, *that* would look too brazen. I must confine myself to the two and a half pages prescribed as the maximum extent—and of that allowance already perhaps have used up one half at the least. Shocking! is it not? So much the sterner is the demand through the remaining ground for exquisite brevity.

Rushing therefore at once *in medias res*, I observe to the reader that, although it is thoroughly impossible to give him a guide upon so vast a wilderness as the total area of our English language, for, if I must teach him how to pronounce, and upon what learned grounds to pronounce, 40,000 words, and if polemically I must teach him how to dispose of 40,000 objections that have been raised (or that *may* be raised) against these pronunciations, then I should require at the least 40,000 lives (which is quite out of the question, for a cat has but nine)—seeing and allowing for all this, I may yet offer him some guidance as to his guide. One sole rule, if he will attend to it, governs in a paramount sense the total possibilities and compass of pronunciation. A very famous line of Horace states it. What line? What is the supreme law in every language for correct pronunciation no less than for idiomatic propriety?

'*Usus*, quem penes arbitrium est et jus et norma loquendi:'

usage, the established practice, subject to which is all law and normal standard of correct speaking. Now, in what way does such a rule interfere with the ordinary prejudice on this subject? The popular error is that, in pronunciation, as in other things, there is an abstract right and a wrong. The difficulty, it is supposed, lies in ascertaining this right and wrong. But by collation of arguments, by learned investigation, and interchange of *pros* and *cons*, it is fancied that ultimately the exact truth of each separate case might be extracted. Now, in that preconception lies the capital blunder incident to the question. There *is* no right, there *is* no wrong, except what the prevailing usage creates. The usage, the existing custom, *that* is the law: and from that law there is no appeal whatever, nor demur that is sustainable for a moment.

FOOTNOTES:

[52] Amongst the Spaniards there *is*.

XV. THE JEWISH SCRIPTURES COULD HAVE BEEN WRITTEN IN NO MODERN ERA.

Now, observe what I am going to prove. First A, and as a stepping-stone to something (B) which is to follow: It is, that the Jewish Scriptures could not have been composed in any modern æra. I am earnest in drawing your attention to the particular point which I have before me, because one of the enormous faults pervading all argumentative books, so that rarely indeed do you find an exception, is that, in all the dust and cloud of contest and of objects, the reader never knows what is the immediate object before the writer and himself, nor if he were told would he understand in what relation it stood to the main object of contest—the main question at stake. Recollect, therefore, that what I want is to show that these elder Jewish Scriptures must have existed in very ancient days—how ancient? for ancient is an ambiguous word—could not have been written as a memorial of tradition within a century or two of our æra. To suppose, even for the sake of answering, the case of a forgery, is too gross and shocking: though a very common practice amongst writers miscalled religious, but in fact radically, incurably unspiritual. This might be shown to be abominable even in an intellectual sense; because no adequate, no rational purpose could be answered by such a labour. The sole conceivable case would be, that from the eldest days the Jews had been governed by all the Mosaic institutions as we now have them, but that the mere copying, the mere registration on tablets of parchment, wood, leather, brass, had not occurred till some more modern period. As to this the answer is at once: Why should they not have been written down? What answer could be given? Only this: For the same reason that other nations did not commit to writing their elder institutions. And why did they not? Was it to save trouble? So far from that, this one privation imposed infinite trouble that would have been evaded by written copies. For because they did not write down, therefore, as the sole mode of providing for accurate remembrance, they were obliged to compose in a very elaborate metre; in which the mere *pattern* as it were of the verse, so intricate and so closely interlocked, always performed thus two services: first, it assisted the memory in mastering the tenor; but, secondly, it checked and counterpleaded to the lapses of memory or to the artifices of fraud. This explanation is well illustrated in the 'Iliad'—a poem elder by a century, it is rightly argued, than the 'Odyssey,' ergo the eldest of Pagan literature. Now, when the 'Iliad' had once come down safe to Pisistratus 555 years B.C., imagine this great man holding out his hands over the gulf of time to Homer, 1,000 years before, who is chucking or shying his poems across the gulf. Once landed in those conservative hands, never trouble yourself more about the safety of the 'Iliad.' After that it was as safe as the eyes in any Athenian's head. But before that time there *was* a great danger; and this danger was at all surmounted (scholars differ greatly and have sometimes cudgelled one another with real unfigurative cudgels as to the degree in which it *did* surmount the danger) only by the metre and a regular orchestra in every great city dedicated to this peculiar service of chanting the 'Iliad'; insomuch that a special costume was assigned to the chanters of the 'Iliad,' viz., scarlet or crimson, and also another special costume to the chanters of the 'Odyssey,' viz., violet-coloured. Now, this division of orchestras had one great evil and one great benefit. The benefit was, that if locally one orchestra went wrong (as it might do upon local temptations) yet surely all the orchestras would not go wrong: ninety-nine out of every hundred would check and expose the fraudulent hundredth. *There* was the good. But the evil was concurrent. For by this dispersion of orchestras, and this multiplication, not only were the ordinary chances of error according to the doctrine of chances multiplied a hundred or a thousand fold, but also, which was worse, each separate orchestra was brought by local position under a separate and peculiar action of some temptation, some horrible temptation, some bribe that could not be withstood, for falsifying the copy by compliments to local families; that is, to such as were or such as were not descendants from the Paladius of Troy. For that, let me say, was for Greece, nay, for all the Mediterranean world, what for us of Christian ages have been the Crusades. It was the pinnacle from which hung as a dependency all the eldest of families. So that they who were of such families thirsted after what they held aright to be asserted, viz., a Homeric commemoration; and they who were not thirsted after what had begun to seem a feasible ambition to be accomplished. It was feasible: for various attempts are still on record very much like our interpolations of Church books as to records of birth or marriage. Athens, for instance, was discontented with Homer's praise; and the case is interesting, because, though it argues such an attempt to be very difficult, since even a great city could not fully succeed, yet, at the same time, it argues that it was not quite hopeless, or else it would hardly have been attempted. So that here arises one argument for the main genuineness of the Homeric text. Yet you will say: Perhaps when Athens tried the trick it was too late in the day: it was too late after full daylight to be essaying burglaries. But it would have been easy in elder days. This is true; but remark the restraint which that very state of the case supposes. Precisely when this difficulty became great, became enormous, did the desire chiefly become great, become enormous, for mastering it. And when the difficulty was light, when the forgery was most a matter of ease, the ambition was least. For you cannot suppose that families standing near to the Crusades would have cared much for the reputation. As an act of piety they would prize it; as an exponent of antiquity they would not prize it at all. For, in fact, it would argue no such thing, until many centuries had passed. You see, however, by this sketch the *pros* and the *cons* respecting the difficulty of transmitting the 'Iliad' free from corruption, if at once it was resigned to mere oral tradition. The alterations were more and more tempting; but in that ratio were less and less possible. And then, secondly, there were the changes from chance or from changing language. Apply all these considerations to the case of the Hebrew Scriptures, and their great antiquity is demonstrated.

XVI. DISPERSION OF THE JEWS, AND JOSEPHUS'S ENMITY TO CHRISTIANITY.

Look into the Acts of the Apostles, you see the wide dispersion of the Jews which had then been accomplished; a dispersion long antecedent to that penal dispersion which occurred subsequently to the Christian era. But search the pages of the wicked Jew, Josephus,[53] who notices expressly this universal dispersion of the Jews, and gives up and down his works the means of tracing them through every country in the southern belt of the Mediterranean, through every country of the northern belt, through every country of the connecting belt, in Asia Minor and Syria—through every island of the Mediterranean. Search Philo-Judæus, the same result is found. But why? Upon what theory? What great purpose is working, is fermenting underneath? What principle, what law can be abstracted from this antagonist or centrifugal motion outwards now violently beating back as with a conflict of tides the original centripetal motion inwards? Manifestly this: the incubating process had been completed: the ideas of God as an ideal of Holiness, the idea of Sin as the antagonist force—had been perfected; they were now so inextricably worked into the texture of Jewish minds, or the Jewish minds were now arrived at their *maximum* of adhesiveness, or at their *minimum* of repulsiveness, in manners and social character, that this stage was perfect; and now came the five hundred years during which they were to manure all nations with these preparations for Christianity. Hence it was that the great globe of Hebraism was now shivered into fragments; projected 'by one sling of that victorious arm'— which had brought them up from Egypt. Make ready for Christianity! Lay the structure, in which everywhere Christianity will strike root. You, that for yourselves even will reject, will persecute Christianity, become the pioneers, the bridge-layers, the reception-preparers, by means of those two inconceivable ideas, for natural man—sin and its antagonist, holiness.

In this way a preparation was made. But if Christianity was to benefit by it, if Christianity was to move with ease, she must have a language. Accordingly, from the time of Alexander, the strong he-goat, you see a tendency—sudden, abrupt, beyond all example, swift, perfect—for uniting all nations by the bond of a single language. You see kings and nations taking up their positions as regularly, faithfully, solemnly as a great fleet on going into action, for supporting this chain of language.

Yet even that will be insufficient; for fluent motion out of nation into nation it will be requisite that all nations should be provinces of one supreme people; so that no hindrances from adverse laws, or from jealousies of enmity, can possibly impede the fluent passage of the apostle and the apostle's delegates—inasmuch as the laws are swallowed up into one single code, and enmity disappears with its consequent jealousies, where all nationalities are absorbed into unity.

This last change being made, a signal, it may be supposed, was given as with a trumpet; now then, move forward, Christianity; the ground is ready, the obstacles are withdrawn. Enter upon the field which is manured; try the roads which are cleared; use the language which is prepared; benefit by the laws which protect and favour your motion; apply the germinating principles which are beginning to swell in this great vernal season of Christianity. New heavens and new earth are forming: do you promote it.

Such a *complexus* of favourable tendencies, such a meeting in one centre of plans—commencing in far different climates and far different centres, all coming up at the same æra face to face, and by direct lines of connection meeting in one centre—the world had never seen before.

FOOTNOTES:

[53] 'The wicked Jew,' Josephus, as once I endeavoured to show, was perhaps the worst man in all antiquity; it is pleasant to be foremost upon any path, and Joe might assuredly congratulate himself on surmounting and cresting all the scoundrels since the flood. What there might be on the other side the flood, none of us can say. But on *this* side, amongst the Cis-diluvians, Joe in a contest for the deanery of that venerable chapter, would assuredly carry off the prize. Wordsworth, on a question arising as to *who* might be the worst man in English history, vehemently contended for the pre-eminent pretensions of Monk. And when some of us assigned him only the fifth or sixth place, was disposed to mourn for him as an ill-used man. But no difficulty of this kind could arise with regard to the place of Josephus among the ancients, full knowledge and impartial judgment being presupposed. And his works do follow him; just look at this: From the ridiculous attempt of some imbecile Christian to interpolate in Josephus's History a passage favourable to Christ, it is clear that no adequate idea prevailed of his intense hatred to the new sect of Nazarenes and Galilæans. In our own days we have a lively illustration of the use which may be extracted from the Essenes by sceptics, and an indirect confirmation of my own allegation, against them, in Dr. Strauss (*Leben Jesu*). The moment that his attention was directed to that fact of the Essenes being utterly ignored in the New Testament (a fact so easily explained by *my* theory, a fact so *utterly* unaccountable to *his*) he conceived an affection for them. Had they been mentioned by St. John, there was an end to the dislike; but Josephus had, even with this modern sceptical Biblical critic, done his work and done it well.

XVII. CHRISTIANITY AS THE RESULT OF PRE-ESTABLISHED HARMONY.

If you are one that upon meditative grounds have come sincerely to perceive the philosophic value of this faith; if you have become sensible that as yet Christianity is but in its infant stages—after eighteen centuries is but beginning to unfold its adaptations to the long series of human situations, slowly unfolding as time and change move onwards; and that these self-adapting relations of the religion to human necessities, this conformity to unforeseen developments, argues a Leibnitzian pre-establishment of this great system as though it had from the first been a mysterious substratum laid under 'the dark foundations' of human nature; holding or admitting such views of the progress awaiting Christianity—you will thank us for what we are going to say. You may, possibly for yourself, when reviewing the past history of man, have chanced to perceive the same—we are not jealous of participation in a field so ample—but even in such a case, if the remark (on which we are now going to throw a ray of light) should appeal to you in particular, with less of absolute novelty, not the less you will feel thankful to be confirmed in your views by independent testimony. We, for ourselves, offer the remark as new; but, in an age teeming with so much agility of thought, it is rare that any remark can have absolutely evaded all partial glimpses or stray notices of others, even when *aliud agentes*, men stumble upon truths, to which they are not entitled by any meritorious or direct studies. However, whether absolutely original or not, the remark is this—Did it ever strike you, reader, as a most memorable phenomenon about Christianity, as one of those contradictory functions which, to a thing of human mechanism, is impossible, but which are found in *vital* agencies and in all deep-laid systems of truth—that the same scheme of belief which is the most settling, freezing, tranquillizing for one purpose, is the most unbinding, agitating, revolutionary in another? Christianity is that religion which most of all settles what is perilous in scepticism; and yet, also, it is that which most of all unsettles whatever may invite man's intellectual activity. It is the sole religion which can give any deep anchorage for man's hopes; and yet, also, in mysterious self-antagonism, it is the sole religion which opens a pathless ocean to man's useful and blameless speculations. Whilst all false religions neither as a matter of fact *have* produced—nor as a matter of possibility *could* have produced—a philosophy, it is a most significant distinction of Christianity, and one upon which volumes might be written, that simply by means of the great truths which that faith has fixed when brought afterwards into collision with the innumerable questions which that faith has left undetermined (as not essential to her own final purposes), Christianity has bred, and tempted, and stimulated a vast body of philosophy on neutral ground; ground religious enough to create an interest in the questions, yet not so religious as to react upon capital truths by any errors that may be committed in the discussion. For instance, on that one sea-like question of free agency, besides the *explicit* philosophy that Christianity has bred amongst the Schoolmen, and since their time, what a number of sects, heresies, orthodox churches have *implicitly* couched and diffused some one view or other of this question amongst their characteristic differences; and without prejudice to the integrity of their Christian views or the purity of their Christian morals. Whilst, on the other hand, the very noblest of false religions (the noblest as having stolen much from Christianity), viz., Islamism, has foreclosed all philosophy on this subject by the stupid and killing doctrine of fatalism. This we give as one instance; but in all the rest it is the same. You might fancy that from a false religion should arise a false philosophy—false, but still a philosophy. Is it so? On the contrary: the result of false religion is no philosophy at all.

Paganism produced none: the Pagans had a philosophy; but it stood in no sort of relation, real or fancied relation, to their mythology or worship. And the Mahometans, in times when they had universities and professors' chairs, drew the whole of their philosophic systems from Greece, without so much as ever attempting to connect these systems with their own religious creed. But Christianity, on the other hand, the only great doctrinal religion, the only religion which ties up—chains—and imprisons human faith, where it is good for man's peace that he should be fettered, is also the only religion which places him in perfect liberty on that vast neutral arena where it is good for him to exercise his unlimited energies of mind. And it is most remarkable, that whilst Christianity so far shoots her rays into these neutral questions as to invest them with grandeur, she keeps herself uncommitted and unpledged to such philosophic problems in any point where they might ally themselves with error. For instance, St. Austin's, or Calvin's doctrine on free agency is so far Christian, that Christian churches have adopted it into their articles of faith, or have even built upon it as a foundation. So far it seems connected with Christian truth. Yet, again, it is so far separate from Christian truth, that no man dares to pronounce his brother heretical for doubting or denying it. And thus Christianity has ministered, even in this side-chapel of its great temple, to two great necessities: it has thrown out a permanent temptation to human activity of intellect, by connecting itself with tertiary questions growing out of itself derivatively and yet indifferent to the main interests of truth. In this way Christianity has ministered to a necessity which was not religious, but simply human, through a religious radiation in a descending line. Secondly, it has kept alive and ventilated through every age the direct religious interest in its own primary truths, by throwing out secondary truths, that were doubtfully related to the first, for polemical agitation. Foolish are they who talk of our Christian disputes as arguments of an unsound state, or as silent reproaches to the sanity or perfect development of our religion. Mahometans are united, because the only points that could disunite them relate generally to fact and *not* to doctrinal truths. Their very national heresies turn only on a ridiculous piece of gossip—Was such a man's son-in-law his legitimate successor? Upon a point so puerile as this revolves the entire difference between the heterodoxy of Persia and the orthodoxy of Turkey. Or, if their differences go deeper, in that case they tend to the utter extinction of Islamism; they maintain no characteristic or exclusive dogma; as amongst the modern Sikhs of Hindostan, who have blended the Brahminical and Mahometan creeds by an incoherent *syncretismus*; or, as amongst many heretics of Persia and Arabia, who are mere crazy freethinkers, without any religious determination, without any principle of libration for the oscillating mind. Whereas *our* differences, leaving generally all central truths untouched, arise like our political parties, and operate like them; they grow out of our sincerity, and they sustain our sincerity. That interest *must* be unaffected which leads men into disputes and permanent factions, and that truth *must* be diffusive as life itself, which is found to underlay a vast body of philosophy. It is the cold petrific annihilation of a moral interest in the subject, by substituting a meagre interest of historical facts, which stifles all differences; stifles political differences under a despotism, from utter despair of winning practical value to men's opinions; stifles religious differences under a childish creed of facts or anecdotes, from the impossibility of bringing to bear upon the το positive of an arbitrary legend, or the mere conventional of a clan history—dead, inert letters—any moral views this way or that, and any life of philosophical speculation. Thence comes the soul-killing monotony (unity one cannot call it) of all false religions. Attached to mere formal facts, they provoke no hostility in the inner nature. Affirming nothing as regards the life of truth, why should they tempt any man to contradict? Lying, indeed, but lying only as a false pedigree lies, or an old mythological legend, they interest no principle in man's moral heart; they make no oracular answers, put forth no secret agitation, they provoke no question. But Christianity, merely by her settlements and fixing of truths, has disengaged and unfixed a world of other truths, for sustaining or for tempting an endless activity of the intellect. And the astonishing result has thus been accomplished—that round a centre, fixed and motionless as a polar tablet of ice, there has been in the remote offing a tumbling sea of everlasting agitation. A central gravitation in the power of Christianity has drawn to one point and converged into one tendency all capital agencies in all degrees of remoteness, making them tend to rest and unity; whilst, again, by an antagonist action, one vast centrifugal force, measured against the other, has so modified the result as to compel the intellect of man into divergencies answering to the line of convergence; balancing the central rest for man's hopes by everlasting motion for his intellect, and the central unity for man's conscience by everlasting progress for his efforts.

Now, the Scholastic philosophy meddled chiefly with those tertiary or sub-dependent truths; such, viz., as are indifferent to Christianity by any reaction which they can exert from error in their treatment, but not indifferent as regards their own original derivation. Many people connect Scholasticism with a notion of error and even of falsehood, because they suppose it to have arisen on the incitement of Popery. And it is undeniable that Popery impressed a bias or *clinamen* upon its movement. It is true also that Scholasticism is not only ministerial to Popery, but in parts is consubstantial with Popery. Popery is not fully fleshed and developed apart from the commentaries or polemical apologies of Aquinas. But still we must remember that Popery had not yet taken up the formal position of hostility to truth, seeing that as yet Protestantism was only beginning its first infant struggles. Many Popish errors were hardened and confirmed in the very furnace of the strife. And though perilous errors had intermingled themselves with Popery, which would eventually have strangled all the Christian truth which it involved, yet that truth it was which gave its whole interest to the Reformation. Had the Reformation fought against mere unmixed error, it could not have been viewed as a reforming process, but as one entirely innovating. So that even where it is most exclusively Popish, Scholasticism has often a golden thread of truth running through its texture; often it is not Popish in the sense of being Anti-Protestant, but in the elder sense of being Anti-Pagan. However, generally speaking, it is upon the neutral ground common to all modes of Christianity that this philosophy ranges. That being so, there was truth enough of a high order to sustain the sublimer motives of the Schoolmen; whilst the consciousness of supporting the mixed interests, secular and spiritual, of that mighty Christian church which at that time was co-extensive with Christianity in the West, gave to the Schoolmen a more instant, human, and impassioned interest in the labours of that mysterious loom which pursued its aerial web through three centuries.

As a consequence from all this, we affirm that the parallel is complete between the situation on the one side of the early Greek authors, the creators of Greek literature in the age of Pericles, and, on the other side, of the Christian Schoolmen; (1) the same intense indolence, which Helvetius fancied to be the most powerful stimulant to the mind under the reaction of *ennui*; (2) the same tantalizing dearth of books—just enough to raise a craving, too little to meet it; (3) the same chilling monotony of daily life and absence of female charities to mould social intercourse—for the Greeks from false composition of society and vicious sequestration of women—for the scholastic monks from the austere asceticism of their founders and the 'rule' of their order; (4) finally the same (but far different) enthusiasm and permanent elevation of thought from disinterested participation in forwarding a great movement of the times—for the one side tending to the unlimited aggrandisement of their own brilliant country; for the other, commensurate with what is conceivable in human grandeur.

This sketch of Christianity as it is mysteriously related to the total body of Philosophy actual or possible, present or in reversion, may seem inadequate. In some sense it *is* so. But call it a note or '*excursus*,' which is the scholarlike name for notes a little longer than usual, and all will be made right. What we have in view, is to explain the situation of the Greeks under Pericles by that of the Schoolmen. We use the modern or Christian case, which is more striking from its monastic peculiarity, as a reflex picture of the other. We rely on the moulding circumstances of Scholasticism, its awakened intellect, its famishing eagerness from defect of books, its gloom from the exile of all feminine graces, and its towering participation in an interest the grandest of the age, as a sort of *camera obscura* for bringing down on the table before us a portraiture essentially the same of early Greek society in the rapturous spring-time of Pericles.

If the governing circumstances were the same in virtue, then probably there would be a virtual sameness in some of the results: and amongst these results would be the prevailing cast of thinking, and therefore to some extent the prevailing features of style. It may seem strange to affirm any affinities between the arid forms of Scholastic style and the free movement of the early Grecian style. They seem rather to be repelling extremes. But extremes meet more often than is supposed. And there really *are* some remarkable features of conformity even as to this point between the tendencies of Christian monachism and the unsocial sociality of Paganism. However, it is not with this view that we have pressed the parallel. Not by way of showing a general affinity in virtues and latent powers, and thence deducing a probable affinity in results, but generally for the sake of fixing and illustrating circumstances which made it *physically* impossible that the movement could have been translated by contagion from one country to the others. Roads were too bad, cities too difficult of access, travellers too rare, books too incapable of transmission, for any solution which should explain the chain of coincidences into a chain of natural causations. No; the solution was, that Christianity had everywhere gone ahead spontaneously with the same crying necessities for purification, that is, for progress. One deep, from North to South, called to another; but the deeps all alike, each separately for itself, were ready with their voices, ready without collusion to hear and to reverberate the cry to God. The light, which abides and lodges in Christianity, had everywhere, by measured steps and by unborrowed strength, kindled into mortal antagonism with the darkness which had gathered over Christianity from human corruptions. But in science this result is even more conspicuous. Not only by their powers and energies the parallel currents of science in different lands enter into emulations that secure a general uniformity of progress, run neck and neck against each other, so as to arrive at any killing rasper of a difficulty pretty nearly about the same time; not only do they thus make it probable that coincidences of victory will continually occur through the rivalships of power; but also through the rivalships of weakness. Most naturally for the same reason that they worshipped in spirit and in truth, for the same reason that led them to value such a worship, they valued its distant fountain-head. Hence their interest in the Messiah. Hence their delegation.

XVIII. THE MESSIANIC IDEA ROMANIZED.

The Romans, so far from looking with the Jews to the Tigris, looked to the Jews themselves. Or at least they looked to that whole Syria, of which the Jews were a section. Consequently, there is a solution of two points:

1. The wise men of the East were delegates from the trans-Tigridian people.

2. The great man who should arise from the East to govern the world was, in the sense of that prophecy, *i.e.*, in the terms of that prophecy interpreted according to the sense of all who circulated and partook in—or were parties to—the belief of that prophecy, was to come from Syria: *i.e.*, from Judea.

Now take it either way, observe the sublimity and the portentous significance of this expectation. Every man of imaginative feeling has been struck with that secret whisper that stirred through France in 1814-15—that a man was to come with the violets. The violets were symbolically Napoleonic, as being the colour of his livery: it was also his cognizance: and the time for his return was *March*, from which commence the ever memorable Hundred days. And the sublimity lies in the circumstances of:

1. A whisper running through Christendom: people in remotest quarters bound together by a tie so aerial.

2. Of the dread augury enveloped in this little humble but beautiful flower.

3. Of the awful revolution at hand: the great earthquake that was mining and quarrying in the dark chambers beneath the thrones of Europe.

These and other circumstances throw a memorable sublimity upon this whisper of conspiracy. But what was this to the awful whisper that circled round the earth (ἡ οικουμενη) as to the being that was coming from Judea? There was no precedent, no antagonist whisper with which it could enter into any terms of comparison, unless there had by possibility been heard that mysterious and ineffable sigh which Milton ascribes to the planet when man accomplished his mysterious rebellion. The idea of such a sigh, of a whisper circling through the planet, of the light growing thick with the unimaginable charge, and the purple eclipse of Death throwing a penumbra; that may, but nothing else ever can, equal the unutterable sublimity of that buzz—that rumour, that susurrus passing from mouth to mouth—nobody knew whence coming or whither tending, and about a being of whom nobody could tell what he should be—what he should resemble—what he should do, but that all peoples and languages should have an interest in his appearance.

Now, on the one hand, suppose this—I mean, suppose the Roman whisper to be an authorized rumour utterly without root; in that case you would have a clear intervention of Heaven. But, on the other hand, suppose, which is to me the more probable idea, that it was not without a root; that in fact it was the Judæan conception of a Messiah, translated into Roman and worldly ideas; into ideas which a Roman could understand, or with which the world could sympathize, viz., that *rerum potiretur*. (The plural here indicates only the awful nature, its indeterminateness.)

I have, in fact, little doubt that it *was* a Romanized appropriation or translation of the Judæan Messiah. One thing only I must warn you against. You will naturally say: 'Since two writers among the very few surviving have both refuted this prophecy, and Josephus besides, this implies that many thousands did so. For if out of a bundle of newspapers two only had survived quite disconnected, both talking of the same man, we should argue a great popularity for that man.' And you will say: 'All these Roman people, did they interpret?' You know already—by Vespasian. Now whilst, on the one hand, I am far from believing that chance only was the parent of the ancient ευστοχια, their felicitous guessing (for it was a higher science), yet, in this new matter, what coincidence of Pagan prophecy, as doubtless a horrid mistrust in the oracles, etc., made them 'sagacious from a fear' of the coming peril, and, as often happens in Jewish prophecies—God when He puts forth His hand the purposes attained roll one under the other sometimes three deep even to our eyes.

XIX. CONTRAST OF GREEK AND PERSIAN FEELING IN CERTAIN ASPECTS.

Life, naturally the antagonism of Death, must have reacted upon Life according to its own development. Christianity having so awfully affected the το + of Death, this + must have reacted on Life. Hence, therefore, a phenomenon existing broadly to the human sensibility in these ages which for the Pagans had no existence whatever. If to a modern spectator a very splendid specimen of animal power, suppose a horse of three or four years old in the fulness of his energies, that saith *ha* to the trumpets and is unable to stand *loco* if he hears any exciting music, be brought for exhibition—not one of the spectators, however dull, but has a dim feeling of excitement added to his admiration from the lurking antagonism of the fugacious life attached to this ebullient power, and the awful repulsion between that final tendency and the meridian development of the strength. Hence, therefore, the secret rapture in bringing forward tropical life—the shooting of enormous power from darkness, the kindling in the midst of winter and sterility of irrepressible, simultaneous, tropical vegetation—the victorious surmounting of foliage, blossoms, flowers, fruits—burying and concealing the dreary vestiges of desolation.

Reply to the fact that Xerxes wept over his forces, by showing that in kind, like the Jewish, the less ignoble superstition of Persia—which must in the time of Balaam, if we suppose the Mesotam meant to have been the tract between the Euphrates and the Tigris, have been almost coincident with the Jewish as to the unity of God—had always, amidst barbarism arising from the forces moulding social sentiment, prompted a chivalry and sensibility far above Grecian. For how else account for the sole traits of Christian sensibility in regard to women coming forward in the beautiful tale of the Armenian prince, whose wife when asked for her opinion of Cyrus the Conqueror, who promised to restore them all to liberty and favour (an act, by the way, in itself impossible to Greek feelings, which exhibit no one case of relinquishing such rights over captives) in one hour, replied that she knew not, had not remarked his person; for that *her* attention had been all gathered upon that prince, meaning her youthful husband, who being asked by the Persian king what sacrifice he would esteem commensurate to the recovery of his bride, answered so fervently, that life and all which it contained were too slight a ransom to pay. Even that answer was wholly impossible to a Grecian. And again the beautiful catastrophe in the tale of Abradates and Panthea—the gratitude with which both husband and wife received the royal gift of restoration to each other's arms, implying a sort of holy love inconceivable to a state of Polygamy—the consequent reaction of their thought in testifying this gratitude; and as war unhappily offered the sole chance for displaying it, the energy of Panthea in adorning with her own needle the habiliments of her husband—the issuing forth and parting on the morning of battle—the principle of upright duty and of immeasurable gratitude in Abradates forming 'a nobler counsellor' than his wife's 'poor heart'—his prowess—his glorious death—his bringing home as a corpse—the desolation of Panthea—the visit and tears of the Persian king to the sorrowing widow stretched upon the ground by the corpse of her hero—the fine incident of the right hand, by which Cyrus had endeavoured to renew his pledges of friendship with the deceased prince, coming away from the corpse and following the royal touch (this hand having been struck off in the battle)—the burial—and the subsequent death of Panthea, who refused to be comforted under all the kind assurances, the kindest protection from the Persian king—these traits, though surviving in Greek, are undoubtedly Persian. For Xenophon had less sensibility than any Greek author that survives. And besides, abstracting from the writer, how is it that Greek records offer no such story; nothing like it; no love between married people of that chivalric order—no conjugal fidelity—no capacity of that beautiful reply—that she saw him not, for that *her* mind had no leisure for any other thought than one?

XX. OMITTED PASSAGES AND VARIED READINGS.

1.—DINNER.

In London and other great capitals it is well known that new diseases have manifested themselves of late years: and more would be known about them, were it not for the tremulous delicacy which waits on the afflictions of the rich. We do not say this invidiously. It is right that such forbearance should exist. Medical men, as a body, are as manly a race as any amongst us, and as little prone to servility. But obviously the case of exposure under circumstances of humiliating affliction is a very different thing for the man whose rank and consideration place him upon a hill conspicuous to a whole city or nation, and for the unknown labourer whose name excites no feeling whatever in the reader of his case. Meantime it is precisely amongst the higher classes, privileged so justly from an exposure pressing so unequally upon *their* rank, that these new forms of malady emerge. Any man who visits London at intervals long enough to make the spectacle of that great vision impressive to him from novelty and the force of contrast, more especially if this contrast is deepened by a general residence in some quiet rural seclusion, will not fail to be struck by the fever and tumult of London as its primary features. *Struck* is not the word: *awed* is the only adequate expression as applied to the hurry, the uproar, the strife, the agony of life as it boils along some of the main arteries among the London streets. About the hour of equinoctial sunset comes a periodic respite in the shape of dinner. Were it not for that, were it not for the wine and the lustre of lights, and the gentle restraints of courtesies, and the soothing of conversation, through which a daily reaction is obtained, London would perish from excitement in a year. The effect upon one who like ourselves simply beholds the vast frenzy attests its power. The mere sympathy, into which the nerves are forced by the eye, expounds the fury with which it must act upon those who are acting and suffering participators in the mania. Rome suffered in the same way, but in a less degree: and the same relief was wooed daily in a brilliant dinner (*cœna*), but two and a half hours earlier.

The same state of things exists proportionately in other capitals—Edinburgh, Dublin, Naples, Vienna. And doubtless, if the curtain were raised, the same penalties would be traced as pursuing this agitated life; the penalties, we mean, that exist in varied shapes of nervous disease.

2.—OMITTED PASSAGES FROM THE REVIEW OF BENNETT'S CEYLON.

Mr. Bennett personally is that good man who interests us the more because he seems to be an ill-used one. By the way, here is a combination which escaped the Roman moralist: *Vir bonus*, says he, *malâ fortunâ compositus*, is a spectacle for the gods. Yet what is that case, the case of a man matched in duel with the enmity of a malicious fellow-creature—naturally his inferior, but officially having means to oppress him? No man is naturally or easily roused to anger by a blind abstraction like Fortune; and therefore he is under no temptation to lose his self-command. He sustains no trial that can make him worthy of a divine contemplation. Amongst all the extravagancies of human nature, never yet did we hear of a person who harboured a sentiment of private malice against Time for moving too rapidly, or against Space for being infinitely divisible. Even animated annoyers, if they are without spite towards ourselves, we regard with no enmity. No man in all history, if we except the twelfth Cæsar, has nourished a deadly feud against flies[54]: and if Mrs. Jameson allowed a sentiment of revenge to nestle in her heart towards the Canadian mosquitoes, it was the race and not the individual parties to the trespass on herself against whom she protested. Passions it is, human passions, intermingling with the wrong itself that envenom the sense of wrong. We have ourselves been caned severely in passing through a wood by the rebound, the recalcitration we may call it, of elastic branches which we had displaced. And passing through the same wood with a Whitehaven dandy of sixty, now in *Hades*, who happened to wear a beautiful wig from which on account of the heat he had removed his hat, we saw with these eyes of ours one of those same thickets which heretofore had been concerned in our own caning, deliberately lift up, suspend, and keep dangling in the air for the contempt of the public that auburn wig which was presumed by its wearer to be simular of native curls. The ugliness of that death's head which by this means was suddenly exposed to daylight, the hideousness of that grinning skull so abruptly revealed, may be imagined by poets. Neither was the affair easily redressed: the wig swung buoyantly in the playful breezes: to catch it was hard, to release it without injuring the tresses was a matter of nicety: ladies were heard approaching from Rydal Mount: the dandy was agitated: he felt himself, if seen in this condition, to be a mere *memento mori*: for the first time in his life, as we believe, he blushed on meeting our eye: he muttered something, in which we could only catch the word 'Absalom': and finally we extricated ourselves from the cursed thicket barely in time to meet the ladies. Here were insufferable affronts: greater cannot be imagined: wanton outrages on two inoffensive men: and for ourselves, who could have identified and sworn to one of the bushes as an accomplice in *both* assaults, it was not easy altogether to dismiss the idea of malice. Yet, because this malice did not organize and concentrate itself in an eye looking on and genially enjoying our several mortifications, we both pocketed the affronts. All this we say to show Mr. Bennett how fully we do justice to his situation, and allow for the irritation natural to such cases as his, where the loss is clothed with contumely, and the wrong is barbed by malice. But, for all *that*, we do not think such confidential communications of ill-usage properly made to the public.

In fact, this querulous temper of expostulation, running through the book, disfigures its literary aspect. And possibly for our own comfort we might have turned away from a feature of discontent so gloomy and painful, were it not that we are thus accidentally recalled to a grievance in our Eastern administrations upon which we desire to enter a remark. Life is languid, the blood becomes lazy, at the extremities of our bodily system, as we ourselves know by dolorous experience under the complaint of *purpura*; and analogously we find the utility of our supreme government to droop and languish before it reaches the Indian world. Hence partly it is (for nearer home we see nothing of the kind), that foreign adventurers receive far too much encouragement from our British Satraps in the East. To find themselves within 'the regions of the morn,' and cheek to cheek with famous Sultans far inferior in power and substantial splendour, makes our great governors naturally proud. They are transfigured by necessity; and, losing none of their justice or integrity, they lose a good deal of their civic humility. In such a state they become capable of flattery, apt for the stratagems of foreign adulation. We know not certainly that Mr. Bennett's injuries originated in that source; though we suspect as much from the significant stories which he tells of interloping foreigners on the pension list in Ceylon. But this we *do* know, that, from impulses easily deciphered, foreigners creep into favour where an Englishman would not; and why? For two reasons: 1st, because a foreigner *must* be what is meant by 'an adventurer,' and in his necessity he is allowed to find his excuse; 2ndly, because an Englishman, attempting to play the adulatory character, finds an obstacle to his success in the standard of his own national manners from which it requires a perpetual effort to wean himself: whereas the oily and fluent obsequiousness found amongst Italians and Frenchmen makes the transition to a perfect Phrygian servility not only more easy to the artist, and less extravagantly palpable, but more agreeable in the result to his employer. This cannot be denied, and therefore needs no comment. But, as to the other reason, viz., that a foreigner *must* be an adventurer, allow us to explain. Every man is an adventurer, every man is *in sensu strictissimo* sometimes a knave.

You might imagine the situation of an adventurer who had figured virtually in many lives, to resemble that of the late revered Mr. Prig Bentham, when sitting like a contrite spider at the centre of his 'panopticon'; all the lines, which meet in a point at his seat, radiate outwards into chambers still widening as they increase their distance. This *may* be an image of an adventurer's mind when open to compunction, but generally it is exactly reversed; he sees the past sections of his life, however spacious heretofore, crowding up and narrowing into vanishing points to his immediate eye. And such also they become for the public. The villain, who walks, like Æneas at Carthage, shrouded in mist, is as little pursued by any bad report for his forgotten misdeeds as he is usually by remorse. In the process of losing their relation to any known and visible person, acts of fraud, robbery, murder, lose all distinct place in the memory. Such acts are remembered only through persons. And hence it is that many interesting murders, worthy to become cabinet gems in a museum of such works, have wasted their sweetness on the desert air even in our time, for no other reason than that the parties concerned did not amplify their proportions upon the public eye; the sufferers were perhaps themselves knaves; and the doers had retreated from all public knowledge into the mighty crowds of London or Glasgow.

This excursus, on the case of adventurers who run away from their own crimes into the pathless wildernesses of vast cities, may appear disproportionate. But excuse it, reader, for the subject is interesting; and with relation to our Eastern empire it is peculiarly so. Many are the anecdotes we could tell, derived from Oriental connections, about foreign scamps who have first exposed the cloven foot when inextricably connected with political intrigues or commercial interests, or possibly with domestic and confidential secrets. The dangerousness of their characters first began to reveal itself after they had become dangerous by their present position.

Mr. Bennett mentions one lively illustration of this in the case of a foreigner, who had come immediately from the Cape of Good Hope; so far, but not farther, he could be traced. And what part had he played at the Cape? The illustrious one of private sentinel, with a distant prospect perhaps of rising to be a drum-major. This man—possibly a refugee from the bagnio at Marseilles, or from the Italian galleys—was soon allowed to seat himself in an office of £1,000 per annum. For what? For which of his vices? Our English and Scottish brothers, honourable and educated, must sacrifice country, compass land and sea, face a life of storms, with often but a slender chance of any result at all from their pains, whilst a foreign rascal (without any allegation of merit in his favour) shall at one bound, by planting his servility in the right quarter and at the fortunate hour, vault into an income of 25,000 francs per annum; the money, observe, being national money—yours, ours, everybody's—since at that period Ceylon did not pay her own expenses. Now, indeed, she does, and furnishes beside, annually, a surplus of £50,000 sterling. But still, we contend that places of trust, honour, and profit, won painfully by British blood, are naturally and rightfully to be held in trust as reversions for the children of the family. To return, however, and finish the history of our scamp, it happened that through the regular action of his office, and in part perhaps through some irregular influence or consideration with which his station invested him, he became the depositary of many sums saved laboriously by poor Ceylonese. These sums he embezzled; or, as a sympathizing countryman observed of a similar offence in similar circumstances, he 'gave an irregular direction to their appropriation.' You see, he could not forget his old Marseilles tricks. This, however, was coming it too strong for his patron, who in spite of his taste for adulation was a just governor. Our poor friend was summoned most peremptorily to account for the missing dollars; and because it did not occur to him that he might plead, as another man from Marseilles in another colony had done, 'that the white ants had eaten the dollars,' he saw no help for it but to cut his throat, and cut his throat he did. This being done, you may say that he had given such a receipt as he could, and had entitled himself to a release. Well, we are not unmerciful; and were the case of the creditors our own, we should not object. But we remark, besides the private wrong, a posthumous injury to the British nation which this foreigner was enabled to commit; and it was twofold: he charged the pension-list of Ceylon with the support of his widow, in prejudice of other widows left by our meritorious countrymen, some of whom had died in battle for the State; and he had attainted, through one generation at least, the good faith of our nation amongst the poor ignorant Cinghalese, who cannot be expected to distinguish between true Englishmen and other Europeans whom English governors may think proper to exalt in the colony.

Cases such as these, it is well known to the learned in that matter, have been but too frequent in our Eastern colonies; and we do assert that any single case of that nature is too much by one. Even where the question is merely one of courtesy to science or to literature, we complain heavily, not at all of that courtesy, but that by much too great a preponderance is allowed to the pretensions of foreigners. Everybody at Calcutta will recollect the invidious distinctions (invidious upon contrast) paid by a Governor-General some years ago to a French *savant*, who came to the East as an itinerant botanist and geologist on the mission of a Parisian society. The Governor was Lord William Bentinck. His Excellency was a radical, and, being such, could swallow 'homage' by the gallon, which homage the Frenchman took care to administer. In reward he was publicly paraded in the *howdah* of Lady William Bentinck, and caressed in a way not witnessed before or since. Now this Frenchman, after visiting the late king of the Sikhs at Lahore, and receiving every sort of service and hospitality from the English through a devious route of seven thousand miles (treatment which in itself we view with pleasure), finally died of liver complaint through his own obstinacy. By way of honour to his memory, the record of his three years' wanderings has been made public. What is the expression of his gratitude to the English? One service he certainly rendered us: he disabused, if *that* were possible, the French of their silly and most ignorant notions as to our British government in India and Ceylon: he could do no otherwise, for he had himself been astounded at what he saw as compared with what he had been taught to expect. Thus far he does us some justice and therefore some service, urged to it by his bitter contempt of the French credulity wherever England is slandered. But otherwise he treats with insolence unbounded all our men of science, though his own name has made little impression anywhere: and, in his character of traveller he speaks of himself as of one laying the foundation-stone of any true knowledge with regard to India. In particular he dismisses with summary contempt the Travels of Bishop Heber—not very brilliant perhaps, but undoubtedly superior both in knowledge and in style to his own. Yet this was the man selected for *fêting* by the English Governor-General; as though courtesy to a Frenchman could not travel on any line which did not pass through a mortifying slight to Englishmen.

3.—GILLMAN'S COLERIDGE.

Variation on the opening of 'Coleridge and Opium-eating.'

What is the deadest thing known to philosophers? According to popular belief, it is a door-nail. For the world says, 'Dead as a door-nail!' But the world is wrong. Dead may be a door-nail; but deader and most dead is Gillman's Coleridge. Which fact in Natural History we demonstrate thus: Up to Waterloo it was the faith of every child that a sloth took a century for walking across a street. His mother, if she 'knew he was out,' must have had a pretty long spell of uneasiness before she saw him back again. But Mr. Waterton, Baptist of a new generation in these mysteries, took that conceit out of Europe: the sloth, says he, cannot like a snipe or a plover run a race neck and neck with a first-class railway carriage; but is he, therefore, a slow coach? By no means: he would go from London to Edinburgh between seedtime and harvest. Now Gillman's Coleridge, vol. i., has no such speed: it has taken six years to come up with those whom chiefly it concerned. Some dozen of us, Blackwood-men and others, are stung furiously in that book during the early part of 1838; and yet none of us had ever perceived the nuisance or was aware of the hornet until the wheat-fields of 1844 were white for the sickle. In August of 1844 we saw Gillman.

4.—WHY SCRIPTURE DOES NOT DEAL WITH SCIENCE ('PAGAN ORACLES').

The Fathers grant to the Oracles a real power of foresight and prophecy, but in all cases explain these supernatural functions out of diabolic inspiration. Van Dale, on the other hand, with all his Vandalish followers, treats this hypothesis, both as regards the power itself of looking into the future and as regards the supposed source of that power, in the light of a contemptible chimera. They discuss it scarcely with gravity: indeed, the very frontispiece to Van Dale's book already announces the repulsive spirit of scoffing and mockery in which he means to dismiss it; men are there represented in the act of juggling and coarsely exulting over their juggleries by protruding the tongue or exchanging collusive winks with accomplices. Now, in a grave question obliquely affecting Christianity and the course of civilization, this temper of discussion is not becoming, were the result even more absolutely convincing than it is. Everybody can see at a glance that it is not this particular agency of evil spirits which Van Dale would have found so ridiculous, were it not that he had previously addicted himself to viewing the whole existence of evil spirits as a nursery fable. Now it is not our intention to enter upon any speculation so mysterious. It is clear from the first that no man by human researches can any more add one scintillation of light to the obscure indications of Scripture upon this dark question, than he can add a cubit to his stature. We do not know, nor is it possible to know, what is even likely to be the exact meaning of various Scriptural passages partly, perhaps, adapted to the erring preconceptions of the Jews; for never let it be forgotten that upon all questions alike, which concerned no moral interest of man, all teachers alike who had any heavenly mission, patriarchs or lawgivers conversing immediately with God, prophets, apostles, or even the Founder of our religion Himself, never vouchsafe to reveal one ray of illumination. And to us it seems the strangest oversight amongst all the oversights of commentators that, in respect to the Jewish errors as to astronomy, etc., they should not have seen the broad open doctrine which vindicates the profound Scriptural neglect of errors however gross in that quality of speculation. The solution of this neglect is not such as to leave a man under any excuse for apologizing or shuffling. The solution is technical, precise, and absolute. It is not sufficient to say, as the best expounders do generally say, that science, that astronomy for instance, that geology, that physiology, were not the kind of truth which divine missionaries were sent to teach; that is true, but is far short of the whole truth. Not only was it negatively no part of the offices attached to a divine mission that it should extend its teaching to merely intellectual questions (an argument which still leaves the student to figure it as a work not indispensable, not absolutely to be expected, yet in case it *were* granted as so much of advantage, as a *lucro ponatur*), but in the most positive and commanding sense it *was* the business of revelation to refuse all light of this kind. According to all the analogies which explain the meaning of a revelation, it would have been a capital schism in the counsels of Providence, if in one single instance it had condescended to gratify human curiosity by anticipation with regard to any subject whatever, which God had already subjected to human capacity through the ample faculties of the human intellect.

5.—VARIATION ON A FAMOUS PASSAGE IN 'THE DAUGHTER OF LEBANON.'

The evangelist, stepping forward, touched her forehead. 'She is mortal,' he said; and guessing that she was waiting for some one amongst the youthful revellers, he groaned heavily; and then, half to himself and half to *her*, he said, 'O flower too gorgeous, weed too lovely, wert thou adorned with beauty in such excess, that not Solomon in all his glory was arrayed like thee, no nor even the lily of the field, only that thou mightest grieve the Holy Spirit of God?' The woman trembled exceedingly, and answered, 'Rabbi, what should I do? For, behold! all men forsake me.'

Brief had been the path, and few the steps, which had hurried her to destruction. Her father was a prince amongst the princes of Lebanon; but proud, stern, and inflexible.

THE END.

FOOTNOTES:

[54] 'Against flies'—whence he must have merited the anger of Beelzebub, whom Syrians held to be the tutelary god of flies; meaning probably by 'flies' all insects whatever, as the Romans meant by *passer* and *passerculus*, all little birds of whatsoever family, and by *malum* every fruit that took the shape and size of a ball. How honoured were the race of flies, to have a deity of the first rank for their protector, a Cæsar for their enemy! Cæsar made war upon them with his stylus; he is supposed to have massacred openly, or privately and basely to have assassinated, more than seven millions of that unfortunate race, who however lost nothing of that indomitable pertinacity in retaliating all attacks, which Milton has noticed with honour in 'Paradise Regained.' In reference to this notorious spirit of persecution in the last prince of the Flavian house, Suetonius records a capital repartee: 'Is the Emperor alone?' demanded a courtier. 'Quite alone.' 'Are you sure? Really now is nobody with him?' Answer: '*Ne musca quidem.*'